3147240037005~

W9-CSD-749

WITHDRAWN

DUE

Your Sister in the Gospel

Your Sister in the Gospel

The Life of Jane Manning James,
a Nineteenth-Century Black Mormon

QUINCY D. NEWELL

OXFORD
UNIVERSITY PRESS

OXFORD
UNIVERSITY PRESS

Oxford University Press is a department of the University of Oxford. It furthers
the University's objective of excellence in research, scholarship, and education
by publishing worldwide. Oxford is a registered trade mark of Oxford University
Press in the UK and certain other countries.

Published in the United States of America by Oxford University Press
198 Madison Avenue, New York, NY 10016, United States of America.

© Oxford University Press 2019

CIP data is on file at the Library of Congress
ISBN 978–0–19–933866–5

1 3 5 7 9 8 6 4 2

Printed by Sheridan Books, Inc., United States of America

For my family
and in loving memory of
Jane Adair Brownlie
May 15, 1922–August 3, 2017

CONTENTS

ACKNOWLEDGMENTS

I am so grateful for the assistance of friends, colleagues, institutions, and perfect strangers who went out of their ways to help me bring this book into being and make it immeasurably better. I was lucky to study with David W. Wills and Laurie F. Maffly-Kipp. This book would never have seemed possible to me without their support and mentorship, even long after I moved on from their courses. Long before I started writing Jane's biography, the Wason family welcomed me to Salt Lake and Darius Gray and Margaret Blair Young welcomed me to the study of African American Mormons. Brittany Chapman Nash shared the historical gem that tipped me over the edge into writing this book. She has continued to share generously of her immense knowledge. Judith Weisenfeld took an early interest in this project and her curiosity, openness, and intellectual contributions to the study of African American religious history challenged, encouraged, and guided me. W. Paul Reeve and John Turner reviewed my initial book proposal and helped at key moments in my research and writing, providing documents, suggesting fruitful research angles, and expressing enthusiasm about this project. Paul Reeve, in particular, was a wonderful collaborator in my final months of writing. He generously shared his own work and the primary sources he had unearthed, patiently explained the intricacies of the nineteenth-century priesthood restriction and other topics, and in his capacity as manuscript reviewer, thoughtfully critiqued the whole book. This volume is far better for his and the second (anonymous) reviewer's comments. Amy Tanner Thiriot, whose work also involved Jane, shared her formidable genealogical and historical research skills with me, helping me untangle complicated family trees and trace the faint historical tracks of Jane's relations. Kate Holbrook, Jenny Reeder, Alan Morell, and Mark Staker all helped illuminate obscure historical details that allowed me to write a richer account of Jane's life and times. J. Spencer Fluhman and Patrick Q. Mason answered my often haphazard questions about LDS history, culture, and practice with grace and good humor. Louis Duffy, the great-great-grandson of Jane, shared copies of Jane's patriarchal blessings with me and granted permission for them to be published in this book. Bob Russell, who literally wrote the book on the history of Jane's hometown of Wilton, Connecticut, was incredibly helpful in my efforts to trace Jane's early life. Doris Soldner, who researched Jane's family for the New Canaan Historical Society, generously responded to my letter with encouragement and good humor.

Brittany Chapman Nash, Kate Holbrook, Judith Weisenfeld, David Wills, Philip Barlow, David Howlett, Amy Koehlinger, and Matt Harris invited me to speak about Jane at various points, thus providing opportunities and deadlines for thinking through various aspects of Jane's biography. Laurel Thatcher Ulrich offered a generous critique of one talk that helped me think about Jane's life in a more interesting, complicated way.

Travis Cowell, Judy Barry, A'Nova Ettien, Sandra Kline, Patricia McGuire, Celia Moore, Miriam Moore, Melinda Newell, Robert Newell, Erika Simeon, and Kathy Stone-DeBerry all read an almost-complete draft of the manuscript and helped me make the book clearer and more readable. I didn't follow all of their advice, but I certainly benefited from their generous attention to this story. I have been lucky to have two wonderful writing groups while working on Jane's biography: at the University of Wyoming, Erin Forbes, Teena Gabrielson, and Frieda Knobloch read and commented on many drafts of the first pieces of this book. At Hamilton College, Jennifer Ambrose, Celeste Day Moore, and Benj Widiss read the vast majority of the book in its early stages. I am lucky to count the people in both of these groups as valued colleagues and dear friends.

Throughout this project, I had the good fortune to work with excellent staffs at libraries, archives, and historical societies all over the country. I am grateful for the assistance of the wonderful people who work at the University of Utah's J. Willard Marriott Library, Utah State University Libraries' Special Collections and Archives, Brigham Young University Library's L. Tom Perry Special Collections, the LDS Church History Library and Family History Library, University of Wyoming's Coe Library (especially Kaijsa Calkins), Hamilton College's Burke Library (especially Kristin Strohmeyer), the Utah State Historical Society, Multnomah County (Oregon) Libraries, University of Connecticut Library's reference desk, New Canaan (Connecticut) Historical Society, Wilton (Connecticut) Public Library, and Ohio History Connection. I'm also grateful to the volunteers at the Portland, Oregon, Family History Center, for making me welcome there. Matt Page and employees of the Library of Congress, Princeton University Rare Books and Special Collections, the Utah State Historical Society, and the Division of Rare and Manuscript Collections at Cornell University Library provided the vast majority of the images used in this book. I appreciate their assistance. The LDS Church History Library also provided images of Isaac James and a woman believed to be Jane James. Those images are in the public domain, but the folks in the LDS Church's intellectual property division asked that I include the following disclaimer: "This material is neither made, provided, approved, nor endorsed by Intellectual Reserve, Inc. or The Church of Jesus Christ of Latter-day Saints. Any content or opinions expressed, implied or included in or with the material are solely those of the owner and not those of Intellectual Reserve, Inc. or The Church of Jesus Christ of Latter-day Saints."

When I began working on this book, I was on the faculty at the University of Wyoming. When I finished, I was on the faculty of Hamilton College. I am thankful for the material support that both institutions provided and for the wonderful people I have had the opportunity to work with in both places. I completed this book while on a full-year sabbatical supported in part by a grant from the Louisville Institute. I am grateful for the time and mental space that grant made possible, and I am especially indebted to those colleagues who took the time to support my grant applications with letters of recommendation.

This book is dedicated to my family. Their love and support mean the world to me.

WHO'S WHO IN JANE'S STORY

The people listed here appear in at least two different chapters in this book. Everyone is listed in alphabetical order by last name. Women who used multiple surnames are listed under their birth name, with their married name in parentheses.

Philes Abbett: Jane's maternal grandmother. (Spelling of her name varied. It was pronounced "Phyllis.")

Elijah Abel: African American Mormon convert and one of the few black men known to have been ordained to the LDS priesthood.

Henrietta Bankhead: Daughter of Esther and Henry Leggroan, granddaughter of Sylvester and Mary Ann Perkins James, Jane's great-granddaughter.

Elvira Stevens Barney: White LDS physician who penned a partial account of Jane James's life for the *Deseret News* in 1899.

Amanda Chambers: African American Mormon who arrived in Salt Lake City in 1870; wife of Samuel Chambers.

Samuel Chambers: African American Mormon who arrived in Salt Lake City in 1870; husband of Amanda Chambers.

George Parker Dykes: Captain of Jane's ten from Mount Pisgah, Iowa, to Winter Quarters. Jane and Isaac James stayed with Dykes's family in Winter Quarters.

Harriet Jacobs: African American woman who escaped slavery in North Carolina and wrote about her experience in the book *Incidents in the Life of a Slave Girl*.

Ellen Madora James: Jane's fifth child, born in 1852 or 1853. Ellen Madora sometimes used the pseudonym "Nellie Kidd."

Isaac James: Jane's first husband and the father of all of her children except her first.

Isaac James (Junior): Jane's sixth child, stillborn in 1854.

Jesse Jereboam James: Jane's seventh child, born in 1857.

Mary Ann James (Robinson): Jane's third child, the couple's first daughter, born in 1848.

Miriam James (Williams): Jane's fourth child, born in 1850.

Silas James: Jane's second child, her first with Isaac James, born in 1846.

Sylvester James: Jane's first child, born in about 1839; his father's identity is unknown.

Vilate James (Warner): Jane's eighth, and last, child, born in 1859. ("Vilate" is pronounced similarly to "Violet.")

Edward ("Ned") Leggroan: African American Mormon from Mississippi, husband of Susan Leggroan and father of several children including Henry Leggroan.

Henry Leggroan: Son of Edward "Ned" Leggroan and Susan Leggroan, married Jane's granddaughter Esther Jane James.

Susan Leggroan: African American Mormon from Mississippi, wife of Edward "Ned" Leggroan and mother of several children including Henry Leggroan.

Angeline Manning: Jane's sister, probably younger.

Isaac Lewis Manning: Jane's brother, probably older.

Peter Manning: Jane's brother, probably younger.

Philes Manning: Jane's mother. Jane referred to her as Philes; she appears in some records as Eliza.

Sarah Manning (Stebbins): Jane's sister, probably older. Mother of Mary Stebbins.

Edward Martin: Salt Lake photographer who made the likenesses of Isaac James and an African American woman believed to be Jane James.

William McCary: Enigmatic figure, variously identified as African American and Native American, who floated in and out of the LDS movement in the late 1840s. McCary married Lucy Stanton and with her built and led a small schismatic movement in the late 1840s.

Emily Partridge (Young): One of Joseph Smith's plural wives who worked in the Smith home; later married Brigham Young.

Frank Perkins: Jane's second husband.

Mary Ann Perkins (James): Frank Perkins's daughter. Mary Ann Perkins married Sylvester James and became Jane's daughter-in-law.

Elizabeth Jefford Drake Roundy: LDS convert from England to whom Jane dictated her autobiography.

Patty Sessions: Midwife who delivered several of Jane's children, and member of Jane's ten from Mount Pisgah, Iowa, to Winter Quarters.

Elias Smith: Probate court judge in Salt Lake City who granted a divorce decree to Jane and Isaac James.

Emma Smith: First wife of Joseph Smith.

Hyrum Smith: Older brother of Joseph Smith and Patriarch of the LDS Church.

Joseph Smith: Founder and first prophet of the Church of Jesus Christ of Latter-day Saints; employed Jane in Nauvoo.

Joseph F. Smith: Nephew of Joseph Smith, son of Hyrum Smith. Served as a member of the Quorum of the Twelve Apostles and then as the sixth LDS Church President, 1901–1918.

Lucy Stanton (McCary): LDS daughter of white Mormon converts who married William McCary and helped build and lead a schismatic movement in the late 1840s.

Mary Stebbins: Jane's niece, daughter of Sarah Manning (Stebbins).

John Taylor: Third LDS Church President, 1880–1887.

Cato Treadwell: Philes Manning's second husband, Jane's stepfather.

Charles Wesley Wandell: Missionary who baptized Jane as a member of the LDS Church and led a group of converts from southwestern Connecticut to Nauvoo.

Josephine Williams: Daughter of Miriam James (Williams), Jane's granddaughter.

Brigham Young: Second prophet of the LDS Church. Employed Jane and her family in Nauvoo and Salt Lake.

Zina Diantha Huntington Young: Prominent LDS women's leader, plural wife of Joseph Smith and Brigham Young, and third president of the LDS Relief Society.

Introduction

Jane Elizabeth Manning James has haunted me for more than a decade. This is not a traditional haunting; I have never glimpsed of her ghostly visage on a stormy evening, nor have I heard her humming a tune in the dark of night. Instead, she crept into my research, slowly taking over my work on nineteenth-century African American and Native American Mormons, showing up unexpectedly in my primary sources, requiring my attention. Jane James's haunting is friendly. She wishes me no harm. She just wants to be remembered.

A free black woman born in Connecticut in the early 1820s, Jane entered domestic service at a young age, moved to Illinois as a young adult, and then joined the mass movement of Americans into the trans-Mississippi American West in the late 1840s. She raised a large family and was active in her community until her death in 1908. Most importantly for historians, Jane's life is comparatively well documented, which made it easy for her to haunt me: she left multiple accounts narrating her personal history, some of which were published during her lifetime, and she appears in many other sources, including other people's diaries, meeting minutes, and church and government records. Nevertheless, Jane's story is left out of books on African American history, American women's history, and the history of the American West. I think that's because she was Mormon.[1]

Consider one of Jane's contemporaries, a woman we know as Bridget "Biddy" Mason. Born into slavery, Bridget was the legal property of Robert Marion Smith, who took her and other enslaved people to Utah in 1847 and then to California in 1851. In 1855, Bridget sued for her freedom and that of her extended family in order to keep Smith from moving them all to Texas. She prevailed, winning the freedom of fourteen people in all. Bridget chose the surname Mason and established a successful medical practice in the Los Angeles area. She purchased land, built a home for her family, and was a leader in the group that established the Los Angeles branch of the First African Methodist Episcopal Church. Mason died in 1891.[2]

Although Mason left a far smaller paper trail than Jane, scholars include her story in histories of African Americans, American women, and the American

West both because it is important and because it fits the larger tales we want to tell.[3] Jane's story, in contrast, does not seem all that important at first glance, and it does not appear to fit the themes of the grand narratives of American history. Although modern historians may acknowledge the radicalism of the early Church of Jesus Christ of Latter-day Saints (the LDS, or Mormon, Church), they generally see Mormonism as a socially and politically conservative institution that has subjected women and people of color to discrimination and oppression. It is true that women's power in the church has been systematically eroded over the course of its history, and the ideology of white supremacy has certainly influenced the distribution of power, the attitudes of members, and the practice of the faith. Still, the story is more complex than this simple account acknowledges. In some times, and some places, women have wielded considerable power within the church; in some ways, people of color have found liberation in the church instead of oppression. But Jane's membership in the LDS Church leads many observers to see her as a dupe or a victim, someone who was deluded by false promises or exploited by a dishonest institution. While Mason's story illustrates the move from slavery to freedom, Jane seems to go in the opposite direction, choosing to affiliate with a religious organization that treats her as a second-class citizen. Mason's story shows women acting independently and successfully in the public sphere; Jane submitted to the will of the white men who led her church. Mason's story provides an example of a black woman actively nurturing community institutions in the West; Jane seems only to have contributed to the construction of a semitheocratic society that privileged white men. Nevertheless, both Biddy Mason and Jane James played roles in the histories of African Americans, American women, and the American West. To understand American history, we need both stories.

Jane's story is important because it troubles the waters in our grand narratives. Jane's life expands our understanding of nineteenth-century African American history beyond the standard narratives of slavery and freedom, the founding of black churches, and even the long fight for civil rights. Jane's story illuminates geographic regions (rural Connecticut, urban Utah) and religious options (Congregationalism, Mormonism) not often discussed in African American history. Jane's life broadens our sense of nineteenth-century American women's lives as well. Jane was not active in the big social and political causes of her day—she did not agitate for abolition, temperance, suffrage, or any of the other causes in which women's activism figured so prominently. Yet her entire life was shaped by her identity as a woman and the struggle to conform to the gender norms of her community. Jane's experience demonstrates how those norms limited her opportunities and made her vulnerable to attack, even as they offered some kinds of support and community not available to men. Finally, Jane's story improves our understanding of the history of the nineteenth-century American West by increasing our knowledge of African Americans' lives in the region.

Although the West has been a place of refuge for countless religious groups over the course of American history, we have rarely included African Americans among those who went west for religious reasons. Recognizing Jane's religious motivations in moving to the Salt Lake Valley helps us begin to tell that part of the story. Grappling with Jane's presence also helps us acknowledge the ways race shaped western societies: Jane's experience demonstrates that even when those societies were overwhelmingly white, they still wrestled with the construction and meaning of whiteness and other racial identities. When we include Jane and people like her—people who work against the grain of our standard narratives—the stories we tell about American history become more complicated, more nuanced, and more interesting.

Attentive readers will have noticed that after the opening paragraph I have referred to Jane almost exclusively by her first name. This is a deliberate choice, and not one easily made. For African Americans living in the shadow of slavery, surnames could be a mark of independence and self-ownership. But for women, surnames could also mark a different kind of ownership—that of their husbands. Jane Elizabeth Manning James used three different surnames over the course of her long life: she was born into the Manning family, and she married Isaac James and Frank Perkins. She used "Jane Manning" (and sometimes added her middle initial or her full middle name) until her first marriage, but thereafter the only people who used this name were those who considered her marriage irrelevant. She used "Jane E. James" and variants of that name ("Jane James," "Jane E. M. James," and so on) throughout most of the rest of her life, with the exception of a few years when she was married to Frank Perkins and employed "Jane Perkins" on an inconsistent basis. Jane did not demonstrate a strong attachment to the Manning name: she rarely mentioned her father, and she did not revert to her birth name after divorcing Isaac James. So I use Jane's first name throughout this book because it is the name that she used most consistently, and because I want to keep the focus on her, rather than on the men whose names sometimes marked her as "theirs."[4] This choice has the added benefit of making the story easier to read.

I was instantly intrigued by Jane's story when I first encountered it. Jane's short autobiography, written sometime between 1902 and 1908, showed early Mormonism from a different angle than I had ever seen. Until recently, Jane has been almost invisible in histories of Mormonism, because she is neither white nor male, and the prototypical Mormon has always been a white man. The LDS Church has been characterized as "democratic" because, unlike many religious institutions, it makes ordinary men members of its priesthood. But Jane was a woman, and women could not hold the priesthood. (They still cannot.) And Jane married an African American man, who was not allowed to hold the priesthood because of his race. Thus, although the priesthood looked universal from the point of view of white men, Jane's story revealed the ways in which that democratic structure was actually quite hierarchical. People of African descent were also prohibited from participating in most temple ceremonies. For many Mormons the temple is at the core of LDS practice, but Jane was not allowed to perform the rituals she believed were crucial to her salvation. Instead, her faith centered on other kinds of intense religious experiences that she described in her autobiography: speaking in tongues, faith healings, and moments of direct communication with God through dreams, visions, and trance states.[5] Through Jane's eyes, I saw a form of Mormonism that de-centered priesthood and temple rituals and focused instead on supernatural religious experiences and a sense of divine favor that flowed from those experiences.

Unsurprisingly, I am not the only person to be interested in Jane's story. More and more Latter-day Saints have become aware of Jane since LDS Church leaders received a revelation in 1978 extending the priesthood to "all worthy male members of the church," a revelation that also resulted in the lifting of the restriction that had kept Jane out of many temple ceremonies. In part because of this revelation, some Latter-day Saints became more interested in their church's early black members. They started researching and writing about Jane and others—but especially about Jane, whose life was better documented than many nineteenth-century African Americans'. Jane also attracted attention because she had been a domestic servant in the home of Joseph Smith, the founder of the church, and her memories were prized sources about the last years of his life. Jane's connection to Smith, I think, is one reason for the explosion of Latter-day Saint representations of her in the late 1990s and early 2000s: as Mormons approached the 2005 bicentennial of their founder's birth, talking about Jane was a way to talk about Joseph.

As a scholar of American religious history, I often find these popular representations of Jane James deeply discomfiting. The stereotypes of blackness, the "traditional" constructions of femininity, and the selective presentations of fact that they often employ make me squirm. They flatten Jane's experience, tidying up the messiness of her life. By packaging her up in a neat little box, such representations diminish Jane's humanity. They make her easier for Mormons to adopt as a role model, but they also make her less interesting as an historical subject. They also reduce Jane to her Mormonism: her religious commitment to Joseph Smith and the church he founded takes center stage and outshines all the other facets of Jane's story.[6]

I am under no illusions: this book is also a representation of Jane's life. It is likely to inform future stories about Jane. I am not a member of the LDS Church, and my interests diverge from those of people who tell Jane's story either to promote the faith of Latter-day Saints by praising "Aunt Jane's" steadfast faith, or to tear down the church by using Jane to point out its hypocrisy and racism. Still, I come to Jane's story with an agenda as much as anyone else does: I find it fascinating for what it tells us about religion and race in nineteenth-century

America, and especially for the ways Jane gives us a new perspective on race in Mormonism. As a nineteenth-century African American Mormon woman, Jane was unusual, but Joseph Smith and Brigham Young were also anomalous in their own ways. Attending to Jane's life helps us understand how race and gender shaped religious experiences in the nineteenth century as well as how religious experience shaped racial and gender identities.

I take seriously religious studies scholar Eddie Glaude's argument that "African American religion emerges in the encounter between faith, in all of its complexity, and white supremacy," and I tell the story of Jane's religious experience as one of African American—and women's—religion, shaped by overlapping and intersecting systems of oppression. My goal is not only to thoroughly document Jane's life; it is also to show what life was like for someone like Jane: a black person, a woman, a person on the outside of the power structures that shaped society. In the chapters that follow, I present Jane's story in all its messy detail. Jane was a black woman, born to a mother who grew up in slavery. Jane's literacy seems to have been limited: as far as we know, she did not leave any documents in her own hand. All of these facts mean that the historical traces of Jane's story are somewhat fainter than we might like. Although she spent much of her life near the epicenter of the LDS Church, she did not attract the kind of attention that white men and women did. Her life before she joined the church is even less documented. Much of this story, then, is conjectural: I have combined the few documents that do exist with evidence about the lives of Jane's peers—African Americans, women, Latter-day Saints—to flesh out the possibilities and follow the suggestions of the evidence. Where the sources are inconclusive, I imagine the possibilities and discuss the most plausible scenarios. Although such speculation may frustrate readers who want "just the facts, ma'am," the glimpses that these educated guesses offer us into Jane's experience are worth it. Relatively few African Americans joined the LDS Church during Jane's lifetime, and even fewer made the treks to Nauvoo, Illinois, and to Utah's Salt Lake Valley. Tracing Jane's life reveals some of the less-frequently trodden paths sometimes open to nineteenth-century African American women (and men). Jane's story expands our understanding of the range of possibilities for African Americans, and especially African American women, in the nineteenth century—and, as a result, it may help expand our sense of possibility in our time as well.[7]

I hope that you will not just take my word for it: I have included Jane's three most extensive narratives of her life in the Appendix. With the permission of Jane's great-great-grandson, I have also included the two patriarchal blessings Jane received, making these texts publicly available for the first time. Jane meditated on the words of these two blessings, given to her personally by the brother and the nephew of Joseph Smith, and they shaped her religious practice. Primary sources like these are the raw materials out of which historians create the stories we tell. Although I have silently corrected the spelling, grammar, capitalization, and punctuation of primary sources throughout the body of this book for ease of reading, I have left the texts of the primary sources in the appendix as close as possible to the original documents. I invite you to bring your own analyses of these sources to the conversation about Jane and the histories in which she participated.

1

When a Child

(*ca. 1820–1843*)

Jane was a survivor. It ran in her family. Jane's grandmother was captured in Africa, endured the Middle Passage, and lived out her days in slavery. But she raised at least two daughters to adulthood and lived to know her grandchildren. Jane's mother was enslaved from birth but as an adult she claimed her freedom, owned a home, and raised a family. Jane learned from these women, and she thrived in ways that surpassed their most lofty expectations. From what we can piece together of Jane's family history and her early life, nothing portended the unusual path she would follow. Born in Connecticut, Jane would become a Mormon and move first to Illinois and then to Utah. She would come to know, work for, and worship with many of the most prominent men and women in the Church of Jesus Christ of Latter-day Saints (the LDS, or Mormon, Church). And, though she would be excluded from most temple rituals during her lifetime, in the century after her death she would become an important example of faith for Mormons worldwide.

The vast majority of Africans who were enslaved in British North America had been transported from West Africa on British ships. Most were taken to the Caribbean or the southern colonies, but some were sent north. Jane's grandmother eventually arrived in Wilton, Connecticut, where she was owned by Ebenezer Abbott. She might have arrived in New England directly from Africa, but she may also have landed first in another part of the British Empire—Barbados or Jamaica, for example—before being sold northward. Abbott called her Gin; Jane knew her grandmother as Philes. Jane's mother, who was also called Philes but sometimes used the name Eliza, was born into slavery in 1785. David Hermon Van Hoosear, a local historian of Wilton and the great-great grandson of Abbott, wrote that Abbott gave the young Philes to his daughter Sarah when Sarah married Uriah S. Grummon in 1801. Grummon accused the teenaged Philes of "pilfering his wine," among other offenses, and sold her to a man living in Stamford, about thirteen miles away.[1]

In 1784, the Connecticut legislature had passed a law mandating that enslaved people born after March 1 of that year be freed at the age of twenty-five.[2] The provisions of the law were carefully crafted so that enslaved people who were, in the legislature's estimation, too old to support themselves, would remain enslaved, and thus be the responsibility of the slave-owner. Connecticut lawmakers didn't want freed slaves to become a burden on the public. By virtue of her 1785 birthdate, then, the younger Philes was freed by 1810, while Jane's grandmother remained legally enslaved for the rest of her life. Philes's imminent emancipation may have been Uriah and Sarah Grummon's true motive for selling her; by the time Abbott gave them the girl, they only had about ten years to take advantage of her labor. Selling the teenager would have allowed the Grummons to realize a small financial gain from a person they viewed as a rapidly depreciating asset.

Jane did not speak of her father, Isaac Manning, and his presence in her life is not well documented. Van Hoosear asserted that Isaac was from Newtown, Connecticut, about eighteen miles north of Wilton. He might have met Philes in the Wilton area, where he may have had relatives, or perhaps they met in Stamford. Regardless of where or how they met, Philes and Isaac became a couple and soon began having children. Although Van Hoosear claimed they had "eight or ten children," only five left traces in the historical record.[3]

Jane was probably born in her family's home in Wilton, Connecticut, on a spring day in the early 1820s. Either her grandmother or her aunt likely attended the birth. If an African or African American midwife was available, she might also have been called to assist. Childbirth was becoming more medicalized in the United States around this time: increasingly, male medical practitioners were replacing female midwives and birth attendants when women gave birth. But these trends manifested first among wealthy white families, worlds away from Philes and her baby daughter. Instead, if Jane's grandmother was able to help her daughter give birth, the event likely was marked by West African traditions. Many West Africans, likely including Jane's grandmother, understood pregnancy and childbirth to be "very dangerous and unpredictable times for the woman" giving birth. Jane's grandmother would have taught Philes to perform "complex rituals" to ward off danger both before and after the birth, including adorning newborn children with fetishes and appeasing evil spirits with food offerings.[4]

Some elder—Jane's mother or father, her grandmother, or possibly another older relative—named the new baby "Jane Elizabeth," perhaps at a naming ritual a short time after the birth. Her surname, Manning, came from her father. She joined a brother and a sister, Isaac Lewis and Sarah, in the growing Manning family. Over the next few years, Jane's mother gave birth to at least two more children, Angeline and Peter. Some of the names the Manning children bore appear to have honored their parents (Isaac, after his father; Elizabeth, a variant of a name her mother used); other names are a mix of Biblical (Sarah, Peter) and European names (Jane, Angeline, Lewis).[5]

In the 1820s just surviving the first year of life was an accomplishment, particularly for a black child. Just over a fifth of the black girls born in the United States that decade died before reaching their first birthday. Statistically, Jane's life expectancy at birth was just under thirty-five years. But Jane was tenacious. She also had the advantage of a slightly higher standard of living than many black infants at the time: in 1822, Jane's father purchased a piece of land in Wilton on which the Mannings would build their own home.[6]

We have no record of Jane's baptism in any local church during her childhood, even though most of the churches in Wilton practiced infant baptism. Jane's mother had been baptized in the Wilton Congregational Church in 1795 as the "colored servant" of Ebenezer Abbott. Perhaps this ritual demonstrated to Philes the Congregational Church's complicity in her enslavement, and in rebellion she refused to have her own children baptized. Or perhaps she and Isaac simply did not attend church regularly. If that was the case, Philes and Isaac were like many Americans—and especially, like many African Americans— at the time. Jane was born at a time of great religious upheaval in the new American republic. Scholars have dubbed this period of American history, when Americans invested a great deal of energy in religious pursuits, the Second Great Awakening. Retrospectively, we can see that the movement began in rural Connecticut and New Hampshire in the 1790s. Philes's baptism, in fact, may have been driven by the religious enthusiasm of the movement. The Awakening moved into Kentucky and Tennessee in the same decade and then swept through Central New York in the 1820s and 1830s. The movement took different forms in different places. New England, before Jane was born, experienced a subdued awakening: church membership went up, prayer circles formed, and missionary activity rose. To the west, the Awakening was more raucous: extended camp-meeting revivals featured preaching marathons and enthusiastic manifestations of the Holy Spirit including jerking, barking like dogs, and other behaviors that many white, middle-class Protestants considered scandalously undignified. In central New York, the religious creativity of the Second Great Awakening led to the flourishing of new variations on Christianity, including the founding of a movement known as Mormonism that would later attract Jane's attention.[7]

In Connecticut, the revivalism of the Second Great Awakening helped temper what some people saw as the potentially disastrous effects of the separation of church and state in the young nation. In fact, disestablishment, as this development was called, may have strengthened revivalism in Connecticut and elsewhere. The First Amendment to the US Constitution mandated that Congress should "make no law respecting an establishment of religion, or prohibiting the free exercise thereof." But in the early nineteenth century, Americans understood these statements to apply only to the federal government, *not* to the states. As a result, some states continued to support specific religious bodies well into the nineteenth century. In Connecticut, the Congregational Church, a denomination that traced its history to the Puritans, was the state church until the legislature finally yielded to pressure to disestablish in 1818. This legislative development dismayed prominent Congregational ministers like Lyman Beecher (father of Harriet Beecher Stowe, Henry Ward Beecher, Catharine Beecher, and ten other children), but Beecher discovered that his fears were unfounded. As he wrote in his autobiography, disestablishment was *"the best thing that ever happened to the State of Connecticut.* It cut the churches loose from dependence on state support. It threw them wholly on their own resources and on God. They say ministers have lost their influence; the fact is, they have gained. By voluntary efforts, societies, missions, and revivals, they exert a deeper influence than they ever could by queues, and shoe-buckles, and cocked hats, and gold-headed canes."[8]

It was during the Second Great Awakening that the black population in the United States began adopting Christianity in significant numbers. When Jane was born, the first African American denominations were just being organized as free black people increasingly left segregated, white-dominated churches and began worshiping in spaces that they themselves controlled. The founding of these denominations combined with several other factors to make Christianity more widely available than ever before to black people in the United States. Still, there were no African American congregations in Wilton in the 1820s. Instead, African Americans in the town worshiped alongside their white neighbors in biracial—though almost certainly racially segregated—congregations. In Wilton, the Second Great Awakening brought with it an uptick in women's social reform activities, often organized through the Ladies' Benevolent Society and similar associations. The Wilton Congregational Church also collaborated with the local Methodists to mount a week-long revival in 1842 that made converts of some two hundred people. These developments may have spurred Jane and her family to become more religiously active, prompting in them the sorts of questions and feelings that moved them toward conversion. But we have no record of their religious activity in the 1820s.[9]

Isaac died in about 1825, when Jane was still a young girl. In 1830, the Federal Census listed Philes Manning as the head of her own household in Wilton. The only males in the house were two boys under ten years old; the other four household members were female. Everyone in the home, according to the census taker, was free and "colored." The loss of Isaac's labor left the Manning family in a difficult economic position, with at least five children to feed, several of them very young and not yet able to earn their keep.[10] There is no clear evidence that Jane maintained any connection to her father's birth family, nor to any other male relatives besides her brothers. As Jane's story comes down to us, women held her family together—women made the family a family. Through her family's enslavement and freedom, it was the women with whom Jane remained connected.

When she dictated her life story in the early twentieth century, Jane did not open with her birth. "When a child only six years old I left my home and went to live with a family of white people," she began. This move may have been prompted by Isaac's death and the Mannings' subsequent economic need. Jane's employers, Joseph and Hannah Fitch, lived about six miles away in New Canaan. We can't know how Jane and the Fitch family found each other, though news of the position and of Jane's availability almost certainly traveled by word of mouth through various networks. Descendants of an old Connecticut family, the Fitches had distant cousins in Wilton who may have facilitated the connection. A more intriguing possibility is a black man named Robert Manning who lived in New Canaan. Could he have been a relative of Jane's father Isaac? Robert and his wife Rose were members of the New Canaan Congregational Church, which also counted Joseph and Hannah Fitch among its members. Jane was the only African American person in the Fitch household. It is possible that Jane was hired as an ordinary domestic servant, but the young age at which she began working for the Fitches suggested that she was indentured to them instead. The terms of indenture contracts varied widely, but Jane's might well have provided some payment to her family as well as assurances that in return for her labor over a fixed number of years, the Fitches would provide Jane with food, clothing, housing, and perhaps even some education. Such an arrangement relieved the financial pressures on Jane's family and ensured that she would learn the domestic skills that would enable her to earn a living as an adult.[11]

According to historian Gayle T. Tate, the duties of a domestic servant like Jane included "washing and ironing; shopping for provisions; preparing, cooking, and serving the meals; making all of the beds; polishing all of the silver; dusting, sweeping, and cleaning all of the rooms; drawing water . . . ; building and banking of fires; and endless 'fetch and carry' errands for the mistress of the house." Domestic service was one of the ways black women could make a life in nineteenth-century Connecticut. But even that niche was being threatened. In nearby New York City, female Irish immigrants were replacing African American women as domestics. New Canaan was more rural, so the rising tide of immigration did not immediately threaten Jane's position, but it's likely that as she grew up she became aware of this potential competition.[12]

The ideology of white supremacy, enacted in segregation, physical violence, socioeconomic discrimination, and myriad other ways, shaped Jane's life profoundly as she grew up. By the time Jane was old enough to understand that she was free, very few people were enslaved in Connecticut. The 1830 census counted twenty-five slaves in the entire state. Still, slavery was legal in Connecticut until 1848, and the legacy of slavery endured long afterward. Samuel St. John, a native of New Canaan who gave a speech about the town's history on Independence Day in 1876, used part of his address to reflect on the ease with which his fellow white citizens forgot about the history of slavery in their town. "Probably few of my auditors have ever reflected upon the fact that we have had slaves in New Canaan, until within a few years," he mused. "Very many families here in the last century, had one or more slaves, and when the State passed its Emancipation Act, it exempted only those born after a certain date, leaving the others still in slavery." For Jane and others whose families were shaped by slavery, this history was more difficult to forget. Samuel St. John continued his discussion of slavery in New Canaan by remembering how the institution was built into the landscape and then hidden in plain sight: "The whipping-post stood at the angle of the road south-east of us (a few feet north of the present lamp post)—and in my boyhood I witnessed the whipping of two men for petty thieving. The physical infliction was trifling, but the moral degradation was truly pitiable. The post remained there many years but its name was changed to sign-post. Public notices were posted upon it." Born in 1813, St. John was nearly Jane's contemporary. She might also have seen the whippings he witnessed. She was surely familiar with the whipping post, not far from where she attended worship services. Jane almost certainly knew people whose punishment was meted out at that site.[13]

The 1830 federal census provides a sense of the racial makeup of New Canaan. Jane was one of twenty black people who lived in the town. Most of the African Americans in New Canaan lived with white families, but there were three households headed by black men, including Robert and Rose Manning's home. Only one enslaved person was counted in the census, a woman whom the census taker estimated was between the ages of fifty-five and one hundred years old. Probably reflecting the employment situation in New Canaan, African American girls and women under the age of twenty-four outnumbered African American boys and men in the same age bracket by almost three to one. Like Jane, the other black girls and young women could find work in the town as domestic servants. But local manufacturing jobs that might have been considered appropriate for black men instead went to white people. Although some black men were able to open their own businesses, most had to look elsewhere for employment.[14]

To six-year-old Jane, the Fitches must have seemed ancient: Joseph had been born in the 1750s; Hannah, a bit younger, was born in 1760. Both had lived through the Revolutionary War. Joseph and Hannah had several children, all grown— parents, aunts, and uncles in their own right. Jane later recalled that she "was raised by [the Fitches'] daughter." She may have been referring to the Fitches' daughter Hannah Mitchell, who was widowed around the time Jane was born. Hannah and her daughter may have moved back into her parents' home sometime thereafter.[15]

In the spring of 1833, Joseph Fitch died unexpectedly and Jane found herself the domestic servant of a widow.[16] Suddenly dependent on the financial support of her children (who would inherit Joseph Fitch's estate), Mrs. Fitch might have found it necessary to economize by eliminating household staff or even moving in with one of her children. Jane's economic future, and that of her family, was uncertain.

In the immediate aftermath of Fitch's death, though, Jane's labor was more necessary than ever to accomplishing the work of the household. Mr. Fitch's body had to be prepared for viewing and later interment. Although Jane may have helped with this task, it was ritual work customarily reserved for those close to the dead. Jane may have been dispatched, instead, to the local carpenter to request the fabrication of a coffin for her late employer. For the next few days, Joseph Fitch's corpse remained in his home. Jane likely helped prepare the room where he was laid out, hanging swaths of black crepe, covering mirrors with white cloth, or perhaps even removing the furniture altogether. Friends and family members called at the Fitch house to see the dead man's body and to sit with the corpse, keeping watch until the burial.[17] Jane prepared food and drink for the mourners, served the guests, and cleaned up after them.

On the day of the funeral, the mourners gathered at the Fitch house. In all likelihood, someone said a prayer or offered a few thoughts to the group. Then, perhaps, they walked with Fitch's body to New Canaan Congregational Church, where the Reverend Theophilus Smith preached a funeral oration over the corpse and community members filed up to the coffin one more time to view the dead man's remains. Whether Fitch's funeral procession included this interlude at the church, its ultimate destination was the grave that had been prepared on Fitch's family land. At this final resting place, Reverend Smith offered prayers and perhaps another meditation. The newly widowed Mrs. Fitch, her children, and her grandchildren watched as the coffin was lowered into the ground. Then Mrs. Fitch stepped forward and tossed a handful of dirt into the open grave.[18] Was Jane there to bear witness to these rituals of leave-taking? Did she walk with Mrs. Fitch, perhaps worried that the old woman might be overcome with grief and exhaustion? Or did she stay behind, cleaning up after the people who had been occupying the house for the last few days, putting the furniture back in order? Perhaps she used their long-awaited absence from the house to get some fresh air or visit with friends for a bit.

Although Jane made no comment on Fitch's character, other historical evidence makes clear that black women working in white households were extremely vulnerable to abuse and exploitation by both masters and mistresses. So Jane might have been glad that Mr. Fitch was finally gone: the loss of her employer may have felt, to her, more like a chance for a new beginning. Perhaps Joseph Fitch was an old tyrant, filling her days with unreasonable demands, impossible to please. Perhaps he made unwanted sexual advances, and she endeavored never to be alone with him. Perhaps he beat her for her transgressions, real or imagined. It's possible that Jane saw Fitch's death as an answer to her prayers, that she, alone or with others, had used folk magic to hurry his demise. Such feelings were not uncommon among domestic servants.[19]

The uncertainty produced by Fitch's death, though, must have weighed on Jane. Joseph Fitch was the man who supported her, who gave his name to the family that clothed her, fed her, and provided something that looked like security and a future for her and her family. Jane's future suddenly looked murky. Yet it appears that Jane stayed with Hannah Fitch, either because her indenture contract required it or because Fitch continued to employ her. Eight years after Joseph Fitch's death, Jane still lived in New Canaan, suggesting that she still worked for Hannah Fitch.[20]

Another major event soon followed Joseph Fitch's death: Jane's first child, Sylvester, was born around 1839. The identity of Sylvester's father, and the circumstances of his conception, were matters on which Jane maintained a defiant silence. Sylvester's existence raised questions: he looked different from Jane's other children, with lighter skin and straighter hair. The woman to whom Jane dictated her life story many decades later, Elizabeth Roundy, tasked with finding out who Sylvester's father was, asked Jane's brother Isaac instead of directing the question to Jane herself. Isaac told Roundy that Sylvester was the son of a white preacher. Sylvester himself told a different story: his granddaughter Henrietta Bankhead remembered that he was the child of a French Canadian man whom she believed was white. As far as we know, Jane herself never spoke of the matter.[21]

The theories that Sylvester's father was white depended on, and partly stemmed from, Sylvester's physical difference from Jane's later children, who were fathered by an African American man, and from Jane herself. But this kind of quick-and-dirty genetic analysis, based on visual evidence, is deeply flawed. Sylvester's father may have been a white preacher, a French Canadian, or even both. But he may also have been a Native American or African American man, or a man of more obviously mixed racial heritage. He could have been a farmer, a merchant, a traveler—or a friend or relative of Jane's employer.

A more difficult question is whether Jane was a willing partner in Sylvester's conception. It is certainly possible that she enjoyed a consensual sexual relationship with a man whose existence is otherwise undocumented, and that Sylvester was the product of that union. Particularly in the antebellum United States, legal marriage was often unavailable to African Americans even if they were free. At least two of Jane's siblings, Isaac and Sarah, entered into marriage-like relationships in Wilton, but no marriage records documented these unions. The same is true of Jane's mother. The lack of documentation, then, does not preclude the possibility that Jane had a socially, if not legally, recognized husband who was Sylvester's father. African Americans also formed relationships that required more limited commitment but were, nevertheless, recognized and sanctioned by their communities. Sylvester may have been the child of such a "sweethearting" or "taking up" relationship. The experience of another black woman who was Jane's contemporary, Harriet Jacobs, offers another suggestive possibility. Born into slavery in North Carolina, as a teenager Jacobs found herself the target of her white master's sexual threats. To protect herself from rape by her master, and to provoke her master into selling her, Jacobs took as her sexual partner a different white man and ultimately gave birth to two children she conceived with him. Like Jacobs, Jane may have entered the sexual relationship that produced Sylvester for strategic reasons, without emotional attachment or the intention to marry.[22]

Jane's silence seems to foreclose any possibility of answering the questions that swirled around her Connecticut-born son. But what happens if we treat Jane's silence as evidence in itself, rather than as the refusal to provide evidence? Jane's refusal to answer questions about Sylvester's father suggests at least the possibility that she was ashamed about Sylvester's conception, an emotional state that probably would not have followed from a socially accepted relationship with Sylvester's father. Again, a comparison to Harriet Jacobs is useful: after escaping slavery, Jacobs confided to the Reverend Jeremiah Durham, a black pastor, "some of the most important events of [her] life," including how she came to have two children. Durham commended Jacobs, telling her, "Your straight-forward answers do you credit," but he warned her, "don't answer every body so openly. It might give some heartless people a pretext for treating you with contempt." For Jacobs, the logic of her decision did not mitigate the shame she felt. "I know I did wrong," she wrote of her decision to have sex with a white man to whom she was not married. Religious Studies scholar Ann Taves suggested that Durham's warning may have been the reason Jacobs later wrote that she "had determined to let others think as . . . they pleased but my lips should be sealed and no one had a right to question me." Jane likewise may have been ashamed of her decision to have sex outside the bounds of marriage, regardless of whether she made the decision freely or it was the only path available to her.[23]

The shame Jane felt might also have been the result of sexual assault: Sylvester may have been the child of rape. Scholar of French and Francophone Studies Sharon Johnson writes that "Reading for rape not only involves analyzing difficult, even gruesome narratives, but also reading in between the lines to interpret euphemisms and code words for rape, the perpetrator's act and/or the victim's demise." In Jane's case, "reading in between the lines" means that we must interpret her silence, a task that should be undertaken with the utmost caution and restraint. For a woman in Jane's position, the incentives to remain silent about sexual violence were powerful. As literature scholar Hazel V. Carby writes, "Rape has always involved patriarchal notions of women being, at best, not entirely unwilling accomplices, if not outwardly inviting sexual attack. The links between black women and illicit sexuality consolidated during the antebellum years had powerful ideological consequences for the next hundred and fifty years." By the time Elizabeth Roundy inquired about the identity of Sylvester's father at the turn of the twentieth century, the "links between black women and illicit sexuality" were cemented in place. In addition, by the time Roundy was asking around, Jane had become a Mormon, among whom the specter of sexual shame was a powerful force. Even powerful white Mormon women generally refused to speak of sexual violence they encountered. Historian Andrea Radke-Moss writes that white Mormon women spoke of the sexual violence they experienced in a late-1830s conflict with non-Mormons "with sadness, resignation, and mostly with silence. . . . Any mention [of sexual assault] might be considered delicate, sensitive, and private or would have invited shame for a woman in a nineteenth-century context."[24]

For Jane, the disincentives to speak about rape were even stronger than they were for white Mormon women. If she was raped, Jane might have told her mother, her sisters, or trusted female friends. But Jane may have chosen to keep her male relatives in the dark, perhaps because she feared that they, too, would shame her—or because she feared for what they might do (or what might be done to them) if they tried to avenge her.[25]

Jane may also have kept silent in order to keep from propping up stereotypes that many black women saw as harmful to African Americans. The portrayal of black women as the victims of white men's sexual aggression was so common as to become a stereotype in the nineteenth century. Even in the twenty-first century, our inclination to suppose that Jane was raped may be rooted in similar stereotypes. As scholar Frances Smith Foster asked a mostly white group of academics: "Why do you want all of us [black women] to have been raped?" In the antebellum United States, depictions of black women as the victims of white men's sexual aggression and, especially, images of enslaved black women as the victims of white male masters' sexual violence, inspired pity among the white consumers of these portrayals and built support for the abolition of slavery. In the twenty-first century such images work in much the same way, inspiring people to work for the redress of the historical wrong of slavery and for the achievement of a more egalitarian, anti-racist society. Portraying Jane as the victim of rape makes the narrative of black women's victimization by white men specific by supplying a particular victim—Jane Manning—in place of the generic "black women." For modern Latter-day Saints this specific narrative makes Jane a survivor of sexual assault, transforming her into a role model for women who have experienced sexual violence and other forms of trauma. In addition, portraying Sylvester as the son of a rapist renders Jane an innocent victim rather than a woman who transgressed norms of sexual morality, and it fashions her as a model of self-sacrificing motherhood because she kept the child conceived in rape and raised him with the same love and care she gave to all her children.[26]

Jane's adamant silence means we can never be certain about the circumstances under which Sylvester was conceived. But we can be reasonably sure that those circumstances were ones for which Jane believed her community would hold her responsible, regardless of whether she actually had the power to affect them, and that they were circumstances that Jane feared would provoke the "contempt" of those around her. Rather than enduring that humiliation, Jane kept silent.

Isaac's memory was that Jane returned to her family's home to give birth to Sylvester. There, she was attended by her mother. It is possible the family brought in a midwife to attend the birth; they enjoyed a slightly higher standard of living than some black families, since they owned property. But it seems likely that Philes cared for Jane during childbirth just as her mother had once cared for her, and that she used the same techniques as Jane's grandmother to assure that both Jane and her baby would be healthy. Jane probably returned to her employment as soon as she was able. But Sylvester would have had to nurse for at least the first few months of his life; Jane may have hoped to keep nursing him for up to three years, the traditional practice in many West African and African American communities. It seems most likely that Jane took Sylvester to work with her, nursing him between tasks, talking to him as she worked. Perhaps once he was weaned, Jane took him back to her mother's house, leaving Sylvester under Philes's care so that she could return to her job without distraction. In 1840 the federal census taker duly noted the presence of one "Free Colored Person—Male—Under 10" in Jane's family home.[27]

On February 14, 1841, Jane became a member of the New Canaan Congregational Church. She did not give a reason for joining; perhaps she simply felt that it was an appropriate step to take as she came of age. It may have been a strategic decision: Hannah Fitch may have expressed some concern about the morality of Jane's behavior when she became pregnant with Sylvester, and joining the church could have been a way to assuage her employer's concerns. It is possible that Jane hoped to gain access to the church's disciplinary system in case she needed to lodge a complaint against Sylvester's father or another local man. Jane may also have found the church's message compelling. Whatever her reasons, Jane was not alone: the church attracted a small but steady stream of members throughout the ministry of Theophilus Smith, who had been the pastor of the church for a decade by the time Jane joined.

Founded in 1733, the New Canaan Congregational Church was over a century old by the time Jane joined (Figure 1.1). In 1801 the Congregationalists and the Presbyterians, who differed more in how their institutions were organized and governed than in their doctrines, signed a document that became known as the Plan of Union. They pledged to cooperate with each other in

OLD CONGREGATIONAL MEETING HOUSE,
NEW CANAAN CT. ERECTED 1752.

Figure 1.1 This engraving of the Old Congregational Church shows the 1752 building in which Jane formally joined the New Canaan Congregational Church. Division of Rare and Manuscript Collections, Cornell University Library.

the evangelization of the growing nation, dividing the land into sections and assigning responsibility for each section to either the Congregational or the Presbyterian Church. This way, they reasoned, their missionaries would not waste resources competing with one another. They made provisions for Presbyterian pastors to lead Congregational churches and vice versa, and for lay people of both denominations to worship together and govern congregations jointly. In Connecticut, one consequence of the Plan of Union was that Congregationalists, the descendants of the Puritans, lost their distinct identity in the minds of the public, and became known as Presbyterians. Jane would later claim in her autobiography that she had joined the Presbyterians as a teenager, but there was no

Presbyterian church in New Canaan or in Wilton. Southwestern Connecticut, where Jane lived, was Congregational territory. Like many, Jane did not distinguish between the two denominations.[28]

The New Canaan Congregational Church that Jane joined in 1841 was the same church Joseph Fitch had belonged to, and that Hannah Fitch still belonged to. The church's records noted that Jane was "propounded the usual time," meaning that Jane's desire to join the church was announced to the congregation at regular intervals for two weeks. Then, on Sunday, February 14, she was "received to the full communion of the church in the usual form." The "usual form" was that prospective members stood in the aisle of the church sanctuary and publicly assented to the church's covenant and confession of faith. If the church members were willing to accept the new person, they stood up to signify their agreement. As Jane stood, Smith read the words the congregation had voted a decade earlier to adopt as their covenant and confession of faith. "In the presence of the Lord and of this assembly," he said, "you do now appear desiring publicly and solemnly to enter into covenant with God and with this church according to the Gospel, professing your full assent to a summary of the faith once delivered to the saints." Smith then proclaimed the ten articles of faith on which the congregation had agreed. "You believe there is one self existent God, infinite, eternal, unchangeable, in his being, wisdom, power, holiness, justice, goodness, and truth," he began. He went on, making his way through sections that described the natures of the trinity and of human beings, the conditions under which humans might be saved, the sacraments (baptism and communion), and the coming resurrection and judgment.[29]

As Smith read each article of the confession, church members sitting in the pews were reminded of their own agreement to these items even as they watched to see whether Jane assented. Finally the pastor concluded: "Thus you believe in your heart and thus you confess before men." As it was written in the church's records, no question mark at the end prompted a response from the prospective church member, but other Congregational churches' confessions framed this statement as a question requiring an answer. Jane must have demonstrated her assent in some way, but perhaps she paused for a moment—took a breath, looked around, gazed at the faces who waited for her answer. Reverend Smith's attendance records show that two hundred seventy-five people were there that day. Perhaps Jane's eyes rested on the handful of black faces in the congregation, probably clustered together in the gallery where they sat apart from the white congregants. Perhaps she glanced at Hannah Fitch. Nearly eight years a widow by that time, Fitch may have been the person in the congregation who had known Jane the longest. Or perhaps Jane was nervous, worried the church wouldn't accept her, eager to get this done. Either way, she agreed to the deal Reverend Smith offered: she covenanted with God and New Canaan Congregational Church, affirming that she believed as they believed, and that she would do as they did. Jane was also baptized that day, finally undergoing the ritual that her parents had not pursued for her when she was a child. Sprinkled on the forehead with consecrated water, the church members believed that Jane was cleansed of her sin and accepted into the family of God.[30]

As Jane began her new life as a member of the Congregational Church, Hannah Fitch was slipping away. Fitch died in December of 1841, not quite a year after Jane's baptism. Jane's commitment to the congregation did not last long after that. As an elderly woman, narrating her life story, Jane recalled that when she joined the "Presbyterian" church, she "did not feel satisfied; it seemed to me there was something more that I was looking for." That "something more" came in an unexpected form: "I had belonged to the Church about eighteen months when an Elder of the Church of Jesus Christ of Latter-day Saints was travelling through our country preached there." The elder was Charles Wesley Wandell.[31]

Born in Cortland, New York, in 1819, Wandell was about Jane's age. He had been baptized into the LDS Church in 1837 and ordained an elder a few months later. As an elder, Wandell held the divine priesthood that Latter-day Saints believed God had restored to earth through the church's founder Joseph Smith. Like Wandell, many male converts to the LDS Church received the priesthood shortly after joining the movement and then quickly received leadership assignments. By his twenty-first birthday, Wandell's biographer wrote, he "was busily engaged in missionary work in New York and New England."[32] By the spring of 1842, Wandell was serving as presiding elder of a branch in Norwalk, Connecticut, a port town just over five miles southeast of New Canaan. As the leader of his small congregation, Wandell's duties included recruiting new members to the upstart religion. Preaching in New Canaan and other towns surrounding Norwalk was one way to do that. The substance of Wandell's missionary preaching is lost to history, but in it Jane found something persuasive, something convincing—something that went beyond and completed what she had found in the Congregational church. As Jane remembered it, the pastor of her church, the Rev. Theophilus Smith, learned that she was interested in hearing Wandell preach and forbade her to attend the event, but she went anyway.

Jane recalled that she "was fully convinced that it was the true Gospel [Wandell] presented and [she] must embrace it." A week later, she was baptized and confirmed as a member of the Church of Jesus Christ of Latter-day Saints. Jane's dry, unemotional explanation for why she accepted the LDS message was typical among converts to Mormonism. Nineteenth-century Mormon converts frequently relied on rationalistic explanations that showed the superiority of Mormonism to other available religious options. Like other converts, Jane found Wandell's message "convincing." The logical next step was to "embrace it."[33]

Jane's brief explanation leaves us to speculate about other factors that may have influenced her decision to leave the Congregationalists for the Mormons. A young religion, Mormonism may have seemed more egalitarian to Jane than the historic, respectable Congregationalism of New Canaan. Mormonism also presented an expansive, inviting vision of a radically different future in which believers played a vital role in building God's kingdom on earth. Congregationalism, on the other hand, represented the status quo, projecting the existing order of society into the future and expecting change only after believers' deaths. Perhaps Jane was attracted to the possibility that Mormonism offered of a future that was different from the past, a home that was not like southwestern Connecticut, perhaps even a social role that transcended the options available to black women in New England.[34]

The Latter-day Saints did not accept Jane's Congregational baptism, because they did not believe anyone other than LDS priesthood holders had the divine authority to perform baptisms. Thus, for the second time in two years, Jane was baptized. Unlike the Congregational church's baptismal ritual, which merely dampened Jane's brow, Mormon baptism required full immersion. Wandell and the elders who assisted him may have built a baptismal pool for this purpose or simply availed themselves of a local water source like the Norwalk River. Jane and Wandell both waded into the water (Figure 1.2). Wandell recited the formula

Figure 1.2 A detail from LDS artist Frederick Piercy's drawing "Ceremony of Baptism," published in 1852, shows a Mormon elder pronouncing the words of the ceremony before immersing the female baptismal candidate.

given in a revelation to the founder of the church, Joseph Smith: "Jane Elizabeth Manning," he said, "Having been commissioned of Jesus Christ, I baptize you in the name of the Father, and of the Son, and of the Holy Ghost. Amen."[35] Holding fast to Wandell's forearm, Jane went under the water and emerged cleansed of her past sins. Immediately afterward, at least one elder laid his hands on her head and prayed that she would receive the gift of the Holy Ghost.

A year later, in 1843, Jane appeared in the New Canaan Congregational Church records again. She had not, in the judgment of her fellow church members, been upholding her end of the covenant to which she assented. "Whereas," the congregation resolved, "Jane E. Manning has without our approbation or consent wholly withdrawn and separated herself from the fellowship of this church and has since gone to a distant part of the country (Nauvoo . . . , Illinois) and thus placed herself beyond the reach of this church to labor farther with her; therefore *Resolved* that we withdraw our watch and care over her, and consider her as no longer a member of this church."[36] Jane was probably unaware of this resolution: she had, as the church members observed, completely separated herself from the congregation, left the state, and effectively turned her back on the Congregational Church. But Jane did not experience this as a rejection of the congregation and the God with which she had covenanted only a short time earlier; rather, she felt, she was embracing the fulfillment of everything she had promised, and everything that had been promised to her. She was making her own beginning.

2

We Walked

(ca. 1842–1843)

After her LDS baptism, Jane went back to her everyday life. She no longer worked for Hannah Fitch, who had died, but she may have been employed by one of Hannah's children. Or she might have picked up odd jobs, filling in when extra help was needed, or taking in laundry. The latter strategy would have allowed Jane to continue nursing Sylvester, ensuring that he got the nutrition he needed even if the older members of Jane's family may have been unsure sometimes where their next meal would come from. When she told her own story many years later, Jane did not discuss these details. Instead, she pointed to an event that, for her, affirmed her decision to be baptized: "About three weeks after [my baptism and confirmation in the LDS Church] while kneeling at prayer the Gift of Tongues came upon me and frightened the whole family who were in the next room."[1] By the 1840s, when Jane was baptized, the LDS Church was well differentiated from the evangelical Protestant churches with which it competed most closely. One of its distinctive characteristics was Mormons' embrace of "spiritual gifts," including the gift of tongues.

Latter-day Saints understood the gift of tongues to come in two forms: *glossolalia*, or speaking in an unknown language (usually thought to be the language of Adam); and *xenoglossia*, or speaking in a foreign language not known to the speaker. They found xenoglossia useful because it enabled missionaries to communicate with potential converts in their own languages, regardless of the missionaries' training. They understood glossolalia, on the other hand, as a sign from God that, as LDS thinker Orson Pratt put it, "assured [believers], not only of the truth of the doctrine, but that they themselves were accepted of God."[2] Jane gave no indication that those who heard her speak in tongues understood her words or recognized them as an identifiable foreign language, so her experience was more likely glossolalia. Either way, the result was a confirmation of her faith.

Although Jane might have been startled to hear strange words coming from her mouth, Latter-day Saints had thoroughly accepted the practice of speaking in tongues. Critics of the movement mocked them for it. The *Painesville (Ohio) Telegraph*, for example, reported in February 1831 that the Saints "are taken with a fit of jabbering that which they neither understand themselves nor anybody else, and this they call speaking foreign languages by divine inspiration." In 1834, church founder Joseph Smith instructed church members that the gift of tongues, though useful for spreading the Latter-day Saint message, was not intended for "the government of the Church." As church leaders interpreted this statement, tongues were useful for missions and for encouragement of the faithful, but the messages received through tongues were not to be taken as authoritative doctrine, nor were they binding on the church as an institution.[3]

Latter-day Saints were not the only ones speaking in tongues in nineteenth-century America. In the United States, glossolalia was most often associated with members of the United Society of Believers in Christ's Second Coming, commonly known as the Shakers. In an 1828 exposé of Shakerism, critic William Haskett described a Shaker meeting:

> The sisters began to talk in "unknown tongues." Then commenced a scene of awful riot. Now was heard the loud shouts of the brethren, then the soft, but hurried note of the sisters, whose gifts were the apostolic gift of tongues. These gently gestured their language, waved themselves backward and forward like a ship on the billows of a ceased storm, shook their heads, seized their garments, and then violently stamped on the floor. The exercise had lost its violence, and exertion grew faint; yet a continued din of frightful yells rendered the scene a scene of confusion, a scene of blasphemy, an awful scene.

Evangelical Christians in the United States and Europe also experienced glossolalia, particularly during revivals, though the phenomenon was relatively rare. Many Protestant leaders dismissed the practice, but some observers tried to discern what they understood to be the Holy Spirit in the midst of the otherwise suspect phenomenon. Horace Bushnell, a well-respected Congregationalist minister, wrote in defense of glossolalia (and, particularly, some of its practitioners) shortly before the Civil War, using anecdotal evidence to argue that tongues and other spiritual gifts might even come upon respectable Christian people:

> Nothing is farther off from the christian expectation of our New England communities, than the gift of tongues. . . . And yet, a very near christian friend, intelligent in the highest degree, and perfectly reliable to me as my right hand, who was present at a rather private, social gathering of christian disciples, . . . relates that, after one of the brethren

had been speaking, in a strain of discouraging self-accusation, another present shortly rose, with a strangely beaming look, and, fixing his eye on the confessing brother, broke out in a discourse of sounds, wholly unintelligible, though apparently a true language, accompanying the utterances with a very strange and peculiarly impressive gesture, such as he never made at any other time; coming finally to a kind of pause, and commencing again, as if at the same point, to go over in English, with exactly the same gestures, what had just been said. . . . The circle were astounded by the demonstration, not knowing what to make of it. The instinct of prudence threw them on observing a general silence, and it is a curious fact that the public in H– have never, to this hour, been startled by so much as a rumor of the gift of tongues, neither has the name of the speaker been associated with so much as a surmise of the real or supposed fact, by which he would be, perhaps, unenviably distinguished. It has been a great trial to him, it is said, to submit himself to this demonstration; which has recurred several times.

Bushnell's remarks indicate the low opinion many American Christians had of glossolalia, and his cautious defense of the practice certainly did not persuade everyone. However, among Latter-day Saints the practice of glossolalia appeared early and was embraced quickly.[4]

In Jane's telling, it is not clear who took fright when she began speaking in tongues. Which family did she mean? She could just as easily have been referring to her employers as to her birth family. Although the Second Great Awakening had witnessed enormous religious creativity in the Northeastern United States, most Christians in the region were not particularly "enthusiastic," in the parlance of the day. The Awakening in the Northeast drew souls into churches, but did not result in emphatic displays of emotion or the kinds of physical manifestations of spiritual fervor that became popular in other regions.[5] Thus, whether it was the Fitches or the Mannings or yet another family who overheard Jane's glossolalia, their fright would have been understandable to her. As Horace Bushnell's account intimates, speaking in tongues was the kind of thing that just wasn't done in southwestern Connecticut.

Jane's family appears to have been baptized and confirmed in the LDS Church around the same time as Jane, but this was just the beginning of their Mormon journey. By the early 1840s, Mormon missionaries had spent years preaching the doctrine of the "gathering," the idea that Latter-day Saints should "gather unto Zion." The practical application of this doctrine called for Mormon converts to leave their homes and physically join the growing Latter-day Saint community centered around Joseph Smith. After their baptisms, Jane and her family, like many converts, prepared to gather: to move to Nauvoo, Illinois, where the church had established its headquarters after mob violence forced Mormons to leave their previous base of operations in Missouri. Charles Wesley Wandell, the missionary who baptized Jane, wrote regular dispatches back to the church in Nauvoo, and in 1843 he reported that "the brethren here are very anxious to emigrate to Illinois; so you may expect to see all of us in Zion this Fall that can possibly get there."[6]

Making the move to Nauvoo required a leap of faith for nearly everyone who decided to gather, but for Jane and her family the choice entailed significantly more risk than it did for white converts. Traveling in the United States was a difficult proposition for black people, even those who were free, educated, and financially comfortable. Whether they were going across town or across the continent, black travelers were vulnerable to anti-black harassment at every stage in their journey, including verbal and physical assault, refusal of service, segregated and inferior accommodations, and unreasonable and unpredictable demands that travelers pay extra for their fares. Jane and her family were no exceptions: as they prepared to relocate to Nauvoo, they must have contemplated the difficulties they would encounter. Traveling with Wandell and the white converts from southwestern Connecticut might insulate Jane and her family from the worst treatment, but the Mannings' white companions could not shield the black converts from every barb.[7]

Jane packed for the trip, assembling her belongings and a few things for Sylvester in a large trunk covered with animal skin—light red, with some white on one side, probably from a pinto horse. The skin helped waterproof the wooden box, fitting it for travel in the hold of a boat. This was standard equipment for a long journey in the 1840s, but it is not likely that Jane would have already owned such an item. She may have purchased it especially for this trip, anticipating her first travel beyond the region where she grew up. Perhaps she acquired it from the Fitch family or another employer as a parting gift in recognition of Jane's many years of service, or as a cast-off item, no longer needed by its original owner. Into the trunk went "clothes of all descriptions mostly new." They were "beautiful clothes," Jane remembered later. She was particular about her appearance and her possessions. They helped her project a sense of herself as a respectable, serious woman. The sturdy trunk and the new clothes suggest that Jane's departure for Nauvoo felt like a turning point in her life, a new beginning.[8]

On September 12, 1843, Jane's family sold their property to Jemima Britto, a white woman who lived in Wilton. Britto got about an acre of land and a "Dwelling house standing therein." Jane's family received forty-five dollars. With that, their last remaining ties to Wilton were severed. Shortly thereafter, the Mannings joined a group of converts from southwestern Connecticut, both black and white, and set out for Illinois. Jane's later recollections of the group's black membership were inconsistent, but the black travelers included, at a minimum, Jane and her son Sylvester; her mother, Philes; her brothers and sisters,

Peter, Isaac Lewis, Sarah, and Angeline; Angeline's baby Julia; Sarah's husband Anthony and their toddler Mary; and Isaac Lewis's wife Lucinda. The group probably also included Jane's stepfather, Cato Treadwell, and it may have included two other black converts from the Wilton area, Henry and Lucinda Tonquin. The first stages of the journey were uneventful and apparently not memorable: Jane said only that they "started from Wilton, Conn., and travelled by Canal to Buffalo, N.Y.," but there was more to it than she described (Figure 2.1). While Jane and her family began their trek in Wilton, they first had to join the rest of the group in Norwalk, where the local branch of the church was located. There they would meet Charles Wandell, who would guide the travelers to Nauvoo. The six- to eight-mile walk from Wilton to the meeting point in Norwalk might have been daunting for the group, given the trunks of possessions and the small children who would have to be carried. They may have hired a stagecoach instead, to take at least some of their group, along with the luggage.[9]

From Norwalk, Wandell's group started for New York City. It was possible to travel all the way by stagecoach in 1843, but the size of the group would have required multiple coaches. It is more likely that the group traveled by sea from Norwalk. There were several packet sloop lines that sailed from Norwalk to New York City; in decent weather, these boats could make the trip in under twenty-four hours. Two steamboats, the *Nimrod* and the *Fairfield*, also regularly carried passengers between Norwalk and New York City starting in the 1830s, making the trip even more quickly than the packet boats.[10]

The boats from Norwalk docked in the East River, so Wandell and his group disembarked in Lower Manhattan. We have no reason to believe that Jane had ever set foot in New York City before 1843. She never discussed her impression of the city, but it was certainly a change from the small towns of Wilton and New Canaan. People and conveyances moved in every direction, a veritable Babel of languages greeted Jane's ears, and she beheld, quite probably, more black people than she had ever before seen in one place. The hustle and bustle of the city might have been exhilarating, or the chaos might have been terrifying. Jane might have gone crazy with worry keeping track of her things, making sure they were properly transferred, wincing every time that beautiful trunk crashed into someone else's luggage or splashed down in a puddle, hoping the skin covering held fast and continued to protect everything inside, all the while keeping an anxious eye on Sylvester and trying to prevent him from wandering off. It is unlikely that the group stopped over in New York City, since any delay would have added to the cost of the trip. Jane might have regretted that her stay in New York was so short; but then again, she might have been relieved to put the city behind her.

The next leg of the journey took the group up the Hudson River to Albany. Their goal was to get to the relatively new Erie Canal, which would allow them fairly easy passage for several hundred miles thereafter. By the 1840s, steamboats

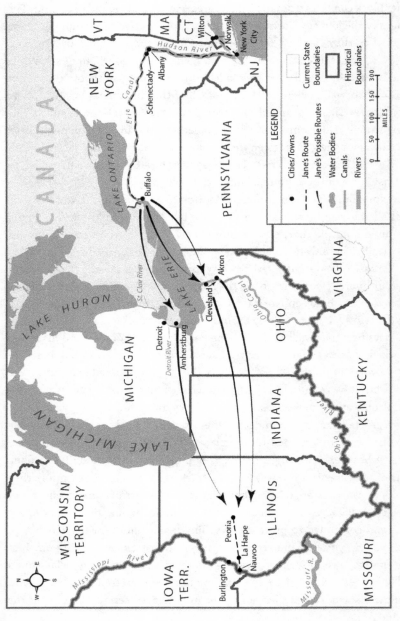

Figure 2.1 Jane and her family traveled with Charles Wesley Wandell and other white converts from Wilton, Connecticut, to New York City, and from there up the Hudson River and west on the Erie Canal to Buffalo. Little is known about the route Jane and her family took to Nauvoo from there. They may have traveled through Canada, re-entering the United States near Detroit, Michigan; or they may have taken a southerly route through Pennsylvania and Ohio. Map by Chelsey Buffington, Center for Spatial Analysis and Research, Portland State University.

were the main form of transportation along the Hudson River. Although disastrous explosions and fires were regular occurrences on steamers, these boats were still the preferred method for this leg of the journey, and almost certainly the means that transported the Mannings to Albany. Wandell's group likely made its way as efficiently as it could across the tip of Manhattan to the base of Cortland Street, where the steamboats to Albany docked, and booked passage on the next departing boat. In September 1843 the "Independent Opposition Line" to Albany advertised fares on "the new and fast sailing steamboat WAVE" at astonishingly low rates. "Passage 50 Cents—Berths 50 Cents—Supper 25 Cents—Forward Deck 25 Cents," the ad trumpeted, promising potential customers that "The Wave being of light draft of water, and making but few landings, passengers will arrive in Albany in good time for the railroads." This was a night line, leaving the dock in Manhattan at 5:00 p.m. and arriving early the next morning. Other boats made the trip during the day. There is a small chance Wandell's group avoided segregated accommodations on their way to New York City, but the Hudson River steamboats routinely separated their passengers by race. The forward deck, to which black passengers were usually restricted, was windy and chilly even on a hot summer's day. It is easy to picture Jane shielding her little boy from the spray of the waves as the boat made its way steadily north, pointing out the sights to Sylvester, and joining him in imagining the grand lives of the people inhabiting the beautiful homes overlooking the water.[11]

Although the eastern terminus of the Erie Canal was in Albany, where Wandell's group disembarked from their steamboat, smart travelers went sixteen miles east to Schenectady to board a canal boat. As a travel guide writer noted in 1841, traveling from Albany to Schenectady by railroad took between one and two hours, while making the same trip on the canal took twelve to fourteen hours. The discrepant travel times were due to the change in elevation between the two sites: Schenectady was 226 feet higher than Albany, so the boat had to go through twenty-seven locks to make the climb. While Wandell's group might have opted to spend a day making the trip by canal, it seems more likely that they took the train or engaged stage coaches to transport them to Schenectady and boarded a canal boat there. Travel guides of the time describe the boats as quite comfortable: "The Canal Packet-boats, by which the traveler to the west continues his journey from Schenectady," wrote Robert J. Vandewater, "are about 80 feet in length and from 8 to 14 wide. A cabin in the forward part of the boat is fitted for ladies, with berths, in a similar style to those of the steamboats on the Hudson. The dining-cabin is about 35 feet in length. The gentlemen's berths are not stationary, but are hung up in the dining-cabin at bedtime by means of hooks fitted for the purpose. Back of the dining-cabin is the kitchen and sleeping-cabin for the hands." Because they were black, Jane and her family almost certainly stayed in the back of the boat, taking their meals in the kitchen and sleeping in whatever space was available. By canal, the distance from Schenectady to Buffalo was

333 miles. If all went smoothly, Jane and her traveling companions spent nearly three full days—sixty-eight hours—on the water, in addition to waiting through layovers in Utica, Syracuse, and Rochester.[12]

When they reached Buffalo, on the shores of Lake Erie, Wandell and his group boarded the steamboat *Bunker Hill*, captained by C. Stanard and bound for Chicago. They would disembark at Cleveland, an intermediate port on the *Bunker Hill*'s route. The passage on Lake Erie took only a day or so: Sally Randall, another Mormon convert who departed upstate New York for Nauvoo at about the same time as Jane's group left Connecticut, wrote to relatives that she and her family "did not leave Buffalo until Monday morning and got to Cleveland Tuesday before noon." That leg of the trip was not without its challenges for Randall and her traveling companions; she continued, "The lake was very rough Monday night. Almost all on board were sick. I was not very sick nor the children, but we had to keep pretty still to keep from it."[13]

But Jane and her family may not have had a chance to deal with the rough waters that Randall experienced. Ohio had stringent laws against black immigration that required black people entering the state to post a $500 bond and produce "free papers" attesting to their status. Perhaps for this reason, Jane and the other black members of the group were not permitted to remain on the boat. Jane recalled in her autobiography that "We were to go to Columbus Ohio before our fares were to be collected, but they insisted on having the money at Buffalo and would not take us farther. So we left the boat." We can reasonably assume that Jane and the other travelers had the money to pay their fare, whether at Buffalo or Columbus. However, they may not have realized that a $500 bond would be required of each of them in addition to the normal fee for passage. It may also be that the steamboat captain or canalboat operator simply refused to carry black passengers, regardless of whether Jane and her family could pay their fares. This setback may have sent some of the less intrepid among the group back home, but many of the black people in Jane's group were determined to press on. Jane arranged for Wandell to take her trunk to Nauvoo, and then she and her family began the long trek overland to western Illinois.[14]

Jane provided almost no information about the route she and her family followed between New York and Illinois. They might have followed the northern shore of Lake Erie, walking through Canada until reaching Detroit. This route would have given Jane and her fellow travelers some respite from the persistent worry that an unscrupulous slavecatcher might kidnap them and sell them into slavery, and some relief from the onerous requirements imposed by the "black codes" of states like Ohio, which had passed entire sets of laws restricting the activities of African Americans within their jurisdictions. If they did go through Canada, the Mannings would have had to rely on the kindness of strangers, but they might well have found a great deal of kindness along their route. They also would have found a significant population of black people, many formerly enslaved fugitives from the United States. According to historian Robin Winks, "By 1840 there were said to be nearly twelve thousand [African American] fugitives" in Canada, many of whom had settled in the farmlands of the southern Canadian border. The British government had taken steps to protect these fugitives from re-enslavement in the United States, though American requests for the extradition of fugitive slaves were occasionally successful. Nevertheless, the early 1840s were a time of growing racial tensions in Canada, and Jane may have observed both cooperation—blacks and whites working together to farm the land and worshiping together in integrated churches—and discord, as when white settlers insisted on segregating their communities or even requested the removal of black people from their midst. Traveling through Canada might have made a significant impression on Jane and her siblings; Jane's brothers Isaac and Peter both moved to London, Ontario, many years later.[15]

If they took the northern route, Jane and her family would probably have crossed back into the United States at Amherstburg, a settlement on the east side of the Detroit River, several miles south of Detroit. Amherstburg had been home to a relatively large number of escaped slaves since the 1820s. *Smith's Canadian Gazetteer*, published three years after Jane's journey, listed Amherstburg's population at 985 in 1846. Of these, according to *Smith's*, 174 were "people of colour." The town boasted five churches, including a Baptist church "for coloured people," and twice as many taverns. (*Smith's* did not report whether the latter establishments were racially segregated.) *Smith's* description made clear that Amherstburg was a bustling town: the list of economic concerns ran the gamut, from "two physicians and surgeons" to "fourteen stores" to "one watchmaker." Amherstburg also had "two butchers," "three bakers," and at least one candlestick maker in the "soap and candle manufactory." But the town also boasted some natural beauty: "The banks of the river," *Smith's* noted, "both above and below the town, but particularly the latter, where the river emerges into Lake Erie, are very beautiful; the sweet-briar bushes, with which the banks are studded, are here remarkably fine." Jane and her family might have had the opportunity to admire these scenic vistas as they crossed the Detroit River. Unless they were able to take a steamer to Detroit, they had to hire a boat to convey them to the American side of the border. As at Buffalo, the boundary between the United States and Canada was largely unsupervised; the transnational crossing was merely a matter of arranging appropriate conveyance.[16]

Alternatively, the group might have headed southwest from Buffalo, along the southern shore of Lake Erie, through a corner of Pennsylvania and then across Ohio. Traveling on foot, the Mannings could more easily escape the notice of authorities who might demand a $500 bond from them. The southern route would have taken them through Cleveland, on the eastern bank of the Cuyahoga River where the river flowed into Lake Erie. In an 1839 guide for tourists, John Calvin Smith described the up-and-coming city: "It is chiefly built upon a plain about 80 feet above the lake; it is very regularly laid out, with wide streets." Smith's title page promised "concise description," and he kept things brief: "Cleveland contains a court-house, a jail, 6 churches, and 2 banks. The population in 1825 was 500; 1830, 1,000; 1834, 4,300; and at the present time estimated at 7,000." By the end of the next decade, the city held 17,034 residents. This explosive growth was explained by Smith's laconic remark: "Its location at the northern termination of the Ohio canal renders it a very important place both for inland and lake navigation." Cleveland's geography contributed to its booming economy and made it a frequent stop on the Underground Railroad. The black community in Cleveland was small but active in abolitionist causes, and for the most part African Americans found allies among their white neighbors in Cleveland.[17] Abolitionist William Wells Brown wrote in 1848, "It is well known that a great number of fugitives make their escape to Canada, by way of Cleveland; and while on the lakes, I always made arrangements to carry them on the boat to Buffalo or Detroit, and thus effect their escape to the 'promised land.' The friends of the slave, knowing that I would transport them without charge, never failed to have a delegation when the boat arrived at Cleveland." There and elsewhere in northern Ohio, Jane and her family might well have come into contact with abolitionists eager to help them and dismayed to discover that this particular group of African Americans was not escaping slavery, but pursuing Mormonism. Anti-Mormonism was strong among American abolitionists, who saw both the young Mormon movement and the considerably older institution of slavery as tyrannical systems that were inimical to human freedom and American democracy.[18]

The southerly route seems more likely, in part because some evidence suggests that Wandell's group split up well after it had passed through Buffalo. It may be that black members of Wandell's group were asked to post a bond, or pay a higher fare, at some point after their arrival in Ohio, and that their inability to meet this demand led the group to part ways. Wandell was brought up on charges in a church court in Nauvoo for "unchristian conduct towards certain colored brethren by leaving them at Cleveland in Ohio." Jane also told the story of her life to a white Mormon woman named Elvira Stevens Barney in 1899, and when Barney recorded the story for the *Deseret News*, she said that Jane had walked from "Eckland, Ohio." Jane may have meant—she may even have said—"Akron"; no place named "Eckland" existed in Ohio at the time, and Wandell's group would have traveled through Akron on the Ohio canal system as they made their way west.[19]

Regardless of precisely where Wandell's group became separated, Jane and her family were faced with a trek of hundreds of miles. "We walked until our shoes were worn out," Jane remembered. Those shoes may well have been purchased in New Canaan, which had specialized in shoemaking after the American Revolution. One of the leading families in New Canaan, the Benedicts, specialized in rough pegged shoes, just the sort of durable footwear that Jane and her family needed for the journey. The leather uppers were attached to the cowhide soles of the shoes with stitches, anchored with a row of wooden pegs just inside the stitching. The Benedict family sold their sturdy shoes locally, but also developed a thriving market in the South, where plantation owners purchased Benedict shoes for their field slaves. Either way, as Jane wore the shoes, they molded themselves to her feet, resulting over time in a very comfortable fit. Even the sturdiest shoes, though, were not designed for a thousand-mile hike. It is not surprising, then, that the shoes did not last the distance. Once the shoes were gone, Jane recalled, "our feet became sore and cracked open and bled until you could see the whole print of our feet with blood on the ground." The injuries to her feet clearly made an impression on Jane: she mentioned them in her conversation with Elvira Barney as well. When she arrived in Nauvoo, she recalled, "my feet were sore and bleeding, and were very painful."[20]

In addition to the physical injury, Jane's pride may have been wounded by the breakdown of her shoes and her feet. Later in her life, Jane emphasized repeatedly that she had never been enslaved, as if she feared that people would assume she had based on her skin color. In her elaborations of her possessions worn out or lost—her shoes, her trunk, her stockings, her dresses—Jane demanded recognition that she was different from enslaved people: her ability to acquire, use, and lose these products marked her as a consumer, not a producer.[21] The condition of Jane's feet was, for her, a source of shame, as if her wounds made her appear more like an enslaved woman. In fact, traveling by foot through Ohio and Illinois with injured bodies, minimal supplies, and deteriorating clothing, Jane and her companions may have looked suspiciously like escaped slaves to those who did not know them.

Like Ohio, Illinois had an onerous black code. In order to enter the state, African Americans were required to have a certificate of freedom, and to register that certificate immediately upon arrival. If they were stopped and failed to produce the appropriate documentation, Jane and her group would have been exposed to the threat of incarceration and forced labor. Indeed, Jane recalled that "When we arrived at Peoria, Illinois the authorities threatened to put us in jail to get our free papers. We didn't know at first what he meant for we had never been slaves, but he concluded to let us go." When Jane protested that she and her companions "didn't know what [the authorities] meant" when they demanded the group's "free papers," she again distanced herself from enslaved people, insisting on her difference from them. In fact, she and her family knew all too well what the authorities were asking for: Jane's mother had been enslaved in Connecticut, and gained her freedom before Jane's birth. Getting certificates of freedom before leaving Connecticut would have been a prudent thing for Jane and her family to do, but this was a difficult, expensive step under the best circumstances. Local opposition to the Mormons may have made it even more difficult for the Mannings to obtain these legal documents from the court in Norwalk. More to the point, Jane and her family probably did not know such papers would be required of them until they were hundreds of miles from Connecticut. By that time, there was no way to marshal testimony about their free status from white people in Wilton and New Canaan whose statements would be accepted by legal authorities.[22]

As Charles Wandell and the other white people in Jane's original group floated along canals and rivers to Nauvoo, Jane and her family "lay in bushes, and in barns and outdoors, and traveled until there was a frost just like a snow, and we had to walk on that frost." For Sally Randall, the white convert from New York, the trip to Nauvoo took about two weeks. Wandell's white converts took a few days longer; but Jane and her family were on the road for about two and a half months. The weather turned from hot, muggy summer to cool, crisp fall. The nights got colder. After they left Peoria, Jane remembered,

> we travelled on until we came to a river and as there was no bridge we walked right into the stream, when we got to the middle the water was up to our necks but we got safely across, and then it became so dark we could hardly see our hands before us, but we could see a light in the distance, so we went toward it and found it was an old Log Cabin. Here we spent the night; next day we walked for a considerable distance and stayed that night in a forest, out in the open air. The frost fell on us so heavy that it was like a light fall of snow. We rose early and started on our way walking through that frost with our bare feet, until the sun rose and melted it away.

Jane narrated these hardships in her autobiography in order to demonstrate God's providence: a threatening official and the group's confusion was paired with the inexplicable but fortuitous decision to let the group go on its way; a river without a bridge with a safe passage through the water; darkness with light and shelter; and frost with the emergence of the sun to melt it. Most strikingly, physical injury was paired with divine healing. When their feet cracked and bled, Jane recalled, "We stopped and united in prayer to the Lord, we asked God the Eternal Father to heal our feet and our prayers were answered and our feet were healed forthwith."[23]

Divine healing was a recurring motif in the accounts the elderly Jane gave of her life. It was also a common practice among early members of the church: church leaders and missionaries, men and women, recent converts and longtime members all participated in and received healings. However, women's roles in healing became more restricted over the course of the nineteenth century, yielding to men's expanding priesthood authority. By the time Jane dictated her autobiography in the first decade of the twentieth century, church leaders had decisively curtailed women's healing activities. An editorial in the church-run *Deseret Evening News* stated, "The ordinance appointed in the Church for the healing of the sick is to be performed by the Elders," or men holding what Latter-day Saints called the "Melchizedek priesthood." According to a revelation that Joseph Smith received in 1835, the Melchizedek priesthood encompassed "power and authority over all the offices in the church in all ages of the world, to administer in spiritual things." The editorial went on: "A Priest, Teacher or Deacon may administer to the sick." These offices—priest, teacher, and deacon—were occupied by men holding the lesser "Aaronic priesthood" which had "power in administering outward ordinances." In fact, the editorial allowed, just as those holding the Aaronic priesthood could administer to the sick, "so may a member, male or female, but," it cautioned, "neither of them can seal the anointing and blessing, because the authority to do that is vested in the Priesthood after the order of Melchizedek." Perhaps as an implicit rebuttal to this suggestion that healing power could only be wielded effectively by those who held the priesthood, Jane told of her own experiences with healing. After describing the healing of her group's feet through the power of prayer, Jane went one step further. "At La Harpe we came to a place where there was a very sick child," she remembered. "We administered to it, and the child was healed." La Harpe was just thirty miles from Nauvoo, and at the time Jane passed through a small community of Mormons lived there. Healings like the one she and her group performed were unremarkable at that time in Mormon history, but Jane added a flourish at the end of the episode to drive her point home: "I found after [that] the elders had before this given it up as they did not think it could live." Jane thus asserted that healing power was not limited to men.[24]

When Sally Randall, the white convert from upstate New York, arrived in Nauvoo, she was unimpressed with the town. Randall wrote tactfully to her family members in New York, "As for Nauvoo, I cannot tell you much about it at present for I have not seen much of it yet." But her fears came flooding out almost immediately: "It is very sickly here at present with . . . fever and ague and measles, and a great many children die with them." Indeed, a few days later one of Sally's sons came down with what she identified as "the ague and fever," an ailment that killed him in about three weeks. Jane and her family arrived two months after Sally, near the end of November. Writing home ten days before Jane's arrival to let her extended family know of her son's death, Sally wrote, "It is not as sickly here as it has been, but there is a good many deaths now. People are coming in very fast. There was a boat load came in yesterday from England." The population of Nauvoo was booming in 1843: the Saints' emphasis on the doctrine of the gathering motivated converts across the United States and in the British Isles to make the journey, and the city grew by leaps and bounds. In 1842, Nauvoo was home to approximately 4,000 people; by two years later, three times that many would call it home.[25]

Randall's description of Nauvoo as a "sickly" place articulated the conventional wisdom of the time. Americans in the mid-nineteenth century determined the healthfulness or sickliness of a place in large part by its environmental characteristics. Nauvoo, constructed on a bend of the Mississippi River, was low and wet, with no natural drainage. Church founder Joseph Smith's official history recorded that "the place was literally a wilderness. The land was mostly covered with trees and bushes, and much of it so wet that it was with the utmost difficulty a footman could get through, and totally impossible for teams" of livestock. Smith made the connection between the wild wetness of the place and its medical character: it "was so unhealthful, very few could live there" when the Saints acquired the site. Even after the Mormons drained the marshy land, Smith wrote, "like all other places on the river, it is sickly in the summer." Indeed, scholar Samuel Morris Brown noted that Nauvoo lost five percent of its population to death every year, and the vast majority of these deaths were due to infection rather than injury or old age. Residents of Nauvoo were particularly susceptible to the disease they knew as *ague*, which they recognized by its symptomatic cycles of fever and chills. Mormons and others believed that miasma caused ague. An environmental hazard widely recognized by nineteenth-century Euro-Americans, miasma was described by Noah Webster as "infecting substances floating in the air; the effluvia of any putrefying bodies, rising and floating in the atmosphere." Unfortunately for the Mormons, Nauvoo was the sort of place prone to miasma, and there was nowhere that was safe: arising from the scummy standing water found in the area, miasma was borne on the very air Nauvoo residents breathed. We now know that ague was what we call malaria, and that it was spread by mosquitoes rather than miasma. But when the Mormons built Nauvoo, they could not distinguish the disease-bearing mosquitoes from the warm, wet, miasma-producing locations those insects frequented.[26]

Despite its sickly nature, observers reported that Nauvoo was bustling with industry: a Methodist minister who visited the city in 1843 reported, "I found all the people engaged in some useful and healthy employment. The place was alive with business—much more so than any place I have visited since the hard times commenced. . . . I could see no loungers about the streets nor any drunkards about the taverns. . . . all were cheerful, polite, and industrious." That whirlwind of activity, though, did not necessarily mean that residents of Nauvoo were prosperous. Sally Randall reflected, "I expect it is a hard place for poor people that have no money to get a living. There is so many poor that depend on their work for a living that they can hardly get enough to be comfortable." Indeed, historian Robert Flanders wrote that "it was expected that an increasing population would bring prosperity to Nauvoo, but the opposite tended to be the case. Large numbers of poor English immigrants, as well as those from the states little better off, drove the per capita wealth of the city down. The heavy demand for goods and services which had been expected to invigorate the economy tended to depress it instead, since the capital to finance both production and consumption was inadequate." Still, the cost of living was not high: Randall reported that "Provisions are very cheap. We can get good pork for four cents a pound, flour for one dollar and fifty cents a hundred, sugar from 8 to 10 cents a pound. Cows are from six to ten dollars." Jane reported in her autobiography that everyone in her family found homes and, likely, employment within a week of arriving in the city. It is notable, though, that the group split up: Jane's family did not purchase property, as they had in Wilton. Instead, they lived with employers, rented rooms, or found homes in one of the communities that surrounded Nauvoo.[27]

This was the place that Jane and her traveling companions found: a city bursting at the seams, with more people arriving every day, houses going up and lots being subdivided so fast that city officials couldn't keep up. A "sickly" city, where waves of malaria swept through regularly and carried off some of the more vulnerable residents. A "hard" place for the poor, barely able to absorb the well-off migrants and lacking in resources to take care of those who had left everything to get to the center of the church's activity. Nauvoo was also, primarily, a white city, not accustomed to welcoming African Americans into its midst. There were a few black people around. Records showed that a black man, Elijah Abel, purchased a lot in December 1839. However, by the time Jane arrived in Nauvoo, Abel had deeded his land to other men in the community and moved to Cincinnati. Another black convert, Isaac James, was still in Nauvoo; he had come from Monmouth County, New Jersey, in about 1841. For Jane, this racial mixture felt familiar: southwestern Connecticut was very similar.[28]

Jane's journey was not over when she reached the Nauvoo city limits. When her family arrived in Nauvoo, she later remembered in her autobiography, "we went through all kinds of hardship, trial, and rebuff." It is unclear what Jane meant by this phrase. Its placement in her narrative clearly indicated that the difficulties occurred *in* Nauvoo, presumably at the hands of other Mormons. Were Jane and her family made to feel unwelcome because of their race? Did their ragged, threadbare appearance put off Latter-day Saints who were already concerned about how to provide for their poor? It is impossible to say exactly what happened. The attitudes of Latter-day Saints on the issues of race and slavery had shifted significantly over the previous decade: although the church did not take a stand on slavery in its early years, Joseph Smith had affirmed his support for the "peculiar institution" in 1835, and the church maintained this position for the rest of the 1830s. In the early 1840s, however, Smith reversed this stance, and the church began denouncing slavery. When he ran for president in 1844, Smith advocated a gradual emancipation and colonization plan that would compensate slaveowners and remove black people from white American society, resettling them in Africa or elsewhere. Mormons' opposition to slavery, however, did not necessarily entail a belief in racial equality. Although

Joseph Smith suggested in private conversation that blacks' inferiority was due to structural impediments imposed by society, he also publicly opposed inter-racial marriage. Smith's followers were not always as nuanced in their views, and many held to common white American prejudices against black people. Jane recalled the Mormon settlement as "our destined haven of rest, the beautiful Nauvoo," but the city did not provide Jane and her family with a refuge from the everyday torment of racism.[29]

Making it to Nauvoo was challenge enough, but once they reached the city, the "rebuff" that Jane and her family faced may have raised doubts about what to do next. Luckily, as Jane remembered it, Orson Spencer directed the group to Joseph Smith's home. Spencer was a white convert from Massachusetts and an alderman in Nauvoo. His social standing may have reassured Jane that she and her family would be welcomed in the city, although they had initially found a cold reception. As Jane remembered it, when the group reached the Smith home, Emma Smith invited them in and Joseph Smith welcomed them. Jane asserted much later that the Smiths were expecting her, because she had written them a letter to notify them that she and her family were on their way.[30] Jane's level of literacy is uncertain: although she claimed to be able to read and write, no document in her hand is known to survive. If she did write, or dictate, a letter to the Smiths, it has not been found. Given the setbacks that delayed the group's arrival in Nauvoo, it seems unlikely that the Smiths actively anticipated the Mannings' appearance, though it is possible that word of a group of black Saints preceded them to Nauvoo from La Harpe or other outlying LDS communities.

Jane emphasized the racial egalitarianism of the Smiths' hospitality, in con-trast to the hostility the group had sensed earlier that day: "Brother Joseph said to some white sisters that was present, 'Sisters, I want you to occupy this room this evening with some brothers and sisters that have just arrived,'" she recalled. Then, gathering his wife Emma and John Bernhisel, another guest at the Smiths' home, Joseph asked Jane to recount the story of the group's journey. In Jane's memory, Joseph was an appreciative audience for her tale: "Brother Joseph slapped Dr. Bernhisel on the knee and said, 'What do you think of that, Dr., isn't that faith?'" Even the distinguished doctor had to admit the group's extraordi-nary fortitude: "Well I rather think it is," he responded. "If it had . . . been me I fear I should have backed out and returned to my home!" The reception Jane and her family received at the Smith home reassured Jane that she had made the right decision. In welcoming her, Joseph Smith proved himself to be the prophet she believed he was. The sense of confirmation that Jane experienced upon meeting Smith was apparent many years later: when Smith entered the room, Jane remembered, "I knew him. Did not have to tell me [who he was] because I knew him. I knew him when I saw him back in old Connecticut in a vision, saw him plain and knew he was a prophet." Smith's hospitality gave Jane to know that she was a valued member of the faith community, despite all of the obstacles that had been placed in the way of her gathering to Nauvoo.[31] In that moment, Nauvoo truly felt to her like a "haven of rest," the place where God had "destined" her to be. She was home.

3

The Beautiful Nauvoo

(1843–1844)

Despite Jane's powerful feeling that she had finally reached the place where she belonged, worry undercut her sense of security and threatened to overwhelm her with despair. "On the morning that my folks all left to go to work, I looked at myself, clothed in the only two pieces I possessed. I sat down and wept," Jane remembered.[1] She had left a position of relative comfort in Connecticut, where her family had a house and Jane, even if she didn't have steady employment at the time, knew the lay of the land. She could feel reasonably confident that she would find another permanent position in the Wilton area, and Sylvester would soon be old enough to contribute to the family economy as well. In Nauvoo, Jane knew nobody except her family and some of the white people who had also come from Connecticut. Foremost among them was Charles Wesley Wandell, who had abdicated his responsibility to make sure Jane and her family made it safely to Nauvoo, and on top of that, had lost Jane's trunk, leaving her with nothing except the clothes on her back. Alone and impoverished, she felt utterly dependent on the kindness of strangers and the providence of God as she made a new beginning for herself in this new place.

In later years, Nauvoo occupied a central place in Jane's imagination. There, she had encountered the founder, prophet, and leader of the Mormons and experienced his kindness firsthand. As she recalled it, Joseph Smith walked in on Jane as she wept. Surprised, or perhaps flustered, to see her crying, he asked why she was weeping. "The folks have all gone and got themselves homes, and I have got none," she responded. "Yes you have," came the reply from Smith. "You have a home right here if you want it. You mustn't cry; we dry up all tears here." Jane remembered that Smith left the room and returned with Emma. "Sister Emma," he said, "here is a girl that says she has no home. Haven't you a home for her?" True to Jane's initial impression of Emma as unfailingly gracious, the prophet's wife responded in the affirmative: "Why yes, if she wants one," was the reply Jane remembered. Joseph responded that Jane did and then left, apparently considering the matter settled. Stepping into a managerial role,

Emma immediately turned to an assessment of Jane's skills: "What can you do?" she asked. Jane responded eagerly. "I said I can wash, iron, cook, and do housework!," she recalled.[2] Indeed, that was the work Jane had done almost her entire life.

This offer of long-term housing and employment may not have been as spontaneous as it seemed: together with his wife Emma, Joseph Smith operated their family home as a "mansion house," a nineteenth-century form of accommodation for travelers. Mansion houses were more genteel than taverns and inns, and they offered a more personalized level of service and more intimate experience than the hotels that had begun to appear in American cities. They were an essential part of the nascent American tourism industry, catering to clients who traveled for edification and recreation. The Smiths' mansion house was some Mormons' first lodging in Nauvoo, but it also accommodated all manner of other travelers passing through the town as well as tourists who made Nauvoo their destination, coming to see the Mormon city for themselves. The Nauvoo Mansion had opened for business not quite two months before Jane arrived. The Smiths already had several domestic employees to help with the day-to-day functioning of the hotel, but they may have seen in Jane Manning the opportunity to expand their workforce.[3]

The Smiths made the mansion house possible by building a large wing on the back of their family home (Figure 3.1). The two-story addition included a large dining room and kitchen on the main floor, with ten guest bedrooms upstairs that would accommodate fourteen people. Jane and Sylvester probably shared a bedroom with the other young women in the Smiths' employ in the southeast corner of the newly constructed wing. The "Servants' Bedroom," on the second floor, was about two hundred square feet, with a stairway connecting it to the "Servants' Living Room" downstairs. There was one window on the south wall, overlooking Water Street, and beyond that, the Mississippi River. On the main floor, the servants' living room opened onto the "Well Room," through which Jane and the others could enter the kitchen and, from there, the dining room. The servants' quarters were separated from the Smith family's living quarters by the space devoted to mansion house guests. Despite the physical separation of their living quarters, Jane and the other servants who lived and worked at the mansion house saw Joseph and Emma Smith regularly. Emma was the manager of the house's day-to-day operations and probably worked alongside Jane as much as she supervised her. In addition to Joseph and Emma, the mansion house was also home to Joseph's mother, Lucy Mack Smith, and the Smiths' four living children, who ranged in age from about five to thirteen at the time of Jane's arrival in Nauvoo.[4]

Although the permanent residents of the Nauvoo Mansion might easily have outnumbered the paying guests most days, the mansion house still had plenty of work to keep Jane busy. Joseph and Emma Smith frequently hosted parties for

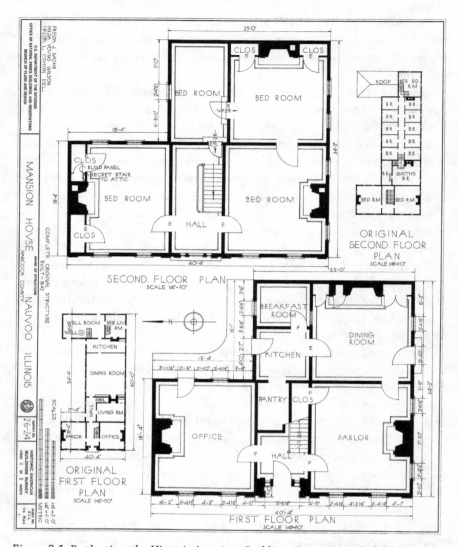

Figure 3.1 By the time the Historic American Buildings Survey recorded the layout of the Nauvoo Mansion in the 1930s, the addition Joseph and Emma Smith had built to accommodate guests had been removed. The "original" first and second floors shown here represent the house as Jane knew it. Historic American Buildings Survey, Mansion House, Main & Water Streets, Nauvoo, Hancock County, IL, 1933, Prints and Photographs Division, Library of Congress, HABS ILL,34-NAU,1-.

members of the church and the community. One well-known event was a party for fifty couples on the afternoon of Christmas Day, 1843. Emma was decked out in a new dress; Joseph wore his military dress uniform, reflecting his position as Lieutenant General of the Nauvoo Legion, the local militia the Mormons had formed. Dinner was served to the entire party, and a band provided music for dancing afterward. Most descriptions are silent on the amount of labor that went into producing this party—labor that had to begin days, if not weeks or months, ahead of time and extended long after all of the guests had gone home. Jane almost certainly had a hand in the washing and ironing of Joseph and Emma's clothes, as well as the preparation of all of the table linens, dishes, and cutlery the party required. She also must have helped with cooking and serving the food. The party's aftermath was nearly as labor-intensive: dishes had to be cleaned, linens had to be washed, and everything had to be restored to order in the house. There was no time for a break when the work of the Christmas party was complete: the Smiths hosted another large party just a week later on New Year's Day, and another to mark their anniversary on January 18. Jane's labor, largely invisible in the historical record, enabled Joseph and Emma Smith to be welcoming, hospitable community leaders in Nauvoo.[5]

Jane probably received little material compensation beyond room and board in exchange for her labor in the Smith home, but years later she remembered her reward coming in the form of intense spiritual experiences. On her first day of work for the family, Jane recalled in her autobiography, she did the laundry. "Among the clothes I found Brother Joseph's robes," she said. "I looked at them and wondered. I had never seen any before, and I pondered over them and thought about them so earnestly that the Spirit made manifest to me that they pertained to the new name that is given the Saints that the world knows not of. I didn't know when I washed them or when I put them out to dry." The Latter-day Saints who heard or read Jane's reminiscence of this episode would immediately recognize the references in her account to temple ceremonies: the "robes" that Jane washed were special clothing that Smith and others wore to participate in these sacred rituals, and the "new name" is given during the endowment ceremony, a ritual that Smith was developing at the time with the help of leading members of the church. Latter-day Saints consider the endowment a crucial ritual step in their religious journey. The endowment ceremony functions as an initiation ritual. Participants review sacred history, make sacred vows, and receive sacred promises and knowledge, including "key words, signs, [and] tokens" and the new name that they will need to reach their eternal home after death. In addition to wearing temple robes for the endowment ceremony, Latter-day Saints are dressed in clothes called "garments," which they subsequently wear daily under their street clothes. Like the new name, the garments mark Latter-day Saints' sacred identities, but they are not displayed publicly.[6]

Jane was so taken with Smith's temple clothing that she shared it with one of the other "hired girls" who worked at the mansion house. Many years later, Maria Jane Johnston Woodward declared that she could "bear testimony that [Joseph Smith] had had his endowments and wore garments, for the woman who washed for the family showed them to me."[7] Jane would not be allowed to

receive her endowment during her lifetime, because church leaders would ultimately decide that her black skin disqualified her from participating in this and
other temple rituals. Telling the story of Joseph Smith's robes at the beginning
of the twentieth century, Jane implicitly protested this ruling, pointing out the
intimate access she had to the church's first prophet and to knowledge of the
closely guarded temple rituals.

Jane was not the only uninitiated Mormon washing temple robes. In 1902,
Woodward told of a time when she was working for Joseph Smith's uncle. "On
one occasion the Prophet [Joseph Smith] wrote a letter to his uncle to meet him
the next morning in Nauvoo, (we were twenty-five miles from there). Mother
Smith, [his wife, Joseph's aunt] . . . was sick and as I was the hired girl I had to get
these clothes and fix them in time for Father Smith to meet the Prophet Joseph
in Nauvoo. Mother Smith told Father Smith to explain to me about this clothing,
what they were for and what they did with them, the reason he had to have them
and have them in good condition, before I got them out, and he did so. That was
the first I knew about endowment clothes." Woodward's reminiscence included
details about the great care with which this clothing was treated. Father Smith's
clothes "were in a chest locked up, inside of a little cotton bag made for the purpose," Woodward recalled. "These clothes were never put out publicly, in the
washing or in any other way. When we washed them we hung them out between
sheets, because we were in the midst of the Gentiles."[8] Jane did not recall any
special information from Emma Smith regarding Joseph's temple robes, but,
like Woodward, she may well have received some instruction in order to explain
the special treatment the clothing required.

The performance of the endowment ceremony would later be confined to
LDS temples, but during Joseph Smith's lifetime, this and other rituals were developed and performed in a room above Joseph Smith's general store in Nauvoo
and in other spaces that were improvised as needed. L. John Nuttall, a secretary to Brigham Young, recorded Young's memory of the first time he experienced the endowment ritual in Nauvoo. "We were washed and anointed, had our
garments placed upon us, and received our new name," Young remembered, "and
after [Joseph Smith] had performed these ceremonies, he gave the key words,
signs, tokens, and penalties. Then, after, we went into the large room over the
store in Nauvoo. Joseph divided up the room the best that he could, hung up the
veil, marked it, [and] gave us our instructions as we passed along from one department to another, giving us signs, tokens, [and] penalties with the key words
pertaining to those signs."[9]

Joseph Smith's mother, Lucy Mack Smith, afforded Jane further access to the
most closely guarded aspects of Mormonism. Jane recalled that "Mother Smith,"
as Lucy was commonly known among the LDS community, "would often stop me
and talk to me. She told me all Brother Joseph's troubles, and what he had suffered
in publishing the Book of Mormon." The history of Mormonism was intimately

tied up with the story of Joseph Smith's translation and publication of the Book of Mormon, which Latter-day Saints believed was a history of the ancient inhabitants of the Americas that recounted the ministry of Jesus in the New World. Smith said he had been visited by an angel who directed him to dig up a set of ancient metal plates from a hill near his home in 1827. With them was a set of "interpreters" known as the Urim and Thummim that Smith would use to translate the plates from "reformed Egyptian" into English. As Lucy Mack Smith described them, the Urim and Thummim were "2 smooth 3-cornered diamonds set in glass and the glass was set in silver bows connected with each other in the same way that old fashioned spectacles are made." Joseph Smith published the book that resulted—the Book of Mormon—in 1830. The church that took the Book of Mormon as scripture was officially organized the same year.[10]

Jane was an appreciative audience for Mother Smith's memories. One morning in the winter of 1843–1844, when she entered Lucy Mack Smith's room, Jane remembered, "she said 'Good morning, bring me that bundle from my bureau and sit down here.' I did as she told me. She placed the bundle in my hands and said, 'Handle this and then put [it] in the top drawer of my bureau and lock it up.'" Once Jane had followed her directions, Smith explained: "'Do you remember that I told you about the Urim and Thummim when I told you about the Book of Mormon?' I answered, 'Yes, Ma'am.' She then told me I had just handled it. 'You are not permitted to see it, but you have been permitted to handle it. You will live long after I am dead and gone. And you can tell the Latter-day Saints that you was permitted to handle the Urim and Thummim.'"[11]

According to Joseph Smith's own history, though, he returned the Urim and Thummim along with the plates to a divine messenger when he was finished translating the book, so Jane joined the church far too late to handle those precious artifacts of the church's founding. Instead, it appears that Joseph Smith and those close to him generalized the term "Urim and Thummim" to refer to "any stones used to receive divine revelations." This included both the interpreters Smith had received with the Book of Mormon plates and other seer stones, some of which Smith had owned even before he began having the visions that would ultimately lead to the founding of Mormonism. In 1830 Smith gave one of these stones to Oliver Cowdery, who had helped transcribe the Book of Mormon as Smith translated it. Cowdery kept that stone until his death in 1850; it was later donated to the LDS Church. But Brigham Young stated in 1853 that "Joseph had 3 [other seer stones] which Emma [Smith] has." It is likely that Lucy Mack Smith used the term "Urim and Thummim" to describe some combination of these stones, and that Jane handled these instruments at Mother Smith's direction. In an 1899 conversation with Elvira Stevens Barney, a white Mormon woman, Jane described the object Mother Smith had allowed her to handle: "The instrument as near as I can describe it, which I handled, was made of some kind of metal, because it was so very heavy. It was firmly attached, one piece upon another.

One piece seemed to be about the size of my wrist," which Barney interjected was "good size and not perfectly round." Jane went on: "The other piece was not so large. These were set upright in a circular base." This description of stones set in an armature sounded more like the original set of interpreters than it did like the "ordinary" seer stones that Jane probably handled. But Jane was careful to quash speculation about the objects to which she had access, telling Barney that Mother Smith "did not say that Joseph used it to translate the Book of Mormon." By quoting Lucy Mack Smith's remark that Jane would be able to "tell the Latter-day Saints that [she] was permitted to handle the Urim and Thummim," Jane made clear the intimate access she had to the foundations of the LDS Church as a trusted member of the Smith household. Handling any of Joseph Smith's seer stones was a privilege few Saints could claim.[12]

Living in the Smiths' home, Jane was privy to some of Mormonism's most explosive secrets. In addition to Jane and Maria Jane Johnston, the staff of the mansion house also appears to have included two sets of sisters: Eliza and Emily Partridge and Maria and Sarah Lawrence. In her autobiography, Jane recalled "sitting discussing Mormonism" with the four women when "Sarah said, 'What would you think if a man had more wives than one?'" Sarah Lawrence's unusual conversational gambit may have been prompted by the rumors swirling in Nauvoo and in the national press about Mormonism's doctrine of "spiritual wifery," which suggested that Joseph Smith was teaching polygamy. Smith and those to whom he taught the doctrine of "celestial marriage" attempted to keep the practice secret to avoid inflaming passions against the church, but the rumors found fertile soil among Americans' deep-seated fears of sexual deviance.[13]

For Jane, the idea of a man having "more wives than one" may have resonated differently than it did for the white women with whom she discussed the idea. Historian Tera W. Hunter has shown that economic, social, and legal circumstances, including slavery and racial discrimination, often led ante-bellum African American men and women to form and dissolve marriage-like relationships without necessarily seeking legal recognition. In addition, because circumstances might force partners to live apart, and because even those who were legally married might lose track of one another when one or the other was sold or otherwise forced to relocate, it was not unheard of for men and women to have multiple concurrent partners—more wives, or husbands, than one. The idea of having more wives than one might therefore have sounded more ordinary—less scandalous—to Jane than to the white people around her. But Sarah Lawrence had not posited any of the circumstances that some-times led black women and men to maintain multiple concurrent marriage-like relationships. For white people who did not recognize the exigencies that led African Americans into what looked like bigamous relationships, the practice of having multiple romantic or marriage-like relationships supported stereotypes of black people as oversexed and incapable of forming "proper" families. Thus, the notion that Sarah Lawrence raised might also have struck Jane as inviting the same kind of public censure that so often denigrated African Americans' intimate relationships. But Jane suppressed any misgivings she may have had and responded positively to Sarah Lawrence's question. "I said, 'that is all right!'" Jane remembered many years later.[14]

Her approbation gave Maria Lawrence an opening to share a secret only a few people knew: "Well, we are all four Brother Joseph's wives!" Indeed, all four had married Joseph Smith in the spring of 1843. Smith had been teaching the doctrine of plural marriage privately to his closest associates for years, but the church's elite had worked hard to keep this element of the religion secret for fear that it would provoke a violent reaction by outsiders and, possibly, also by members of the church. In the Smith household, Joseph Smith's first wife Emma turned out to be the most stubborn obstacle to Joseph's practice of what he secretly preached. Although Emma consented to Joseph's marriages to the Partridge and Lawrence sisters, she "vacillated between reluctant acceptance and determined opposition to the marriages," her biographers wrote. Accounts of both Emma's and Joseph's lives suggest that tensions in the household over plural marriage had eased by the fall of 1843. But Jane might have sensed that something was a bit different in the Smith home. Sharing living space with the Lawrence and Partridge sisters, Jane would have observed the women's comings and goings. She could not have helped but notice when one of them spent the night away from her own bed. As the household laundress, Jane may also have had to clean up the physical evidence of Joseph's conjugal relations with some of his many wives: religious doctrine had physical consequences for bed linens, clothing, and even the handkerchiefs that wiped away the tears provoked by the difficult emotional demands of plural marriage.[15]

Whether Maria's disclosure came as a complete surprise or merely confirmed Jane's suspicions, in Jane's recollection of the conversation she reacted with visible enthusiasm: "I jumped up," she recalled, "and clapped my hands and said, 'That's good.'"[16]

Sarah Lawrence seemed to appreciate Jane's support for plural marriage. "She is all right," Sarah responded. "Just listen, she believes it all now." Had Sarah and Maria planned this conversation? Sarah's comment seemed to convey a decision: Jane could be trusted. Was this conversation an attempt to gauge Jane's commitment to the church, or to Joseph Smith's leadership? The Partridge sisters had certainly been subjected to such tests before their marriages to Joseph Smith. Perhaps these young wives of the prophet were attempting to ensure the continuing safety of Smith's household by assessing the loyalty of its residents. If so, Jane had passed their test.[17]

Was Jane's approval of plural marriage her sincere belief? Or was it what she thought the Lawrence and Partridge sisters wanted to hear? Throughout her life, Jane demonstrated some skill in saying the right thing—sometimes the most expedient thing—in conversations with those who held more social capital than she. She probably began to develop this skill as a young domestic servant: throughout her life, Jane had relied on white people for employment and patronage. One way to curry their favor was to say the things they wanted to hear. The conversation with Joseph Smith's young wives may have been one of those times. Another may have come years later in 1905, when Joseph and Emma Smith's son Joseph Smith III visited Salt Lake City. Joseph Smith III led the Reorganized Church of Jesus Christ of Latter Day Saints (the RLDS Church), a group that had parted ways with the LDS Church after Joseph Smith's death and that interpreted the founding prophet's teachings differently than the group that followed Brigham Young. Joseph Smith III was committed to the belief that his father had not practiced polygamy. In his memoir, Smith recounted a conversation with Jane: "This aged woman made quite a characteristic statement about my mother: 'She was the best woman I ever knew.' Then she added, 'And them was all lies about the Prophet Joseph having any other wives than her!' "[18] It may be that Smith misheard or misremembered Jane's words (after all, he mistakenly remembered her name as "Maria," perhaps confusing her name with that of Maria Jane Johnston). But it may also be that Smith reported the conversation accurately, and that Jane simply acquiesced to her sense that Smith desperately wanted that denial of polygamy from her. It does not seem likely that Jane's memory was faltering: around the same time that Joseph Smith III visited Salt Lake City, Jane dictated her autobiography, in which she told the story of her conversation with the Lawrence and Partridge sisters. It is also unlikely that Elizabeth J. D. Roundy, who recorded Jane's autobiographical statement, mistook her meaning so egregiously as to change the position Jane articulated about plural marriage in that document, though Roundy may have wanted Jane to affirm polygamy as much as Joseph Smith III wanted her to deny it.

Jane's autobiography emphasized the intimacy she enjoyed with the prophet and his family: during the Mannings' first few days in Nauvoo, Jane remembered, "Brother Joseph came in every morning to say good morning and ask how we were." That friendly treatment continued after Jane became a mansion house employee. In 1905, Jane told an interviewer that Joseph Smith "never passed me without shaking hands with me wherever he was. . . . He'd always smile, always just like he did to his children. He used to be just like I was his child." Jane also claimed that Joseph offered to formalize that familial bond by adopting her as a child. As Jane told the story, the proposal came through Emma Smith: "Sister Emma asked me one day if I would like to be adopted to them as their child? I did not answer her. She said, 'I will wait a while and let you consider it.' She waited two weeks before she asked me again. When she did I told her, 'No, Ma'am!'" Jane told and retold this story in her old age, seeking an opportunity to change her answer. "I did not understand or know what it meant," she lamented in her autobiography. "They were always good and kind to me, but I did not know my own mind. I did not comprehend."[19]

In the mid-1840s, the meaning of Emma's offer was anything but obvious. When Jane was baptized a few years earlier, Mormons explicitly discussed baptism as the ritual whereby a convert was adopted into the family of God. What, Jane must have wondered, could Emma and Joseph possibly mean by this offer to adopt an adult woman as their child? But when Jane told this story at the turn of the twentieth century, the meaning of Emma's offer was both apparent and profound. By the early twentieth century, Mormons regularly used the temple ritual of "sealing" to create eternal bonds between family members, taking literally Jesus's promise in the Gospel of Matthew that "whatsoever thou shalt bind on earth shall be bound in heaven." By sealing men and women in marriages and parents and children in adoptions, Latter-day Saints aspired to create a vast heavenly family that included all of humanity, stretching through time and space back to Adam and thence to God himself. Only by being grafted into Adam's family tree, they believed, could humans be recognized as legitimate members of God's family and legal heirs to the heavenly kingdom. According to LDS theology, sealing people together in familial relationships makes possible the salvation of the entire human race. In Emma's offer of adoption, Jane had been given the chance to enjoy an eternal, familial relationship with Joseph Smith and, through him, with all of God's family. Jane was not alone in her ignorance of the import of this offer at the time: historian Gordon Irving wrote that "while sealing was accepted doctrine by 1844, the Saints in general had little chance to become practically acquainted with the sealing doctrine prior to the death of Joseph Smith." Indeed, it is far from certain that any adoption sealings were performed during Smith's lifetime.[20]

Some commentators have suggested that the offer of adoption was actually an offer of plural marriage. This interpretation fits with an understanding of Jane's conversation with the Lawrence and Partridge sisters as a loyalty test, but Joseph Smith's clear opposition to interracial marriage and Emma Smith's abiding dislike of plural marriage make it unlikely. Joseph sought Emma's consent for some of his plural marriages, and some people have suggested that Emma proposed Jane as a plural wife in order to stymie her husband, presenting him with a choice between taking a plural wife he found unacceptable or not taking more plural wives. But by the time Jane arrived in the Smith household, Joseph Smith had stopped marrying new plural wives. Biographers of both Joseph and Emma agree that by the winter of 1843 the couple was getting along better than they had in some time; it seems improbable that Emma would have used Jane to disturb this delicate peace and provoke further confrontation on a subject that clearly caused her great distress. Since Joseph Smith almost certainly did not see Jane as marriage material, it also seems unlikely that Emma proposed adopting Jane in order to eliminate her from the pool of potential plural wives.[21]

By the time Jane told her story about Emma's offer, no witnesses remained to corroborate or contradict her account, and no other evidence has come to light that might clarify this episode. This lack of evidence raises the possibility that Jane fabricated the story. Certainly, by the turn of the twentieth century when she told this story, Jane had little to lose and much to gain if she could persuade church leaders that Joseph Smith had offered to adopt her. However, inventing a story in which Emma Smith played a central role would have been a tactical misstep: Emma had fallen out of favor in the LDS Church by refusing to go to Utah and ultimately casting her lot with the rival RLDS Church. Jane was surely aware of how church leaders felt about Emma Smith; if her goal was adoption into Joseph Smith's family, it is doubtful Jane would have emphasized Emma's role in any strategic fictionalization of the past. Jane's account of her exchange with Emma Smith remained quite consistent over the two decades or so that she repeated it in various venues. Even if that account is unsupported by other evidence, and even if it was ultimately mistaken, the most reasonable conclusion is that Jane was telling the truth about the past as she remembered it.

Emma's offer of adoption may have been related to the fact that neither Jane's biological father nor her stepfather was present in Nauvoo. This fatherlessness, though it did not seem to bother Jane, was a problem in the patriarchal system that Mormons were constructing. As Joseph Smith and his associates began to teach, the Saints needed "Fathers and Mothers in Israel." Those who lacked fathers, whether through paternal death or abandonment; because their fathers had not joined the LDS Church; or because their fathers were insufficiently spiritually advanced, were objects of particular concern. Adoption into what Mormon studies scholar Samuel Brown called a "sacerdotal family," a spiritual lineage centered on the possession and ritual exercise of priesthood power, represented a potential solution to the problem of spiritually orphaned converts.[22]

While Jane declined Emma Smith's offer of adoption, in March of 1844 she received a patriarchal blessing from Hyrum Smith, Joseph's older brother. As the Patriarch of the church, Hyrum served as a father figure to the entire community, and following the example of the great patriarchs of the Hebrew Bible, he bestowed blessings on church members. Sociologists Gary Shepherd, Gordon Shepherd, and Natalie Shepherd write that for early Mormons like Jane, patriarchal blessings "were considered to be the inspired word of God, addressed directly and personally to individual blessing recipients and thus. . . an important form of prophetic revelation." But to early Latter-day Saints, patriarchal blessings also represented a kind of adoption. Jane's patriarchal blessing extended her adoption into the family of God that she had experienced in the ritual of baptism by creating an explicitly patriarchal relationship between her and Hyrum Smith.

The blessing helped Jane keep up with developments in the Latter-day Saint understanding of the nature of spiritual kinship, cementing her membership in the family of God as the Latter-day Saints understood it in the mid-1840s.[23]

It was not uncommon for church members to receive patriarchal blessings at what Latter-day Saints referred to as "blessing meetings." Historian Irene M. Bates describes these meetings as "celebrations which included feasts, and in one instance Lucy Mack Smith, wife of the first patriarch, added her own blessing to that given by her husband." Patriarchal blessings might also be given in somewhat more private contexts, at family meetings or after a dinner gathering of friends. Jane may have received her blessing in any one of these settings. Hyrum Smith placed his hands on her head and, following the prompting of the Holy Spirit, pronounced a blessing on her. Someone else stood by to record Smith's words. Jane would treasure this written record of her blessing for the rest of her life. She also brought her blessing to a church recorder so that the text could be copied into the church's official blessing book, an institutional record of patriarchal blessings that preserved these documents for posterity.[24]

By the time Jane received Hyrum Smith's blessing, she no longer lived with Joseph Smith's family. The Smiths had not lasted long as innkeepers: in January of 1844, Joseph Smith leased the mansion house to a neighbor, Ebenezer Robinson, reserving only three rooms for his family of six and two servants. Jane and Sylvester went to live with her mother, and Jane began searching for work. It was a difficult time to be unemployed in Nauvoo: not only did immigrants continue to pour into the city, but also, Jane recalled later, "there was not much work because of the persecutions" of the Latter-day Saints.[25]

Anti-Mormon sentiment seemed to be growing, and it drew ever closer to Nauvoo. Disaffected church members in the city organized themselves and published one issue of a newspaper called the *Expositor*, which purported to "explode the vicious principles of Joseph Smith, and those who practice the same abominations and whoredoms." Concerned that the publication would provoke mob violence against the Mormons in Nauvoo, Smith persuaded the Nauvoo city council to deem the *Expositor* libelous. Then, in his capacity as mayor of Nauvoo, he ordered the press destroyed. One of the editors of the paper pressed charges against Smith the next day. The day after that, Joseph Smith was arrested for riot. Although the local court ordered his release, the legal wrangling would ultimately result in Smith's imprisonment in the county seat of Carthage. There he would be murdered by an angry mob.[26]

The unrest in the city may well have made it more difficult for Jane to find a new job, particularly because, according to the state's stringent Black Code, Jane should not have been there at all. In 1819, the Illinois legislature had passed laws requiring that before settling in the state, black people had to "produce a certificate of freedom under seal of a court of record, endorsed by the clerk of the court in which [s]he wished to reside, together with information as to [her] family and [her]self." These were the very "free papers" Jane and her family had been unable to produce when they were demanded on the journey from Connecticut to Nauvoo. The Black Code further complicated Jane's search for employment, because it also provided that anyone who hired a black person who did not have her or his free papers would be fined $1.50 for each day of the undocumented person's labor.[27]

The first portion of the patriarchal blessing Jane received from Hyrum Smith spoke to anxieties she probably felt about her material circumstances. Beginning with the promise that she would have "a place . . . in the midst of the people of Zion" and "a place and where to lay [her] head," the blessing went on to promise her "food and raiment and habitations to dwell in" and that she would "be blessed in [her] avocations, that is, in the labor of [her] hands."[28] Smith's words hinted at Jane's difficult financial circumstances, suggesting that she struggled to feed and clothe herself and her young son, and that although she might have had shelter, she had no place to "dwell in," no place to call home.

But after promising that her obedience to God's commands would bring her a measure of temporal security, the blessing turned decisively to the spiritual rewards of that obedience. Hyrum Smith initially promised that if she was obedient, Jane would have "a name in the midst of the people of Zion," perhaps referring to the new names Latter-day Saints received in their endowments "that the world knows not of," but which Jane believed the Holy Spirit had told her about on that first day of her employment by Joseph and Emma Smith. Hyrum Smith went on to promise that "you shall have a knowledge of the mysteries as God shall reveal them, even the mysteries of his Kingdom manifested in his wisdom unto your capacity." He continued, building on this extravagant-sounding promise of divine knowledge by declaring that still greater treasures awaited. Jane had "a promise through the Father of the New World," he said, that was still hidden. That promise, which was linked to Jane's ancestral spiritual lineage, was "sealed up with the sacred records hereafter to be revealed."[29] This portion of the blessing seems to promise Jane exactly the kind of "something more" she sought when she left the Congregational Church in New Canaan to join the Mormons. She had experienced for herself the gifts of the Spirit: she had spoken in tongues and healed through faith, she had received divine knowledge from the Holy Spirit and handled the instruments the prophet had used to receive revelations. But Hyrum Smith promised that the wonders would not cease. God would reveal yet more knowledge, and had made a promise that would find fulfillment when still more scriptures were uncovered.

Sandwiched between these statements about the forthcoming divine promise was a declaration of Jane's lineage. Protestants had long thought of themselves as symbolically grafted into the house of Israel. Early Mormons began to diverge from other Christians by crafting a more literal interpretation of this identity. In the 1830s and early 1840s, Mormons began to believe that they were spiritually or perhaps even biologically connected to the ten tribes of Israel, collectively known as the tribe of Ephraim. The patriarchal blessings Mormons received reflected this growing interest in the Saints' lineage, and over time it became a standard practice for a patriarch to identify people's lineage in the course of giving a blessing. Most Latter-day Saints' patriarchal blessings identified them as descendants of Ephraim, locating them securely in the majority and among the lineage Saints believed to be part of God's chosen people.[30]

Jane, on the other hand, received a "promise through the Father of the New World," that was handed down "in the lineage of Canaan, the Son of Ham" according to the patriarchal blessing that Hyrum Smith gave her. In identifying Jane as a descendant of Canaan, Hyrum Smith reached back to a period of biblical history that predated Ephraim. At the same time, he saddled Jane with all the racial assumptions of nineteenth-century America, connecting her spiritual lineage to the biblical figure of Canaan, whom Noah had cursed to be a "servant of servants" and who white Americans and Europeans identified as one of two biblical ancestors of black people. Smith compounded the racialized references in his blessing of Jane a few sentences later when he reassured her that "he that changeth times and seasons and placed a mark upon your forehead can take it off and stamp upon you his own Image." Smith's reference to the "mark upon [Jane's] forehead" clearly linked her to the biblical figure Cain. Here again, Hyrum Smith drew on white Christians' racial folklore, which held that the dark skin of African-descended people was the mark of Cain and visual proof of black people's descent from the biblical first murderer. Even as he held out the possibility of release from these biblical curses with the suggestion that God might "stamp upon [her] his own Image," Smith invoked the very Bible stories that white Christians used to justify their oppression of black people.[31] Jane was trapped: she could not get a blessing without receiving a curse.

The theme of obedience ran throughout the blessing Hyrum Smith pronounced on Jane. The blessing began, "Behold, I say unto you, Jane, if you will keep the commandments of God you shall be blessed spiritually and temporally." After specifying the forms of those spiritual and temporal blessings, he returned to the idea of obedience: "Now, therefore, I say unto you, Jane: it is through obedience to the Gospel that you are blessed, and it is through a continuation in obedience to the commandments of God, even unto the end of your days, that you may be saved. Shun the path of vice, turn away from wickedness, be fervent unto prayer without ceasing, and your name shall be handed down to posterity, from generation to generation." The blessing appeared to reach its conclusion with a somewhat generic, and optimistic, benediction: "Now, therefore, look and live; and remember the redemption and the resurrection of the just, and it shall be well with you." Smith followed these words with a customary closing, "These blessings and promises I seal upon your head." But then, it seems, he felt moved to offer one more personalized warning: "Behold, I say unto you,

Jane: if thou doest well thou shalt be accepted; if thou doest not well sin lieth at the door." Smith's words here echoed LDS scripture, quoting God's warning to Cain, recalling once again the curses to which Smith believed Jane was heir. Again, Smith closed by sealing on Jane the "blessings and promises" he had pronounced.[32]

It was common in patriarchal blessings of the time that some promises were made conditional on the recipient's faithful belief or action. Still, the strength of the element of contingency in this blessing was striking. The focus on Jane's obedience to God's commandments might be a clue that Jane was not the paragon of moral virtue that she would later portray herself to be. But perhaps this concern about Jane's faithfulness had more to do with how others perceived her than with her actual behavior. It may be that Jane's status as an unwed mother raised eyebrows in Nauvoo, kindling speculation about her sexual activity. Jane's racial difference from her neighbors might have added fuel to the flames, bolstering suspicions about Jane's sexual history with stereotypes about the sexual promiscuity of black women. But the racial stereotypes that informed white Latter-day Saints' views on Jane's sexuality also prescribed a social structure in which Jane's role was to be a "servant of servants," and obedience was a necessary trait for a servant. Moreover, Jane had worked most of her life as a domestic servant, one accustomed to obeying an employer. Thus, we might read the preponderance of statements about obedience in Jane's patriarchal blessing as having to do more with her racial identity and employment history. It is possible that Hyrum Smith's blessing simply focused on applying obedience, a skill Jane had learned and practiced throughout her life, to the arena of faith.[33]

It was customary to pay the patriarch directly for one's blessing, though the payment was more like a gratuity than a fee. By the spring of 1844, Jane probably had no cash with which to remunerate the patriarch. She may have paid in kind, by doing laundry or other domestic service for Hyrum and his family; or, like some Saints, she may have accepted the blessing as a gift and not attempted to compensate the giver. The search for work wore on Jane, and eventually she gave up on Nauvoo. In her autobiography, she recalled that she "saw Brother Joseph and asked him if I should go to Burlington and take my sister Angeline with me?" Just thirty miles upriver from Nauvoo on the other side of the Mississippi, Burlington was "Iowa's preeminent city," even though its population of close to three thousand people made it about a quarter the size of Nauvoo in 1844. The two cities enjoyed a close relationship. Mormons from Nauvoo took pleasure excursions to Burlington on the LDS Church-owned steamboat *Maid of Iowa*. Burlington politicians visited Nauvoo for important civic events. And the Burlington press regularly reported on Mormon affairs. Iowa's Black Code closely resembled that of Illinois, but Jane may have felt that she would have a better chance of finding work there, since Burlington was not receiving boat loads of white immigrants every day with whom Jane would have to compete for employment.[34]

Like Jane, Angeline may also have been out of work and staying with her mother, further stretching the Manning family's meager resources. Going to Burlington together would guarantee both sisters a little more respectability and safety than either would have if she traveled alone. As Jane recalled her conversation with Joseph Smith, he did not speculate on her chances of finding work, but he promised a far more important outcome: "He said yes, go and be good girls, and remember your profession of faith in the Everlasting Gospel, and the Lord will bless you." This blessing, contingent on Jane's faithfulness just like the patriarchal blessing she had received from Smith's brother Hyrum, were the last words Jane remembered hearing from her prophet. As she recalled, "we went and stayed [in Burlington] three weeks then returned to Nauvoo. During this time Joseph and Hyrum were killed."[35]

Joseph and Hyrum Smith had been jailed in Carthage, Illinois, for rioting, the charge that editors of the anti-Mormon *Nauvoo Expositor* pressed in response to the destruction of their press. The guards at the jail allowed a large mob to storm the building; the attackers killed the two brothers and wounded John Taylor, another leader in the church. As historian Robert Flanders wrote, Joseph Smith's followers were "paralyzed with shock and fear." The Mormons' opponents were equally stunned, alarmed by the brazen violence and afraid that Mormons would retaliate in kind for the deaths of their leaders. Thomas Ford, the governor of Illinois, cautioned the Mormons against mistaking the expressions of outrage over the Smiths' murders for support of the movement Joseph Smith led: in a letter to the people of Nauvoo nearly a month after the Smiths' deaths, Ford wrote that "the naked truth is that most well informed persons condemn in the most unqualified manner the mode in which the Smiths were put to death, but nine out of ten [express also] their pleasure that they are dead. . . . The unfortunate victims . . . were generally and thoroughly hated throughout the country, and it is not reasonable to suppose that their death has produced any reaction in the public mind resulting in active sympathy; if you think so, you are mistaken." The Mormons would not make that mistake. They mourned their fallen leaders, vowed vengeance against their enemies, and turned to the task of navigating the days ahead without the men who had brought their church into being and had laid their hands on members' heads in blessing. With the martyrdom of Joseph and Hyrum Smith, the first era of Mormon history had ended. Jane felt like her life was over too: she remembered later that she "liked to a died."[36] She could hardly imagine the changes that would come in the wake of the Smith brothers' deaths.

4

We Got Along Splendid

(1844–1848)

The new beginning Jane had made in Nauvoo, the world of possibility so close she could touch it, came crashing to the ground with Joseph Smith's death in 1844. For Jane, it seemed that Joseph Smith held the power to make the world new again, to create a heaven on earth. His death dashed that hope. Slowly, painfully, she picked up the pieces and found a way to go on. Her son Sylvester needed her. Her sister Angeline was close by, too, and perhaps encouraged her to keep going. Although Jane said she wanted to die when Joseph Smith was killed, the teachers of the church urged her to live.[1]

The LDS Church was still a young organization. It had not established a process for selecting a new leader, so Joseph Smith's death left the church without clear direction. In the spring, hundreds of elders had gone to the northeast on a "political mission" to promote Joseph Smith's campaign for the presidency of the United States. Now they hurried home to discuss the future of the church and discern God's will for the community. Sidney Rigdon, Smith's running mate, returned to Nauvoo from Pittsburgh. Rigdon had been a member of the LDS Church's "First Presidency," the leadership team composed of the prophet and two counselors, but had lost Joseph Smith's confidence in the early 1840s and retained his position near the top of the church's hierarchy only because of the support of other church leaders. Rigdon arrived in Nauvoo in early August and attempted to persuade church members to appoint him as a "guardian" to care for the church until Joseph Smith's resurrection. Only two days before a church meeting appointed to consider Rigdon's plan, Brigham Young arrived and presented an alternate strategy. A guardian was not what the church needed, Young said; Joseph Smith had left the Quorum of the Twelve Apostles, of which Young was the president, with "all the keys and powers" that were necessary to lead the church into the future. Church members voted to support the Quorum of the Twelve Apostles as the leaders of the church. In doing so, they implicitly endorsed the theological claims Young made for the primacy of the priesthood and temple rituals in LDS religious faith and practice.[2] Here was a new beginning for the movement, one that allowed the church to move into an uncertain future.

Jane found a new beginning of her own when she married Isaac James, a black convert from New Jersey. The couple almost certainly met shortly after Jane arrived in Nauvoo in 1843. As two of only a handful of black people in the town, they stood out. They might have encountered one another at any number of occasions, ranging from worship services to work situations. Jane and Isaac's wedding date is uncertain, but the event seems to have taken place after Joseph Smith's death in the summer of 1844 and before the fall of 1845.[3] At the time, Jane was probably a domestic servant in Brigham Young's home, where she had found work after her return from Burlington.

What we know with certainty about Isaac James could fit on a postcard. He was born in Prospertown, New Jersey, probably a few years before Jane in the late 1810s. Located in Monmouth County, Prospertown was in New Jersey's Pine Barrens, a sandy area that supported little agriculture. Mormonism made significant inroads in this region in the late 1830s and early 1840s. In 1839–1840, Joseph Smith himself visited the area on his way to Washington, DC and, one historian wrote, he "is said to have 'sealed a large number.'" Several members of the Ivins family, which was prominent in the region, joined the LDS Church during this period: the Federal Census of 1840 listed the family of LDS convert James Ivins living in Monmouth County's Upper Freehold Township, about five miles from Prospertown. Isaac James may have lived with and worked for James Ivins and his family. The 1840 census record for the Ivins household included two free black people, each between ten and twenty-four years old, one male—who may have been Isaac James—and one female.[4]

James Ivins and his brother Charles traveled to Nauvoo the fall of 1840 with missionary Erastus Snow to investigate the possibility of joining the gathering there. All three men returned east in late November of that year. Snow, whose missionary work at the time centered around southeastern Pennsylvania and central New Jersey, returned to the New Jersey Pine Barrens several times in the spring and summer of 1841. He recorded in his journal that he preached there "to crowded and attentive audiences. I found [them] strong in faith, many having of late been added to them and several families I found about ready to move to Nauvoo in accordance with the commandments." James Ivins and his family, and perhaps Isaac James, were likely among these eager listeners and, indeed, may have joined any one of several groups whose departure for Nauvoo Snow noted in his journal.[5]

Quite apart from his belief in the religious message that Snow presented and its mandate to gather, and regardless of any connection he had with the Ivins family, Isaac might have been very glad to leave New Jersey. Historian Graham Russell Hodges writes that from an economic perspective, in the 1830s black people in Monmouth County had "advanced just beyond a state of bondage," and he characterized the free black community of Upper Freehold in 1839 as "struggling to survive." As a young man just entering his twenties in the late 1830s, Isaac may have preferred to try his luck elsewhere. If Isaac did work for the Ivins family, it may also be that he was happy with the situation he had found with them, and that the possibility of continuing employment with the Ivinses made the prospect of going to Nauvoo more attractive. In early 1842, the LDS Church took a census of its members in Nauvoo. Isaac was listed, and he appeared to be living with James and Mary Ivins.[6]

James and Charles Ivins acquired extensive property holdings in and around Nauvoo and were among the town's more prominent citizens. But the Ivins brothers soon became disillusioned with the town's mayor, and their church's prophet, Joseph Smith. They joined a small group of dissenters in publishing the *Nauvoo Expositor* in 1844, revealing Smith's more scandalous teachings (like polygamy) and seeking reforms in the church.[7] It seems unlikely that Isaac James, who remained loyal to Joseph Smith as the prophet of the church, continued to board with James and Mary Ivins as James Ivins made his way out of the church. With tensions running high, and Mormons on alert for any harbinger of mob attack, working for a dissenting figure would have left Isaac torn between his religious faith and his economic needs. Although there is no way to know with certainty, it is more likely that Isaac worked as a hired laborer and boarded elsewhere when a more comfortable situation presented itself. He may even have gone to Burlington, like Jane, in search of work.

How Jane and Isaac got married, who performed the ceremony, what wording was used, what meaning was imbued in the ritual, is lost to us. We can hazard no more than a few guesses, based on what we know about marriage at the time. Over the first fifteen years of the Latter-day Saint movement, the Mormons departed radically from historical Christian views on marriage, and from accepted Euro-American understandings of marriage. By the time Jane married Isaac, Latter-day Saints in Nauvoo generally believed marriage to be an eternal relationship, rather than one that would end at death. By 1843, this conception of eternal marriage was linked to a ritual act that Mormons referred to as "sealing," a ceremony that would eventually be performed exclusively in LDS temples. Until his death, Joseph Smith developed the Saints' theology of marriage through his participation in wedding ceremonies and through his sermons and revelations. He taught the Mormons that "marriage was an order of the priesthood and without it heaven was unattainable." Further, as religious studies scholar Kathleen Flake noted, the Saints who were married in this way believed that by so doing, they participated in holiness and even divinity. Jane and Isaac's wedding was almost certainly officiated by a priesthood holder, since most men in Nauvoo at the time fit this category. But whether the officiant invoked his priesthood in the ceremony, and whether he sealed upon Jane and Isaac the blessings of priesthood, immortality, eternal life, and a "part in the first resurrection," as was done in other Latter-day Saint weddings of the time, we cannot know. In the absence of evidence to the contrary, it is reasonable to assume that Jane and Isaac got married in the same way that the people around them got married. However, later in her life, Jane believed that she and Isaac had not been sealed in marriage: in 1890 she wrote to Apostle Joseph F. Smith, the son of Hyrum Smith, asking to be sealed in marriage to another African American man without mentioning having been sealed to Isaac James.[8]

As summer turned to fall in the year after Joseph Smith's death, the Mormons continued to labor on the temple that Smith had started to build in Nauvoo, pushing to finish so that they could finally perform the ceremonies their prophet had envisioned as the means to bind the human family for eternity. In early December, the temple was finally ready for the Saints to receive their endowments and be sealed to one another. They went in droves, thronging the temple for the blessings they believed would follow from these rituals. But Jane and Isaac were not recorded among the couples who were sealed in the temple in those heady months. We do not know why Jane and Isaac did not participate in the temple ceremonies that their neighbors were so eager to perform. At the LDS temple in Kirtland, Ohio, the black priesthood holder Elijah Abel had received his washing and anointing, which historian W. Paul Reeve describes as "a temple ceremony designed to ritually wash the initiate clean from the sins and cares of the world." As Reeve notes, this ceremony was the only aspect of temple ritual developed in the 1830s. By the time the Saints performed endowments and sealings in the Nauvoo temple, Abel had left the region and could not participate.[9] The historical record includes no officially announced policy barring black people from the Nauvoo temple; perhaps it was simply that Jane and Isaac's neighbors made them feel unwelcome, or their ecclesiastical leaders discouraged them from attending. Jane was still working in Brigham Young's home, and he may have informed her or Isaac that they should not go into the temple. Or perhaps Jane or Isaac simply felt spiritually unready to participate in ceremonies of such grave import, and decided to wait until later. Whatever the reason, Jane and Isaac did not receive their endowments, they were not sealed to one another, and Sylvester was not sealed to them as a child.

Brigham Young left Nauvoo in February 1846, leading the first wave of Mormons across the Mississippi River into Iowa Territory. The Saints were abandoning the state they believed was complicit in their prophet's murder and were looking forward to a new Promised Land further west (Figure 4.1). Jane was pregnant with her second son, Silas, who would be born in June. She found work in the home of another church leader, Reynolds Cahoon, until she, Isaac, and Sylvester left Illinois later that spring with another wave of migrants. Jane's group benefitted from the warmer, sunnier weather that dried up the muddy roads with which the first group of travelers had to contend, and from the relative abundance of grasses on which their animals could graze. These advantages

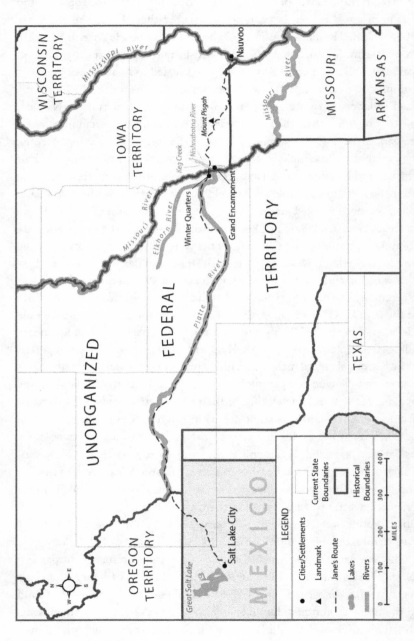

Figure 4.1 Jane and her family, along with many other Mormons, left Nauvoo in the spring of 1846. They traveled to Winter Quarters, in what is now the area of Omaha, Nebraska; they then continued on to the Great Salt Lake Valley in 1847, following the routes shown here. Map by Chelsey Buffington, Center for Spatial Analysis and Research, Portland State University.

made travel much faster and easier than it had been for Brigham Young's group. Jane's company may have caught up with the earlier migrants as soon as the middle of May. "Some Brethren from Nauvoo overtake us. They have been on the road but 3 weeks, we 3 months," midwife and diarist Patty Sessions wrote with some dismay in her journal on May 15, 1846.[10]

A few days later, the entire group paused at a place in Iowa they called Mount Pisgah. "It is a pretty place," opined Sessions. Some of the travelers stayed there, intending to develop the area as a site where later Mormon migrants could rest and resupply before continuing on.[11] Others used the layover to repair equipment; still others went ahead to build bridges and scout the terrain further west. In early June, the travelers began moving again. They were organized into groups of families so that everyone belonged to a "ten," a unit made up of approximately ten heads of families and their dependents. Five tens made a "fifty," and two fifties made a "hundred." Each ten, fifty, and hundred had its own captain to lead it, imposing a quasi-military discipline on the emigrating group that made their travel more orderly and helped ensure that nobody fell behind. Yet their exodus from Nauvoo defied such thorough regimentation: families had left willy-nilly as the opportunity presented itself, rather than waiting to make a methodical exit. As the Mormons made their way westward, they gradually became more orderly, though the full organization of traveling companies would wait until the following year.

George Parker Dykes was captain of the ten to which both Jane's and Patty Sessions's families belonged by the time they left Mount Pisgah. For Jane, Sessions's presence was both convenient and fortuitous, because it meant an experienced midwife was available for the birth of her son, Silas, on June 10, 1846. In Jane's recollection, Silas was born at Keg Creek, Iowa, but according to Sessions's records, the ten was camped somewhat east of Keg Creek on the banks of the Nishnabotna River. Jane did not have a chance to rest from the labor of childbirth; the company continued on its way the following day, and according to Sessions's diary reached Council Bluffs, Iowa, on June 13.[12] There, they created a settlement they called the "Grand Encampment"; some then crossed the Missouri River to a temporary city laid out on a site in what is now the Omaha, Nebraska area that came to be known as "Winter Quarters." Others spread out from the Grand Encampment to sites up and down the Missouri River where they could find food for their livestock and fuel for their fires.

George Parker Dykes volunteered for the Mormon Battalion, a fighting force recruited to assist in the US military effort against Mexico. Although the Latter-day Saints were suspicious of the US government and resentful of the ill treatment they felt they had received from federal officials, they could not turn down the compensation Mormon Battalion volunteers would receive, which would help finance the church's move west. The Battalion assembled near

Council Bluffs in July 1846, and departed on a long march that would eventually take them to the Pacific Ocean. Dykes's subsequent letters to his family and to Brigham Young make clear that Jane and Isaac continued to live with and work for the Dykes family. Dykes added a postscript to an August 1846 letter to Young, asking him to convey a message to his three wives: "Please tell my wife that in all the comforts of life to let Isaac & Jane share bountifully as Isaac is the main pillar now for the family to lean upon. Tell them to hearken diligently to the council of the church & all is well." In October, Dykes reiterated this instruction. Writing to his wives from Santa Fe, he stated, "I want you all to be united & live in peace & let Grandma & Isaac & his family have as good fare as the rest, for Isaac shall yet be rewarded for all his kindness to us not only in the . . . day when [it] . . . is said 'come ye blessed of my Father,' but here in time also. Isaac has done well & I will do as well by him as he has by me." Dykes's words suggest a strong sense of dependence on Isaac and Jane James. Isaac and Jane's labor allowed Dorcas, Cynthia, and Alcina Dykes to live a life of slightly more ease than would otherwise be possible in the rudimentary settlement of Winter Quarters. Perhaps Dykes's persistent reminders to his wives that they should treat the Jameses well were rooted in concern about what might happen if the relationship between his family and the James family soured. Isaac and Jane were not duty-bound to assist the Dykes family; if they felt mistreated, Isaac and Jane might decide to invest their time and energy elsewhere. Still, George Dykes's sense that Isaac James and, by extension, Isaac's family would be rewarded both "here in time" and on Judgment Day is striking, and hints at a progressive attitude toward race relations that may explain why Jane and Isaac chose to stay with the Dykes family after arriving in Winter Quarters, even when George Dykes himself departed with the Mormon Battalion.[13] While Dykes and other men were away, their families and other fellow Mormons regrouped and prepared for the next step in their journey.

Even as the Saints fled Nauvoo, the church continued to develop its understanding of God and humanity. The church's position on race was particularly inchoate at this moment in Winter Quarters. Historians often point to one episode, and one man, in particular as the catalyst for the hardening of racist policies in the church: William McCary. Known by a variety of names, McCary was born into slavery in Natchez, Mississippi. As a boy, he discovered a natural talent for music and mimicry, and he soon became widely known for his talents as an entertainer. He was freed by the early 1840s, and at some point began to present himself as American Indian, rather than black. When he came to Nauvoo in 1846, he played the role of an enigmatic Indian prophet and musician, a strategy that historian Angela Pulley Hudson argued allowed McCary greater freedom than his identity as an African American. He was baptized LDS, and soon married a white woman, Lucy Stanton. The McCarys floated in and out of the LDS community as it moved from Nauvoo to Winter Quarters, but by February of 1847, they were in the Nebraska settlement.[14]

In Winter Quarters, popular perception of William McCary's racial identity was inconclusive. At least some who recorded their impressions seem to have accepted his claims to Indianness while not ruling out blackness. Church secretary Willard Richards, for example, referred to McCary as "the Nigger Indian" on more than one occasion. While Brigham Young and other church leaders seemed inclined, at first, to cautiously accept McCary into the fold, they soon found cause for concern. McCary claimed to be a prophet like Joseph Smith, and he appeared to be contending for more power and authority in Winter Quarters than Brigham Young and his allies were willing to grant. While Young had consolidated his authority sufficiently to lead the Saints as far as the Missouri River, his claim to leadership was not fully settled. Indeed, throughout the years of disruption after Joseph Smith's death, several dissenters led factions out of the church over disputes about doctrine and policy. Sidney Rigdon, Young's initial rival for leadership of the church, headed one of the first groups that positioned itself as an alternative to Young's leadership. Another group, led by James Strang, presented what historian John Turner described as "a viable option for Mormons whose miserable experiences during 1846 cast doubt on either Young's decision-making or revelatory authority." Threats to the leadership of Young and the Quorum of the Twelve Apostles were thus serious matters in Winter Quarters.[15]

McCary's bid for authority was compounded by suggestions of racial and sexual transgression that swirled around the enigmatic figure. Whether McCary was Indian, black, or both, some Saints were uncomfortable with his marriage to Lucy Stanton, because they shared the general American antipathy to interracial marriage. As historian Angela Pulley Hudson noted, McCary came under heightened suspicion because, as one contemporary wrote, "he was 'in favor of holding his meetings of the men and women separately.' It appeared that 'his teaching to the men and to the women was entirely different,' implying spiritual—and perhaps sexual—indecency."[16] Although Latter-day Saints themselves were in the process of radically upending nineteenth-century gender roles and family structures, they were uncomfortable with the idea that William McCary might be experimenting with still other ways of constructing gender norms and configuring families, and that he might be doing so out of sight of white men. McCary's ambiguous racial identity could not have helped matters: stereotypes of black men as oversexualized and animalistic likely underlay some Mormon men's fears that McCary's activities threatened the sexual purity of the women who found his teachings compelling.

Called to meet with Young and the Quorum of the Twelve Apostles, the McCarys focused the conversation on William McCary's identity and white Mormon attitudes about race. The McCarys' complaints demonstrated that

William, like Jane, had experienced "hardship, trial, and rebuff" at the hands of white Mormons. Historian Angela Pulley Hudson wrote that "the appearance before the Twelve was an electric and pivotal moment for the McCarys. But. . . it might not have felt as momentous to [the Twelve]." Indeed, the minutes taken of the meeting reveal a rambling monologue by William McCary that left Young and the Twelve confused at times, indignant at others, and struggling to reassure McCary and his wife that regardless of skin color, as Young put it, "of one blood has God made all flesh." By April, although the Quorum of the Twelve Apostles had issued a public statement against those who threatened to lead followers away from the church, the McCarys had established a base of operations at Mosquito Creek, on the Iowa side of the Missouri River. The number of McCary's followers slowly grew, capitalizing on the Saints' frustration with the leadership of Young and the Twelve and on their fascination with McCary's ambiguous racial identity.[17]

It is hard to tell what Jane might have heard about McCary in Winter Quarters, or about Young's response. As McCary's following grew, he was surely the subject of speculation throughout the LDS settlements. In the spring of 1847, Jane was nursing her infant son and making preparations for another journey to an unfamiliar destination as alarm began to spread among church leaders that McCary was leading Saints into apostasy. Jane must have heard something about the unpredictable McCary as she greeted neighbors before or after worship, phrased as a word of warning from a church authority familiar with the goings-on, or just in conversation with Isaac of an evening. As rumors about the McCarys' activities spread, neighbors in the Mosquito Creek area became openly hostile, and by early summer the couple had fled to Missouri. In the fall of 1847 a local leader named Nelson Whipple went to Mosquito Creek to help restore order. He later recalled that he found that the McCarys had created a sealing ceremony of their own, which he saw as the centerpiece of their apostasy: William McCary, he wrote, "had a number of women sealed to him in his way which was as follows: He had a house in which this ordinance was performed. His wife Lucy Stanton was in the room at the time of the performance, no others were admitted. The form of sealing was for the women to bed with him, in the daytime as I am informed three different times by which they were sealed to the fullest extent."[18]

By the time word of McCary's activities became widespread, Jane and her family had arrived safely in the Salt Lake Valley. What must Jane have thought as these details filtered back to Utah? McCary claimed to be Indian, but it is not clear that white Latter-day Saints were persuaded by his claim. Jane might have reasonably feared that McCary would make things harder in the church for other African Americans. She may have been angry at his irresponsible behavior, or at the white women who reportedly fell under his sway. Perhaps she, like her neighbors, was simply outraged at the scandal of it all, the apparent perversions of what she believed to be the true gospel. For church leaders, the scandal seems to have played an important role in hardening sentiment against interracial marriages, and against the spiritual equality of white and black Mormons.[19]

As they tried to maintain unity, church leaders also prepared the group for the next big trek, this time leaving Iowa and Nebraska for a permanent location in the West. Church leaders began taking stock of resources and organizing groups of people, preparing for departures beginning in the early spring. The Jameses had little to contribute to the overall emigration effort: a survey of resources from February 1847 listed them as having one cow, thirty pounds of meat, and a few garden seeds. Perhaps for this reason, they were assigned to Isaac Haight's ten, which included Daniel Spencer. In the same survey, Spencer reported eight hundred pounds of meat; five bushels of wheat and four of buckwheat; seventeen yokes of oxen, ten cows, and four horses; plus six wagons. In fact, the Jameses were by far the poorest family in their ten. Most families, though certainly not all of them, also listed tools. Several had multiple yokes of oxen, one or more wagons, horses, pounds of flour or meal, and bushels of wheat or corn. It seems likely that the Jameses ultimately drove one of Spencer's wagons, hitched to one of his teams. Or they may have relied on a loan from another member of their company. In the end, though, much of what they traveled with was not their own and would not form the material foundation of their new life once they reached their destination. According to Daniel Spencer, captain of Jane's hundred, the group set out on June 18, 1847. They would spend about three months on the trail.[20]

The Latter-day Saints embarked on their journey west from the Elkhorn River, about twenty-seven miles west of Winter Quarters in the sandhills of what is now eastern Nebraska. Jane's group traveled about fifteen miles along the north side of the Platte River on their first day, and "camped on a beautiful prairie near the River," Isaac Haight recorded. The next day, the group erected a "liberty pole," a tall pole with a white flag on top that symbolized the migrants' freedom. One of several interrelated symbols associated with both freedom and republicanism, the liberty pole was ubiquitous in the early American republic. Historian Arthur Schlesinger wrote that during the American Revolution, "Nothing had dramatized the popular opposition to centralized power so effectively as the Liberty Trees and Liberty Poles. Hence it is not surprising that these symbols outlived the occasion that gave them rise." For the Mormons, raising this well-known symbol was a way to frame their journey as a fight for liberty against the tyranny they felt they had suffered, and to suggest a parallel between their struggles and those of the widely admired American and French revolutionaries.[21]

The group stayed at the river for five nights, waiting for people and supplies to arrive. On the 23rd, they set out again. "The weather being fine," Haight recorded, "we started on our journey over a wide spreading prairie the ground good for roads. We travelled five wagons abreast amounting to five hundred and sixty seven wagons, all in good health and spirits, for the wilderness." The company went twelve miles that day, slightly below the average of twelve and two thirds miles per day that Haight recorded over the course of the trip. Haight kept track of mileage, weather, and road conditions in his journal; he also commented regularly on scenery, the availability of water, wood or other fuel, and food for animals. He documented the fording of rivers, religious instruction (the event, not the content), and notable events: wagon accidents that endangered children or necessitated repairs, for example, as well as friendly encounters with Indians. He did not mention many members of his company by name; only a few of the men made it into the account. Jane and her family were not mentioned, though we know they were there. Jane herself said little about the journey except to note that there were no "serious mishaps, the Lord's blessing was with us and protected us all the way, the only thing that did occur worth relating was when our cattle stampeded, some of them we never did find."[22]

As the summer wore on and the group neared the Great Basin, the weather turned colder. Haight recorded finding ice half an inch thick one morning in early September, as the group camped on the Big Sandy Creek. Two days later, he wrote, "got up in the morning found it snowing then turned to rain." The hostile weather of the high plains would torment other groups of migrants, killing many of them, but Jane's company shivered and hurried on. Two weeks after the morning snow, they were almost there. "[September] 21st came over the mountain 8 miles to the border of the Great Valley and had the pleasure to gaze on the place that is destined to be the future home for the Saints and a resting place from the face of our enemies," wrote Haight. Compared to that first rapturous vision, his report of the group's actual arrival is terse: "22nd arrived safe at the Fort our cattle worn out and all of us tired of travelling." Jane's fatigue was compounded by another factor: she was newly pregnant with her third child, conceived on the journey. This one, a daughter named Mary Ann, would be born in May.[23]

When the Latter-day Saints entered the Great Basin in 1847, they had left the United States behind. At the time, Mexico claimed the Salt Lake Valley and the land around it. The valley, and the lake in the middle of it, were used regularly by local Indian tribes who hunted, fished, and gathered food in the area. It was a gathering spot for people of many different tribal affiliations, as well as for European and Euro-American traders and others with economic or political interests in meeting people of the area.[24] But as Mormons made their way to the Great Salt Lake, the United States government was also pursuing armed conflict against Mexico. The war ended with the Treaty of Guadalupe Hidalgo in 1848. By the terms of the treaty, Mexico ceded nearly a third of its territory to the United States. A large part of what is now the American Southwest, including the present-day state of Utah, was transferred from Mexico to the United States on July 4, 1848. In practical terms, the transfer of sovereignty from Mexico to the United States meant that the Latter-day Saints came under American jurisdiction and the location where they lived became a US territory. The United States had caught up with the Saints once again.

But when Jane and Isaac arrived in the Salt Lake Valley, they did not have the luxury of speculating on the advantages of living under Mexican or United States law. There was work to be done. The advance company, which included Brigham Young, had arrived in late July and laid out the city. There were 135 blocks of ten acres each, with the Temple block at the center. As economic historian Leonard Arrington wrote, "each block was divided into eight home lots of an acre and one-fourth each. . . . Lots around Temple Block were apportioned to members of the Quorum of the Twelve . . . and other lots were distributed by lot." In his journal, Isaac Haight described the situation his ten found when they arrived: "The fort contains 40 acres of land surrounded with houses made of sundried brick built after the Spanish fashion on three sides, and wood houses on the other. We went immediately to work to prepare to build us houses, the Fort not being large enough to contain all the inhabitants. . . . Many built of sundried brick; others of timber. They have to haul for 6 to 15 miles. I put up one of timber and got my family into it the last day of October." The fort to which Haight referred was located about three quarters of a mile southwest of the Temple Block. Jane and Isaac may have camped at the old fort, as many Saints did while they built a more lasting home, or, since the fort was too small to hold everyone, they may have joined the overflow and camped on the Temple Block. Unlike many of the new arrivals, Jane and Isaac did not receive any of the land in the city as an "inheritance," as the Saints referred to the parcels distributed by lot. Still, they found a place in the community: many years later, an early resident of Salt Lake City recalled that the Jameses lived their first four years in Salt Lake in "a house built in the center of the block north of the temple block." Brigham Young, who employed both Jane and Isaac at various times, owned one of the lots on the north side of the block north of the Temple block (Figure 4.2); it is likely that the Jameses' first home in Salt Lake was on his property.[25]

It was a mild winter, during which the Saints busied themselves preparing land for planting crops. According to one historian, the new settlers fenced over 5,000 acres of land, and planted about 1,000 of those with grain. The harvest would be needed to support the nearly 2,000 people who had arrived in the valley that fall, but also to feed those who would begin arriving in the coming summer. In contrast to Nauvoo, which seemed unhealthy because of its swampy land and humid air, the Great Basin was dry, and when the first Mormons arrived in late summer, it was warm. Latter-day Saint William Clayton wrote in 1848 for his audience of Mormon soon-to-be emigrants that the air in the Great Basin "is good and pure, sweetened by healthy breezes from the Salt Lake." Historian Jared Farmer points out the irony: "Unlike freshwater, saltwater did not issue

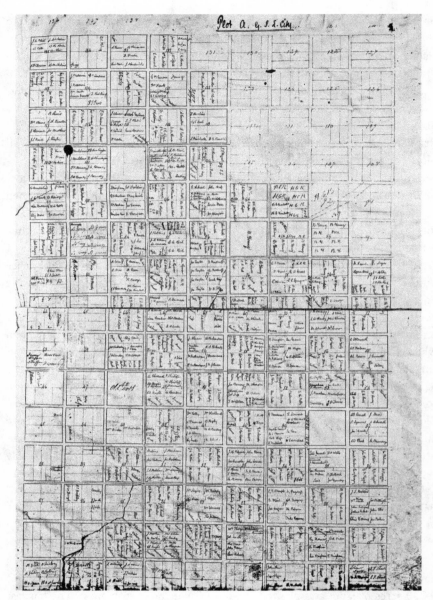

Figure 4.2 Salt Lake City was modeled on the City of Zion that Joseph Smith envisioned before his death, with wide, straight streets and large ten-acre blocks. Much of the land was originally assigned to church leaders; what remained was distributed to church members by lottery. This plat shows the original owners of the lots as they were laid out in the late 1840s. Jane and her family reportedly lived in the middle of the block just north of the temple site—the empty block with Brigham Young's name in the middle—in their early years in Salt Lake, possibly on a portion of the lot assigned to Brigham Young on that block. Used by permission, Utah State Historical Society.

organic contaminants; the Great Salt Lake promoted life precisely because it was lifeless." In October of 1848, just over a year after arriving in the Great Basin, the leader of Jane's hundred, Daniel Spencer, wrote to an acquaintance of the Salt Lake Valley:

> This valley is about 25 by 50 miles; climate last winter much like Massachusetts; the soil quite rich, as it is all made ground from the wash of the hills, which are quite high on all sides and covered with perpetual snow, it is extremely well watered with good water and plenty of mill sites. . . . It has been said by travelers that there never was rain in this valley, but since we have been here it has been tolerably plenty, but not so much so but that we have had to irrigate our land in order to raise our grain. Last winter our herds lived by running at large. Between our mountains in our canyons there is plenty of timber, stone etc. We have not been able as yet to find iron or coal, but we have found gold. We have raised about 100 bushels of wheat, and some 300 bushels of corn this season with other crops common to other countries sufficient for the inhabitants of the valley. The climate is very healthy, the most so of any I was ever in, not excepting old Massachusetts. We have all been well since we came here.

While these descriptions may have been rendered rosier by the Mormon settlers' need to believe they had arrived at their promised Zion, they contrast sharply with descriptions of Nauvoo. The Great Basin seemed to be a place where God would help the Saints to prosper.[26]

Jane's third child was born on May 8, 1848. "Put black Jane to bed with a daughter," Patty Sessions noted in her journal. Isaac and Jane named the infant Mary Ann. Jane's feelings at giving birth to a girl are lost to us. We might imagine some joy: the baby was healthy; Jane would have a daughter to balance out her sons. But that joy may have been tempered by apprehension: girls and women were more vulnerable than men in this society, and black girls occupied a particularly weak position. Harriet Jacobs, a woman enslaved in North Carolina who had strategically selected a white man as a sexual partner to fend off her master's sexual advances, wrote that in 1833 "when they told me my new-born babe was a girl, my heart was heavier than it had ever been before. Slavery is terrible for men; but it is far more terrible for women. Superadded to the burden common to all, *they* have wrongs, and sufferings, and mortifications peculiarly their own." Unlike Jacobs's daughter, Mary Ann James was not born into slavery. Nevertheless, she was born into a society that systematically oppressed black women. Jane may have believed, though, that the Saints were building a new world in the Salt Lake Valley, one where all of God's children would thrive. Perhaps this faith gave Jane hope for her daughter's future as well as her own.[27]

Satisfaction and sadness mingled throughout Jane's autobiography. She recalled the births of her eight children, "all raised to men and women, and all had families but two"; she recalled the good times: "My husband Isaac James worked for Brother Brigham [Young], and we got along splendid accumulating Horses, cows, oxen, sheep, and chickens in abundance." But these good times were not without hard work: "I spun all the cloth for my family clothing for a year or two, and we were in a prosperous condition, until the grasshoppers and crickets came along carrying destruction wherever they went, laying our crops to the ground, stripping the trees of all their leaves and fruit, bringing poverty and desolation throughout this beautiful valley." Although the optimistic descriptions penned by Daniel Spencer and others might have suggested otherwise, the devastating ravages of the grasshoppers and crickets seared the memories of the Utah pioneers. Historian William Hartley documented the settlers' significant problems with crickets and grasshoppers in the 1840s and 1850s. The settlers first encountered the crickets in late May of 1848. Prior to that time, crops were doing well: Mormon John Steele, for example, wrote in mid-April that "wheat, corn, beans and peas are all up and looking grand and grass is 6 inches high." But the crops had to survive killing frosts in May, and then the crickets appeared. Isaac Haight wrote on May 28, "Frost again this morning. Things killed in the garden such as beans, cucumbers, melons, pumpkins, and squash. Corn hurt some and some wheat killed and the crickets are injuring the crops." Patty Sessions wrote on May 30 that the crickets "are taking all before them that they come to." Isaac Haight later summarized, "The crickets destroyed some crops and are eating the heads off the grain as soon as it heads out. The prospects for grain are discouraging."[28]

The Saints tried everything they could think of to protect their crops. They knocked the insects off plants with sticks and other implements; they drove the crickets into fires and tried to drown them in ditches; they drove them away by banging on pots and pans; they smashed them with mallets. Perhaps most gruesomely, having observed that the crickets would eat their own dead, the Saints piled dead crickets at the borders of fields to keep the living ones fed. The two weeks or more that the crickets feasted on the Mormons' crops must have been exhausting for Jane and her family: Jane, Isaac, and Sylvester were surely engaged in the collective effort to drive the plague away, but Silas was nearing his second birthday and Mary Ann was just a couple of weeks old. The Saints were saved that year by great clouds of gulls descending on the fields, sometimes blocking out the sun as they flocked to feast on the insects that were devouring the Mormons' crops. The gulls gorged themselves on the crickets, vomited them up, and then ate more. Hartley noted that this behavior led Mormons to believe that the gulls' "main objective was to kill crickets rather than to feed on them," but pointed out that this is ordinary behavior for the gulls, which disgorge the indigestible parts of their food. Still, the Saints' impression that the gulls were waging war on the crickets boosted their morale and strengthened their conviction that God was watching over them. A June 9 letter to Brigham Young from leaders in Salt Lake exulted: "The sea gulls have come in large flocks from the lake and sweep the crickets as they go; it seems the hand of the Lord is in our favor."[29]

Erastus Snow, the missionary in the Northeast who traveled to Nauvoo and back with the Ivins brothers, had been in the advance company on the trek to the Salt Lake Valley. On August 8, 1847, before Jane's company arrived, Snow noted in his diary that all the Mormons then in the Salt Lake Valley were rebaptized. "This was done," he explained, "because we had as it were entered a new world and wished to renew our covenants & commence in newness of life."[30] The difficulties the Saints endured in their first year in the Salt Lake Valley may have caused some of them to doubt whether they would survive in this new world, but the "miracle of the gulls," as it came to be known, renewed their conviction that God was on their side. Jane did not mention it in her autobiography, but she must have leaned heavily on that sense of divine favor. Her mother and her siblings were no longer with her; instead, she had her husband and her children. Once again, she was making a new beginning.

5

Isaac James, Wife and Children

(1847–ca. 1870)

Although Mormons who emigrated to the Great Basin may have understood their journey as a physical and spiritual passage to a new world, once the settlers built homes and managed to ensure their food supply, life may not have felt much different than it had felt in Nauvoo. In the Great Basin, Mormons worried less about mob violence and more about Indian attacks; they waited longer for news from the eastern United States, and interacted more often with Americans heading west to seek their fortunes. In terms of living arrangements and day-to-day employment, though, Jane's life in the Salt Lake Valley looked quite similar to her life in Nauvoo.

Isaac went to work as Brigham Young's coachman shortly after the family arrived in Salt Lake. It is likely that Jane went to work in his household as well. Seven years later in 1855, the entire family was listed as "Help" in a document that bore the title "List of President B Young's Family residing in the 18th Ward." That ecclesiastical and geographical division, the Eighteenth Ward, included the location of Jane and Isaac's original Salt Lake residence on Young's property. Young owned several residences and parcels of land that were occupied by various branches of his extensive polygamous family. Part of the 1855 document appeared to divide Young's employees up by household, but Jane, Isaac, and their children were not included in that section. Clearly not "wives" or "children," Jane and her family were also excluded from the lists of "Hired help, men" and "Hired help, women." Instead, they were named individually in the "Help" column and enumerated in a column headed "Isaac James, wife & children." It is unlikely that Jane, Isaac, and their children were given precious space in one of Young's domiciles, since Young had not yet made permanent arrangements for the residences of most of his wives and children. Instead, the Jameses probably remained in their own space, working in and around the other properties that Young owned, as needed.[1]

Jane and Isaac had more children during their time working for Brigham Young's family. Miriam was born in 1850; Ellen Madora arrived in 1852 or 1853.

(Despite being only two or three years old, she was still listed as "help" on the 1855 list.) Jane's third son, Isaac, was stillborn in 1854. Her next child, Jesse Jereboam, was born in 1857, and Vilate came in 1859. Jane gave birth at least eight times; seven children survived. Jane's fertility tracked nearly exactly with that of other LDS women of her age who married around the same time: historical demographers have determined that the average number of children born to LDS women who married between 1835 and 1845 was 7.61; and among those women, those between the ages of twenty and twenty-four when they married, as Jane probably was, bore an average number of 8.03 children.[2]

While Brigham Young's family enjoyed a high status in Salt Lake, his wives and children could not afford to live lives of leisure while their servants labored. Instead, Jane probably worked alongside Mary Ann Angell Young and Young's other wives to complete the tasks necessary to keep their households running smoothly. Jane's role in Brigham Young's employ was familiar: it was the same job she had been doing since she was a young girl in Connecticut. Now she trained her daughters in the same tasks: laundry, cooking, cleaning, serving. Jane's sons likely helped Isaac. When he wasn't driving Young's carriage, Isaac was almost certainly caring for horses and doing various kinds of manual labor, from construction and repair to hauling fuel, helping build the temple, and so on. For Jane, whose hallmark religious experience occurred as she was doing laundry for Joseph Smith, this convergence of secular and religious worlds was familiar. Religious studies scholar Jan Shipps has argued that the Saints' early years in the Great Basin were qualitatively different from other times in the church's history because the Latter-day Saints were actively engaged in building what they understood to be the kingdom of God, and that therefore such mundane tasks as ditch-digging took on a quality of holiness that they did not carry before or after this period. Worship, according to Shipps, consisted in building up the kingdom; at least, working on the tasks necessary for the Saints to survive and prosper was seen as religiously equivalent to participating in a worship service. Serving the prophet may have seemed, to Jane, to be yet another instance in which the ostensibly secular and the clearly sacred intermingled.[3]

Not all of Brigham Young's wives were inclined to take an active role in the labor required to keep up their households. Augusta Adams Cobb Young, for example, was perhaps the most well-to-do of the women that Young married, and the one with the greatest expectations of luxury and status afterward. Complaining bitterly about her living conditions, Cobb wrote to her husband: "I have had no wood to bake, wash, or iron with. I could not have Isaac for two hours on Thursday because, forsooth, he had something else to do besides wait on women. May God grant me a negro some day." Young's neglect, Augusta fulminated, would cost him dearly: she demanded a $20 order on a local store, chastising him that "If you had kindly offered to assist me perhaps you might have got off with 10 but the pressure is so great now nothing less than twenty will answer my purpose." Young's domestic squabbles aside, Augusta's letter suggested that Young may have been directly involved in preventing Isaac from splitting wood for her, assigning him tasks other than "wait[ing] on women." But Augusta's irritation may also have arisen from Isaac's own expression of priorities, priorities that did not include performing labor for Young's wives that they could just as well have performed on their own. Many white Mormon women in Utah handled such chores without male assistance. Or perhaps Isaac was simply not willing to perform such labor for Augusta: he may have been reacting to the sense of entitlement to black labor that Augusta articulated in her letter to Young. For Isaac to refuse assistance to Augusta was, at some level, an insistence on his status as a free man—a status that may have felt under attack in 1850s Utah, when Southern converts were arriving in the Salt Lake Valley with large numbers of slaves.[4]

The question of Isaac's status, and that of his family, in Young's household was particularly fraught because of Young's own record on race and slavery in Utah. Utah was organized as a federal territory in 1850 as part of a series of resolutions known as the Compromise of 1850. In the act creating the Utah Territory, Congress explicitly left the issue of slavery unresolved, providing that "when admitted as a State, the said Territory, or any portion of the same, shall be received into the Union, with or without slavery, as their constitution may prescribe at the time of their admission."[5] The Utah Territorial Legislature did not immediately act on the slavery question, leaving citizens to interpret the lack of legislative action as they chose.

In 1852, almost five years after Jane and her family arrived in Utah, the territorial legislature passed a statute entitled "An Act in Relation to Service." This legislation, which Young supported, instituted what amounted to a system of gradual emancipation for slaves. The act converted enslavement to indentured servitude, another form of unfree labor that could easily last a lifetime but, importantly, could not be passed on to an indentured servant's children. The act required the consent of the servant, but as scholars have pointed out, it is difficult to imagine that enslaved people were able to consent meaningfully to the terms of their indentures. The law provided for the transfer of servants from one master or mistress to another (again, requiring the servant's consent) and it laid out the rights and responsibilities of servants toward their masters and mistresses and vice versa. To twenty-first-century eyes, the aspiration to set up a humane system of unfree labor looks hopelessly naïve. But as scholars W. Paul Reeve, Christopher B. Rich Jr., and LaJean Carruth point out, "legislators were trying to codify the entire gambit of 'unfree labor' relationships for all races, not merely black 'servants.' . . . The unfree labor relationships which Utah legislators codified in the 1852 session were quite normal in the early decades of the nineteenth century when Young and other Mormon leaders came of age. Moreover, it made sense in a cash poor territory like Utah to use labor as a medium of exchange."[6]

On January 5, 1852, Young told the assembled members of the Utah Territorial Legislature,

> Thus will a people be redeemed from servile bondage, both mental and physical . . . their thralldom will no longer exist, although the seed of Canaan will inevitably carry the curse which was placed upon them, until the same authority which placed it there, shall see proper to have it removed. . . . Thus, while servitude may and should exist, and that too upon those who are naturally designed to occupy the position of "servant of servants," yet we should not fall into the other extreme, and make them as beasts of the field, regarding not the humanity which attaches to the colored race; nor yet elevate them, as some seem disposed, to an equality with those whom Nature and Nature's God has indicated to be their masters, their superiors.

For Young, Jane and her family were humans "naturally designed to occupy the position of 'servant of servants,'" a scriptural phrase referring to the biblical patriarch Noah's curse on his grandson Canaan.[7] Later, as she petitioned church leaders for temple access, Jane would counter Young's racialized reading of these scriptures obliquely. But that moment of debate over scriptural interpretation was still many years in the future. If Jane expressed an opinion about Young's 1852 pronouncement on God's "natural design" for her and her family, it has not survived.

Jane's and Isaac's positions as servants in Brigham Young's household conferred certain advantages. Young was thin-skinned and irascible, prone to lashing out and quick to see others' faults while remaining blind to his own; but he also knew Jane's and Isaac's names, he could name each of their children, and he needed their help. Jane's various autobiographical statements recounted none of her time in Young's service beyond the bare fact of its existence. We can interpret that silence in many ways: it could have been a traumatic time for her, a time of settling depression that left her blank. Or she may have perceived it as ordinary time, with nothing special on which to remark. Still, it is striking that Jane spoke at such great length about her time in the service of the Smith family, yet was so quiet about her time with the Youngs. Perhaps Young's overt racism, evident in his public comments throughout his tenure as church president, made the contrast to Joseph Smith too stark to articulate. Perhaps the robust practice of polygamy in Brigham Young's family was unsettling to Jane. In her autobiography, she situated her testimony about the truth of plural marriage during her time with Joseph Smith, even though polygamy reached its fullest expression in the lives of the Saints during Jane's time with Brigham

Young. There, Jane might have seen more thoroughly how the practice of plural marriage affected family relations and individual women.[8]

Mary Ann Angell Young had married Brigham Young after the death of his first wife, before Young accepted Joseph Smith's teaching on plural marriage, and she occupied the respected position of a first wife when Young began to take plural wives. Young's other wives—over fifty of them, in all—referred to Mary Ann as "Mrs. Young," "Sister Young," or "Mother Young," acknowledging her status as Young's senior wife. But Mary Ann was a private person who, as one historian wrote, "preferred a more secluded existence." After just over five years of life with Brigham Young and several of his wives and children in Young's official residence in Salt Lake City, Mary Ann moved to another dwelling on the same property, which gave her the luxury of her own space.[9]

Jane's sympathies might have been with Mrs. Young alone, or they might have extended to many of Young's wives. Some of them she knew from Nauvoo: Emily Dow Partridge Young, for example, was one of the women who, Jane said, revealed the secret of plural marriage to her back in Illinois. After Joseph Smith's death, Emily and many others of Smith's plural wives had married Brigham Young, maintaining their status as members of the leading family of Mormonism. But how many of them mourned their opportunity to be a first wife, a sole wife, to conform to the emerging romantic ideal of the time that exalted monogamous marriage as a union of soul mates? Had Jane been privy to some of the bitterness and lingering disappointment that many of Brigham Young's wives felt as she worked alongside them in Salt Lake? By the time she recorded her autobiography, Jane had endured the dissolution of two marriages. The emotional turmoil she might have experienced may have struck her as similar to the ways Brigham Young's wives experienced their plural marriages to this "great man": the feelings of love and allegiance, the disappointment of loneliness, the desperate attempt to reconcile oneself to a lived experience that did not match the romantic ideal, the longing for spiritual solace.[10] Perhaps Jane did not speak much of her time in the Young household because she did not wish to dwell on negative memories; or perhaps doing so seemed politically unwise, given the power Brigham Young's family held in LDS society even well after his 1877 death.

Jane's and Isaac's work for Brigham Young kept food on the table for their growing family and may have provided a measure of status in the religious community, but it was also a stepping stone toward financial stability and even a measure of prosperity. The 1850 federal census of Utah Territory lists Isaac's occupation as "farmer," and the earliest extant tax assessment, in 1856, shows that they had acquired land in the southeast corner of the city, an area then designated as the First Ward (Figure 5.1). They had improved the land—that is, they had built on it—and the assessor noted that they had a timepiece and other personal possessions. The James's assets remained steady from 1856 through

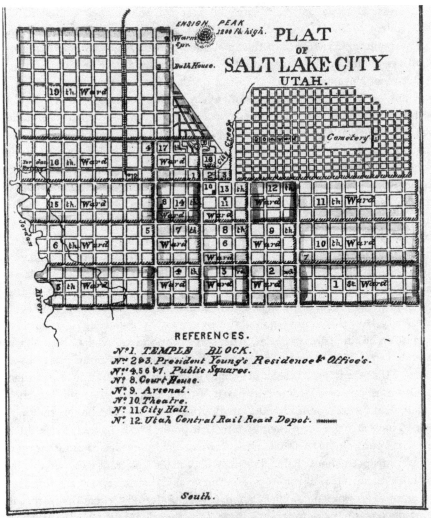

Figure 5.1 This map, made in 1874, shows the original boundaries of Salt Lake City's wards, or local ecclesiastical divisions. Jane and her family lived first in the Eighteenth Ward. In the 1850s, they acquired land in the First Ward (in the southeast corner). In 1870, Jane moved to the Eighth Ward (north and west, toward the center of the city). Used by permission, Utah State Historical Society.

1858: Jesse C. Little, Salt Lake City's tax assessor, valued their land at $200, their timepiece at $10, and the rest of their possessions at $40. One of Jane's earliest biographers wrote that "this small stake probably represented a hand-to-mouth existence, but it seems typical of the families living in [the First] ward."[11]

Between November of 1858, when Little assessed the James family's holdings, and the 1859 assessment, when Little's successor Jeter Clinton performed the same task, the James's taxable assets nearly doubled. Their land was now valued at $275; and they now had two oxen ($75), one cow ($30), one hog ($25), a vehicle ($70), and twenty dollars' worth of furniture. Overall, the value of their possessions rose from $250 to $495. According to this assessment, the Jameses ranked fourteenth out of the thirty-seven households in their ward. That placed them just below the wealthiest third of their neighbors. Part of the increase might have been driven by the change in assessors: Clinton may simply have judged Jane and Isaac's land to be more valuable than Little had found it. But clearly the James family had also acquired more wealth. That change was most apparent in their livestock: over the course of a year, they had accumulated the means to plow fields and move goods, in the oxen; a source of milk, in the cow; and a source of meat in the hog. These animals suggest stability, and even prosperity. How the family acquired these animals is not entirely clear, but one suggestion lies in historian John Turner's observation that Brigham Young had extended over $1,000 credit to Isaac by the mid-1850s. Isaac may have used some of that credit to establish his family's agricultural operation. If so, then the Jameses' prosperity came at the cost of their financial independence: they remained indebted, quite literally, to Brigham Young even though they appear to have struck out on their own by that point. If the Jameses worked for Brigham Young by the late 1850s, it was on a casual, as-needed basis rather than as full-time, permanent "help." Jane may have made this transition possible by establishing herself as a laundress, drawing on skills she learned at a young age. For many black women, taking in laundry was a preferred occupation because it allowed women to work in their own spaces, rather than in the homes of white employers, and it gave them some control over their own schedules.[12]

The livestock listed in the James family's tax assessments not only demonstrated Jane and Isaac's economic stability; it also suggested that the James family ate a relatively nutritious diet. Whereas Jane had begged for milk from another family during her early years in Salt Lake, by the late 1850s the James family had milk and butter from their cow and meat from their hogs. The oxen and cow grazed each day with the community herd, returning at night for milking and bedding down on the Jameses' land. The family's table scraps fed the swine. The Jameses also had chickens that went unlisted in tax assessments, perhaps because they were so common in the city. These creatures contributed eggs to the family diet and ended up as meat on the table or in the soup pot. Livestock require tending, but the James children, who ranged in 1859 from infancy to twenty years old, were more than capable of handling the necessary tasks. It is easy to imagine Silas (thirteen years old in 1860) assigned the job of milking the cow every morning, and Mary Ann (eleven at the time) carrying food out to the pig pen, while Isaac stoked the fire to warm the family's house in the winter and Jane began breakfast preparations for the family. As the days got longer and the hens began to lay, the younger children might have been assigned to collect the eggs. Those the Jameses did not eat could be sold to supplement their income.[13]

The James family's net worth declined slowly over the next few years. In 1860, they only owned one ox, not two; by 1861, they owned no oxen at all. They acquired more hogs, but the total value of these animals dropped to $15 for three. (The one hog they owned in 1859 may have been particularly valuable by virtue of being a pregnant sow and thus likely to deliver, literally, more value.) Even so, the James family was well enough off that they could afford to purchase at least some of their clothing from local vendors rather than sewing it themselves. While Jane later recounted that in her first years in the Salt Lake Valley she "spun all the cloth for my family clothing for a year or two," by fifteen years later Jane had put away her spinning wheel. Leonard Hill, a local merchant, included several entries in his accounts detailing items he sold to members of Jane's family: in 1864, for example, the family paid a total of $10.75 for three pairs of pants for Isaac, a dress for Miriam, a shirt for Jesse, a dress for Jane, a coat for Silas, and a waist (a blouse, or the top part of a dress) for Mary Ann.[14]

The move to the Great Basin separated Jane from a large part of her social and familial network. Her mother, her siblings, and her siblings-in-law all stayed behind in the Midwest. They may have planned to follow Brigham Young west later; Jane and her family may have been in the vanguard because of their close association with Joseph Smith's successor. But the church Young led was hemorrhaging members. Jane's family may have found Young unpersuasive as a prophet, or they may have discerned God calling them in another direction. Or, on a more mundane level, social and economic realities may have made another relocation untenable so soon after the family's move from Connecticut to Illinois. Whatever the reason, Jane must have considered the very real possibility that she would never see her family again. It is a great irony that Joseph Smith worked so hard to create eternal kinship connections linking believers to each other and to the generations that came before and after them, and that Jane's fidelity to Smith's religion removed her from her kinship network, breaking up relationships that might otherwise have supported and sustained her. The black community in Salt Lake became an extension of, and a replacement for, Jane's birth family.

The Jameses were not the only black people in the Salt Lake Valley when they arrived there in 1847, but they certainly stood out. In 1850, the Federal

Census listed fifty black people in the Utah Territory. Of these, twenty-six were described as slaves en route to California. The remaining twenty-four were listed as free. Fifteen lived in Salt Lake County: Jane, Isaac, and their four children; and nine adults and children enslaved by the Bankhead family. Together, these fifteen people comprised two of the 650 households listed in the Salt Lake County census, and not quite half a percent of the entire county population—the remainder of which, according to the census, was white. (A draft of the census shows that there were at least eight additional black people held as slaves in the county, increasing the proportion of people of color in the region by an infinitesimal amount.) When the Jameses moved to Salt Lake City's First Ward in the mid-1850s, they were surrounded by white neighbors. The 1860 federal census counted 212 people in the First Ward; of these, one was listed as "Indian"; Jane's family of nine was marked "black"; and the remaining 202, whose race was literally unmarked on the census forms, were considered white.[15]

These numbers described a reality in which Jane and her family had no option but to interact with white people on a daily basis. Jane and Isaac were employed by white men and women, but they also depended on white people for goods and services ranging from the herd boys who drove the community's livestock to pasture in the mornings and led the animals back in the evenings, to the merchant who sold clothing and other goods to Jane and her family. Jane and Isaac worked alongside white people in church and community projects, from raising money for missions to helping build the city in which they lived. They turned to white midwives when their children were born, white doctors when their children were ill, and white ecclesiastical leaders when they needed spiritual sustenance. Life might have been a little easier for Jane and Isaac if they could have leaned more often on black friends who understood the physical, emotional, and spiritual costs of living surrounded by people who believed, at a fundamental level, that dark skin signified an ancient curse. But black friends were few and far between.

The black Mormon community in Salt Lake grew slowly, one family—sometimes one person—at a time. Some left Utah as soon as they could; others stayed, enmeshing themselves in the social networks of the Valley. Nathan and Susan Bankhead, for example, who had been enslaved by the Bankhead family, left Utah when they gained their freedom, but their son George stayed behind. Black families often established homes near one another and frequently intermarried. For example, a few years after Jane and her family reached the Salt Lake Valley, the family of Frank Perkins arrived in Utah as the property of Reuben Perkins and settled with Reuben's family in Bountiful, north of Salt Lake City. Jane's son Sylvester married Frank Perkins's daughter Mary Ann. Two of Sylvester and Mary Ann's daughters married Henry and Louis Leggroan, sons of Edward and Susan Leggroan, a free black family from Mississippi that moved to Utah in 1870. At least two of Sylvester and Mary Ann's grandchildren,

Jane's great-grandchildren, married the children of George Bankhead. Although Jane had lost contact with her mother, her siblings, and their families when she moved to the Great Basin, as she put down roots in Salt Lake, her family ties extended throughout the region, connecting her to new kin in her new home.[16]

A decade after the Latter-day Saints were driven out of Illinois, church leaders lamented the lack of fervor among the Saints in Utah. Brigham Young entrusted one of his counselors, Jedediah M. Grant, with the task of reinvigorating the Saints' zeal for their religion, and Grant responded by starting a revival. Grant began his fiery preaching in Kayesville, a settlement north of Salt Lake City, and challenged his listeners to demonstrate the renewal of their faith by undergoing rebaptism. Some five hundred Mormons did so, and the revival quickly spread to other LDS communities with the encouragement of the church leadership.[17] The hallmarks of religious revival were all there: the Saints attended additional worship services, formed societies to help keep each other on track, saw visions, and spoke in tongues. But reformers preached a holistic revival, encouraging Latter-day Saints not only to shape up spiritually, but also to clean up literally: to bathe more frequently, to tidy their houses, and to get their finances in order. This fusion of the sacred and the mundane surely seemed familiar to Jane.

By the time it reached Salt Lake, this movement, known to historians as the Mormon Reformation, had become systematized. Scholar Paul H. Peterson writes that in Salt Lake City, "a policy was established to have two home missionaries assigned to each ward. Equipped with a twenty-seven-question catechism to help measure the worthiness of the Saints, the home missionaries assisted families with everything from hygiene and church attendance to obeying the Ten Commandments. Only after some months of missionary-member visits were Saints in the Salt Lake City wards rebaptized in early spring of 1857." By that time, the infrastructure was in place to support the mass rebaptisms. In October 1856, church leader Samuel W. Richards had recorded, "A splendid Font of hewn rock has been built near the Endowment-house, inside the Temple Block wall, and dedicated for use." The effects of the reformation were palpable: "The Territory this season," Brigham Young wrote to a correspondent in California, "has taken an emetic, and the way Lawyers, Loafers, Special Pleaders, Apostates, Officials, and filth has now been cast out, is a caution to all sinners, that here they would be in the wrong place." In other words, the reformation had a winnowing effect, encouraging those not fully devoted to the cause to move along.[18] Jane and her family were committed. Although we do not have explicit records of their rebaptism, we can infer that they participated in the mass baptisms of the reformation because none of them were cut off from the church, a frequent punishment for those who declined to join in the fervor.

Historians have suggested that as the reformation revived the Saints' faith, it also fanned the smoldering embers of conflict between the LDS Church and the US government. That conflict ultimately burst into flames in the Utah War of 1857–1858. Concerned that Brigham Young and his followers did not respect federal authority over the Utah Territory, a newly inaugurated President James Buchanan quickly sent troops to protect the territorial officials he appointed and to ensure that Young did not attempt to remain the territorial governor. For his part, when he received reports that US troops were on their way to Utah, Young declared martial law and ordered the territorial borders sealed. He also mobilized the Utah Territorial Militia, known as the Nauvoo Legion. The Legion's main task was to harass the federal troops, attempting to slow their progress, diminish their efficacy, and decrease their morale.[19]

As Young and Buchanan both attempted to negotiate a face-saving peace through various proxies—Young because he knew the Saints could not stand up to US military might, and Buchanan because Congress was grumbling about the expense of funding an expedition against the Mormons—the Latter-day Saints, fearing a military assault, temporarily abandoned Salt Lake City and more northerly settlements for points further south. Instead of planting crops in the spring of 1858, Jane and Isaac packed up their family's belongings, as did their neighbors. On April 1, the exodus began. The snows were still in the mountains; the roads were almost certainly muddy, slowing the procession of Saints to a crawl. Displaced Mormons formed temporary encampments near Provo (some forty miles southeast of Salt Lake) and beyond, where they waited for an end to the hostilities. Young began preparations to build multiple homes for his family in Provo, even as he continued to angle for a peaceful settlement to the conflict. At the end of June, three months after the Latter-day Saints had begun their evacuation and after several months of strategic negotiations, the US army marched through an abandoned Salt Lake City. They built Camp Floyd about forty miles southwest of Salt Lake, and left the city alone. Young initiated the Saints' return to Salt Lake immediately, taking a carriage overnight in order to arrive back at his official residence on July 1. As one historian put it, the Saints returned to the city as "survivor[s] but not as . . . victor[s]."[20]

The Utah War exacted a heavy toll on the Latter-day Saints. The church suspended immigration from Europe, and the church leadership prohibited members from selling food or ammunition to outsiders. The abandonment of Salt Lake City interrupted agricultural activities, raising the prospect that the Saints would go hungry that winter. As is often the case, the economic burden imposed by these factors fell most heavily on the poorest members of the church. Somehow, Jane and Isaac found a way through the economic disruption of 1857 and 1858: their net worth, as it was figured on annual tax assessments, rose in 1858 and 1859. Jane and Isaac may have been able to bolster their economic position by drawing on the credit Brigham Young extended to Isaac to purchase assets from economically distressed Saints at bargain prices, or perhaps they were simply able to steward their resources more carefully than others.[21]

The Utah War shaped the Latter-day Saints' relationship to the federal government for decades to come. Historian William P. MacKinnon wrote, "The 1857–1858 conflict was the single biggest factor in shaping Utah's unique reaction to the Civil War when it began three years later." Separated geographically from the rest of the United States, and alienated from the nation because of what they perceived as a history of persecution most recently manifested in the Utah War, the Mormons, according to historian Richard E. Bennett, "were not drawn into taking sides in the war. While it was true that Utah remained loyal to the Union and when called upon even equipped small regiments to defend government property during the war, the Mormon view was essentially one of neutrality."[22]

Mormons expected the conflict to fulfill a revelation given to Joseph Smith that they considered a prophecy: "For behold," the revelation said, "the Southern States shall be divided against the Northern States, and the Southern States will call on other nations, even the nation of Great Britain, as it is called, and they shall also call upon other nations, in order to defend themselves against other nations; and then war shall be poured out upon all nations." Prompted by the 1832 nullification crisis, in which South Carolina refused to recognize a tariff imposed by the federal government, this revelation seemed to the Saints to predict the Civil War with uncanny accuracy. The text went on to predict that both sides would be destroyed, leaving the Saints "avenged of their enemies," and, as the Mormons read it, the revelation commanded them not to interfere: "Wherefore, stand ye in holy places, and be not moved, until the day of the Lord come; for behold, it cometh quickly, saith the Lord. Amen."[23]

There is no evidence that Jane or any other African American Mormon publicly disputed the LDS Church's apocalyptic expectation that the North and South would annihilate one another. Privately, however, they may have expressed more partisan views of the conflict. Sam, one of the black men enslaved by the Bankhead family, reportedly followed news of the war closely and remarked frequently, "I sure hope the South gets licked."[24] Jane may have hoped that Utah would take a more aggressive stance against the Confederacy, and she may have hoped that her son would have a chance to fight for the cause. She was related to formerly enslaved people, and friends with many who had been brought to Utah Territory as slaves. She was the mother of free black children who, like Jane and every other black person in the United States, were vulnerable to enslavement as long as the 1850 Fugitive Slave Law—a particularly draconian piece of federal legislation that required free states to cooperate in recovering escaped slaves—was on the books. Jane's sensitivity about her status as a free woman lasted the rest of her life: she gave that element of her personal history extra emphasis when she dictated her autobiography. For Jane, the eradication of slavery was personal.

In the fall of 1861, the leader of the Utah Territorial Militia issued orders "to quietly revive the military throughout the Territory." In response, Brigadier

General Franklin D. Richards ordered each regiment in the Second Brigade "to update rolls and conduct an inspection." Richards wrote an explanation to accompany his orders: "No particular danger is now felt that requires these orders to be issued, but the present is the first proper time that has presented itself, since our Territory was occupied by a Government Mob, to put our Militia in a state of self defense." He noted that the militia might be called upon to participate in the Civil War, and explained that he wanted the troops prepared for any eventuality. In response to Richards's orders, Nauvoo Legion units tallied their membership and supplies. Just after Christmas in 1861, Sylvester James, Jane's firstborn son, was recorded as a member of the Second Battalion of the Second Brigade of the First Regiment of infantry of the Nauvoo Legion, armed with a rifle and ten rounds of ammunition.[25]

Since membership in the Legion was legally restricted to white men, and informally restricted to Latter-day Saints, Sylvester's participation was significant. He was about twenty-two years old at the time, and the inventory of his supplies showed that he was ill-prepared for military service. A volunteer force, the Utah Territorial Militia required that its members—both officers and enlisted men— provide their own uniforms, rations, and weapons. Each man was expected to have "at least forty rounds of lead, powder, and percussion caps at all times," at least four times the amount Sylvester had. Sylvester was far from alone in his lack of supplies: about half of the men in his battalion had no ammunition at all, and nearly that many had no weapon. Nearly a quarter of those who had some ammunition did not have the minimum required forty rounds.[26] Sylvester's battalion was not called into active duty, so his lack of supplies never put him in harm's way.

Although the Emancipation Proclamation, which President Abraham Lincoln issued on January 1, 1863, provided the legal framework for freeing enslaved people in the South, it only applied to those states that had joined the Confederacy. It was the Thirteenth Amendment, ratified in December 1865, that definitively abolished slavery and indentured servitude throughout the United States. But even before these landmark governmental actions, Congress exercised its authority over Utah by abolishing slavery in US territories in the summer of 1862. In doing so, the federal government nullified the "Act in Relation to Service" that Brigham Young and the Utah Territorial Legislature had passed, demolishing the framework they had created to structure labor relations between former slaves and former slaveowners. For Jane, this too was a fulfillment of Joseph Smith's prophecy: in 1905, she would tell an interviewer, "Things came to pass what he prophesied about the colored race being freed. Things that he said has come to pass."[27]

The 1832 revelation that Saints interpreted as foretelling the Civil War, though it did predict slave rebellion, did not mention slaves being freed. Jane may have been retrospectively reading the prediction of freedom for African Americans into that revelation, or she may have been referring to an 1833 revelation in which God promised redemption and the end of persecution to his people. That revelation described the "laws and constitution of the people" as items God had "suffered to be established" and that "should be maintained for the rights and protection of all flesh, according to just and holy principles; that every man may act. . . according to the moral agency which I have given unto him." It continued: "Therefore, it is not right that any man should be in bondage one to another. And for this purpose have I established the Constitution of this land, by the hands of wise men whom I raised up unto this very purpose, and redeemed the land by the shedding of blood."[28] Most Latter-day Saints did not appear to have referred to this revelation in thinking about slavery, but Jane's statement may point us to an alternative strand of interpretation that remained largely invisible during Brigham Young's presidency.

The close of the Civil War heralded a new era for the United States marked, in part, by a long struggle for African Americans' civil rights. Living in Utah, Jane was insulated from much of the turmoil that attended the end of the war, though the act abolishing slavery in US territories and later the Thirteenth Amendment clearly had an impact on her black friends and family, some of whom were finally released from indentured servitude. Some used their newfound freedom to leave the Utah Territory. Others stayed put, but exercised their freedom by altering their labor arrangements. Jane no longer had to contemplate the awful possibility that she or someone she knew would be captured and sold into slavery.

Jane had her likeness made sometime after the end of the Civil War, historians believe. The photograph that survives is small, two and three-sixteenths inches across and three and three-eighths inches high (Figure 5.2). The subject of the photograph, an African American woman, looks directly into the camera. As was customary at the time, she is not smiling, but her expression is kind. Her hair is pulled back, and she is dressed neatly, with subtle embellishments to her ensemble: hoops adorn her ears, and the sleeves of her relatively simple, dark dress are decorated with tassels. A modest white collar sets off her face. Although the design of the dress is fairly plain, the lustrous reflection of light on the folds of the skirt hints at the rich fabric with which it was made. The woman sits nearly erect, leaning almost imperceptibly to her left to rest her elbow on a side table covered with a cloth that has a design as elaborate as the woman's dress is simple. In her right hand, which rests in her lap, she holds a white handkerchief, echoing her white collar. The photograph was made in the studio of Edward Martin, an English convert about Jane's age. In Salt Lake, Martin worked as a "sign, carriage, and ornamental painter" and got into the photography business in 1865. He had no pretensions about being a great artist; he advertised "Now is your chance to get LIKENESSES CHEAP!" and asked that "Bishops Give Notice" of Martin's services to their congregations. "I am selling CARD and other PICTURES at EXTREMELY LOW PRICES," his advertisement continued, "and receiving for them the Produce

Figure 5.2 Scholars believe the woman in this *carte de visite* photograph is Jane James. Edward Martin's studio may have produced several copies of this image that Jane could have used like calling cards; they may also have been purchased by white residents of Salt Lake City for display in their own homes. Courtesy of the Church History Library of the Church of Jesus Christ of Latter-day Saints.

of the Field, Orchard, or Garden, at Current Prices; Cash not refused." Martin's studio also produced the likeness of an African American man (Figure 5.3). Someone wrote on the photograph, "Isaac. for many years in the service of Pres Young." Although not definitive, this caption helps identify the subject as Isaac James and, in turn, adds weight to the identification of the African American woman in the other photograph as Jane James.[29]

The props and poses used in these photos were the same as those of white people photographed in Martin's studio. Indeed, the formal similarities of these likenesses to photographs of other white Mormons of the time period make it tempting to characterize Jane and Isaac's photographs as a way in which they participated, and were included, in the predominantly white society of Salt Lake City without regard to their racial difference. Photographs like these were all the rage in the United States at the time, and likenesses of family members were *de rigueur* among middle-class white Americans. For Jane and Isaac, having likenesses made may have been part of an effort to keep up with their

Figure 5.3 The handwritten caption on this *carte de visite* photograph identifies the subject as "Isaac. for many years in the service of Pres Young." This description matches Isaac James. The fact that this photograph was also taken in Edward Martin's studio helps strengthen the identification of the subject in Figure 5.2 as Isaac's wife Jane. Courtesy of the Church History Library of the Church of Jesus Christ of Latter-day Saints.

neighbors: by sitting for photographs, and displaying the resulting likenesses in their home, Jane and Isaac could minimize the racial divide that separated them from white residents of Salt Lake City. As historian Laura Wexler writes, during this era the middle-class "hall table and the parlor were accumulating photographs at an impressive rate. . . . The resulting accumulation of images helped to make, not merely to mirror, the home. . . . As Nathaniel Hawthorne observed in his notebooks, when his wife Sophia rearranged the parlor and put a table with books and pictures at its center, their new house in Lenox became a home." Jane and Isaac may have had an additional reason to get photographs taken after the close of the Civil War. Wexler observes that "both Sojourner Truth and Harriet Jacobs documented the fact of their legal freedom with photographic portraits." Although Jane had never been enslaved, she may have been making a similar statement about her family's free status by paying Martin's studio to photograph her and her husband.[30]

But we should be careful not to read too much into these images. We have no information about why Jane and Isaac's photos were made—if, indeed, these were photos of Jane and Isaac, as they seem to be. We also do not know how these images circulated. Edward Martin might have offered Jane and Isaac the opportunity to have their likenesses made for free in exchange for the right to sell copies of their photographs. Nineteenth-century Americans bought and displayed innumerable photographs once technology made it possible to reproduce large numbers of images at low cost. Literature scholar Teresa Zackodnik writes that Americans purchased photographs of famous people and of "oddities (Siamese twins, thin men, dwarfs)." They also consumed images of anonymous African Americans, images that sometimes displayed the scars their subjects had received from brutal overseers. Zackodnik argues that photos like these helped define racial "types," displaying African American bodies like scientific specimens for the consumption of white Americans. Jane and Isaac's images may have served this purpose, converting them into racial types for their white neighbors to study and display.[31] Brigham Young might have commissioned these photographs as part of an ongoing effort to enumerate the members of his family and extended household. Jane and Isaac might have intended to use their *cartes de visite* to help drum up business, presenting themselves as respectable middle-class people whom potential clients could trust to work in their homes. Or perhaps Jane and Isaac decided to spend some of their money to have their likenesses made to celebrate their freedom and mark their entry into the new world that Joseph Smith had prophesied.

Desired to Do Right

(1870–1877)

Although, as Jane later said, "we got along splendid," all was not well in the James household. Jane's marriage ended, officially, near the close of March 1870. The Honorable Elias Smith, a judge in the Salt Lake County Probate Court, issued the divorce decree during the court's March term. The one-page, handwritten decree explains that Jane had initiated the proceedings and that Isaac had joined the petition on the 23rd of March. This was not, it appeared, a long, drawn-out process. Instead, Jane and Isaac had agreed that it was time to end their marriage. The court concurred. "Upon investigation," Smith wrote, "it was fully and satisfactorily made to appear, that the said parties could not live together in peace and union in the marital relations and that their welfare and happiness required that they should be separated from each other." Smith granted custody of the couples' minor children, Ellen Madora, Jesse, and Vilate, to Jane, and ordered that she retain the family house and the land on which it stood, with the exception of a section at the north end of the lot. Jane also got to keep the household goods: furniture, beds, a mirror, and so on. Isaac was ordered to pay an unspecified sum of court costs.[1]

Although the terms of Smith's ruling meant that Jane did not owe Isaac a cent, documents filed two months later indicated that she paid him $500 for most of the family real estate. This may have been a way to comply with the judgment of a church court, which frequently became involved in cases like the Jameses'. In a review of an earlier divorce case decided by Elias Smith, the LDS Salt Lake High Council affirmed Smith's decision to grant the couple's house to the husband, but ruled that the wife should be paid three hundred dollars and allowed her to remain in the house until she received the money from her former husband. A church court may have reached a similar verdict in Jane and Isaac's case.[2]

Probate courts are generally concerned with the settlement of estates and the disposition of wills, not with the dissolution of marriages and other such matters involving the living. But Latter-day Saints in Utah had expanded purview of probate courts to civil and criminal matters of all kinds. The federal district courts, to which most such matters would normally be referred, were understaffed in the territory's early years, and federal judges were appointed by the government in Washington, DC. Probate judges like Elias Smith, on the other hand, were locals and almost always Mormons. They could be counted on to uphold community standards and to understand local mores. This was particularly important for the Latter-day Saints as they attempted to retain the practice of plural marriage, which the federal government was intent on eradicating. But even for those Saints who did not practice polygamy, probate courts often seemed a safer or more accessible space than courts administered by federal appointees.[3]

Although Latter-day Saints believed firmly in the eternal nature of marital bonds, they also placed few obstacles in the way of those who sought to end their marriages. The first territorial legislative assembly in 1852 had passed a law that permitted divorce for all the same reasons it was allowed in other regions of the United States: impotence, infidelity, desertion, inebriation, criminality, and abuse. To these, the legislature added another, relatively unusual, cause: divorce was permitted "when it shall be made to appear to the satisfaction and conviction of the court, that the parties cannot live in peace and union together and that their welfare requires a separation." Attorney Lisa Madsen Pearson and historian Carol Cornwall Madsen noted that "only six other states and territories had a similar law." Judge Smith clearly borrowed from the legislature's language as he wrote Jane and Isaac's divorce decree. In 1870, eighty-two civil divorces were granted in the territory; thirty-one of them, including Jane and Isaac's, were in Salt Lake County. According to the statistics compiled by the federal commissioner of labor, that worked out to a little less than one divorce for every thousand residents of the territory. This frequency was much higher than the surrounding states and territories, perhaps because Utah's divorce laws were so liberal. Even so, many divorces in Utah Territory were obtained through ecclesiastical processes rather than the civil judiciary and were thus not counted in these statistics. For polygamous wives, no civil divorce was available. Instead, plural wives and their husbands seeking relief appealed directly to the church president, the only ecclesiastical official empowered to dissolve a plural marriage. During his tenure as church president, Brigham Young granted 1,645 divorces, averaging about sixty-five per year.[4]

At this remove, it is impossible to know why Jane and Isaac felt they could not, or should not, remain married. Judge Smith stated that they "could not live together in peace and union" and so for the sake of "their welfare and happiness," they had to separate. These broad statements cover a multitude of possibilities, ranging from financial disagreements to suspicions of marital infidelity. It may be that Jane's continuing commitment to the LDS Church was causing tension. LDS women were expected to conform to the same norms of femininity as other

Protestant women in the Victorian era: purity, piety, passivity, and domesticity. In frontier Utah, they also had to be industrious: producing goods at home, stepping in as store clerks and bookkeepers so that their husbands could attend to more strenuous work in the fields, and otherwise generating economic value to allow the Latter-day Saints to become independent of the eastern United States. Motherhood was also a key component of LDS femininity, a physical and spiritual obligation. Jane was able to meet all of these obligations, and in her autobiography she emphasized her adherence to LDS standards of femininity.[5]

For Isaac, though, the situation was different. The ideal of masculinity for LDS men rested on two pillars: priesthood and plural marriage. Although a few black men had been ordained during Joseph Smith's lifetime, Isaac was not one of them. When Brigham Young declared that men of African descent could not hold the priesthood, any hope Isaac might have had of meeting LDS standards of masculinity disappeared. Even if Isaac wanted to take a plural wife, it was impossible to get permission to do so without holding the priesthood. So although Jane could be a "real" woman, according to LDS standards, Isaac could not be a "real" man. The emasculation of black men in the LDS Church paralleled the emasculation of black men in American society following the Civil War, but carried with it specific religious consequences: without priesthood, Isaac could not bless any of the couple's children when they were born, nor could he provide blessings for his family members when they were ill. Instead, the family had to depend on white neighbors and ecclesiastical leaders for these services. Isaac's inability to perform these basic priesthood duties, and the family's subsequent reliance on white men, may have introduced intolerable tensions in Jane and Isaac's marriage.[6]

Jane and Isaac may also have disagreed on the path forward for their family. In 1869, the transcontinental railroad was completed at Promontory Point in Utah. Isaac may have seen this development as a chance for a better future: not only was it now easier to leave Utah, but a black man had a chance at a good career as a railroad porter. Jane, evidently, preferred to stay put. While the Saints were expanding their reach in the United States, establishing outposts throughout the West and sending representatives both around the nation and around the globe, her community was in Salt Lake. Isaac ultimately decided to try his luck elsewhere. Two years after the divorce, he sold his remaining property, dissolving the last financial ties that held him in Salt Lake.[7]

Some months after her divorce, Jane relocated to the Eighth Ward. North and west of her former home, the Eighth Ward was closer to the center of the city. The move made economic sense: without Isaac, it's unlikely Jane could have maintained the agricultural operation that the family's First Ward home made possible. In the Eighth Ward, Jane was closer to people who might hire her to do laundry, or purchase the soap she made and sold. Jane would formalize this move the following year, filing the paperwork to exchange her property in the

First Ward for property in the Eighth Ward. Jane's move to the Eighth Ward also made social sense: here, she was closer to Amanda and Samuel Chambers, an African American Mormon couple who had just moved to Salt Lake City that year. The Chambers lived just a couple blocks away from Jane's new home, and Amanda attended women's meetings with Jane.[8] The move may also have satisfied a religious desire to be closer to the temple that was rising in the center of the city. Jane's new home was only seven blocks or so away from the temple site, and she may have hoped that she eventually would be able to visit that sacred building regularly.

In 1875 Emily Dow Partridge Young, whom Jane had known in Nauvoo as one of Joseph Smith's wives and who later married Brigham Young, recorded a brief visit from Jane in her journal: "Jane James came in today. She has had considerable trouble since she has been in the valley. Her husband left her for a white woman (a fortune teller) and she has buried several of her children. All have their troubles, whether black or white." Since the divorce decree contains no hint of this fortune teller, it seems unlikely that she was the cause, or even the catalyst, for the dissolution of Jane's marriage. If she had been, Judge Smith almost certainly would have listed Isaac's infidelity or abandonment as the main reason for granting a divorce. It seems more likely that Isaac entered a relationship with the fortune teller sometime after the divorce was finalized. Even so, in hindsight Jane might still have suspected that his motive in agreeing to, or perhaps even provoking, the divorce had something to do with the fortune teller. Emily's report suggested that Jane was attempting to convey the magnitude of the difficulties she had faced in the previous three decades or so, during some of which time Jane had been working for Emily's husband and family. The diary in which Emily reported this conversation is full of melancholy, hardship, and complaint: the deaths of family members and friends, the hardships of perceived poverty, the loneliness that crept in when children grew up and moved away, and the difficulties of physical illness preoccupied her. Emily's own dismal outlook may have determined the tone of her report about Jane James's life, or perhaps Jane shaped her remarks in such a way as to fit the general tenor of her Emily's mood.[9]

By the time Jane sat in Emily Dow Partridge Young's home and lamented Isaac's departure, fortune telling had become a national craze. Historian Jamie L. Pietruska notes that "fortune-tellers' advertisements became a regular feature in urban dailies nationwide" in the early 1870s. Fortune tellers occupied socially marginal positions in the United States: according to Pietruska, they were "often poor and working-class immigrant and African American women, and occasionally white middle-class women and men." Refiguring their outsider identities as exotic and mysterious, fortune tellers provided their clients an opportunity to go "slumming" and indulge in "escapism tinged with exoticism." But the sensational allure of an interracial relationship like the one Jane reported between her ex-husband and the white fortune teller would have been a scandal in the 1870s both within the LDS community and outside it. Legislators in the colony of Maryland passed a law prohibiting marriage between "freeborn English women" and "Negro slaves" in 1664, inaugurating a stream of legislation against interracial marriages in the American colonies that continued unbroken through the legislative history of the nineteenth-century United States. The Utah Territorial Legislature passed a law in 1852 banning sexual relations between black and white people, and until his death in 1877 Brigham Young repeatedly articulated his strident opposition to the prospect of "amalgamation"—interracial relationships between black and white people. Historian Paul Reeve notes that this stance situated Young squarely "in the mainstream of racial thought for his day." Whether Jane intended to stir up the racial animus that Young and others so readily voiced when it came to interracial sexual activity, her marking of the fortune teller as white certainly added an additional layer of disgrace to an already scandalous story.[10]

It was bad enough that the woman with whom Jane believed Isaac had associated himself was a fortune teller, an occupation that broadcast the woman's questionable moral character. In 1867, the *New York Times* published an editorial describing fortune tellers in its title as "A Growing and Dangerous Class" and decrying the corrupting influence of the practice of fortune telling on the general population. In 1895, folklorist Henry Carrington Bolton gave a talk to the Baltimore Branch of the American Folk-Lore Society, asserting: "Notwithstanding the high average of intelligence in these United States, quite a number of fortune-tellers ply their trade with certain success in most of our larger cities; the daily press teems with the advertisements of these charlatans, who style themselves 'clairvoyants,' 'spiritualists,' and 'test-mediums,' but more commonly 'astrologers.'" Bolton's suggestion that the American public ought to know better than to be taken in by such figures reinforced his characterization of fortune tellers as "charlatans," scam artists of questionable character.[11]

Fortune tellers' methods varied widely: they "read horoscopes, palms (including thumbs and fingernails), cards, tea leaves, and character (using phrenological techniques). Fortune-telling practices varied regionally, from the African American conjure tradition in the South to the 'calculating' tradition of Chinese fortune-tellers in the West who based their predictions on tortoise shells, coins, dominoes, or characters printed in a book." The various forms of divination associated with fortune tellers hearkened back to Joseph Smith and his use of seer stones, as well as his less savory practice of digging for buried treasures supposedly guarded by spirits and detectable through spiritual means. Brigham Young spoke publicly on multiple occasions of a "wicked" fortune teller in the orbit of early Mormonism, so perhaps Jane felt that members of Young's family would be more likely to attach a negative judgment to the woman with whom Isaac left if Jane identified her as a fortune teller. Jane may also have identified fortune tellers with Lucy Stanton, the white woman who married the formerly enslaved William McCary and with him led a small schismatic movement when the Saints were in Winter Quarters. The movement was most notable, and scandalous among Mormons, for its interpretation of sealing rituals as requiring women to have sex with McCary. The McCarys had long since left the LDS Church, but Lucy Stanton's parents had remained with the fold and cared for their daughter's children. Lucy herself had returned to the community in 1869, joining her parents and children south of Salt Lake City in Springville, Utah. Whether Jane had this scandalous interracial couple in mind as she lamented her ex-husband's departure, it is impossible to know. But the associations are intriguing.[12]

The day after Jane's divorce became final, the Relief Society, an LDS women's organization, was reorganized in the First Ward, where she lived at the time. The first Relief Society had been founded in Nauvoo. When Latter-day Saints arrived in Utah, the women again created Relief Societies, but these groups appear to have declined after the Utah War. In the late 1860s and early 1870s, Mormon women once again organized themselves, meeting regularly and channeling their energies into work for the poor and needy. Jane joined the Relief Society in the First Ward when it was organized, and when she moved to the Eighth Ward a few months later, she also joined that ward's Relief Society. These women's organizations provided Jane with spiritual and financial support as she navigated her new life as a single mother.[13]

She would need the support: Jane's divorce from Isaac was the beginning of a long string of losses. In May, her three-month-old grandson Joseph died of pneumonia. His mother, Jane's daughter Mary Ann, lived in Corinne, well to the north of Salt Lake City. Corinne had been founded the previous year in cooperation with the Union Pacific Railroad Company. Its founders envisioned it as a trading center for the Intermountain West, centrally located and, crucially, dominated by non-Mormons and therefore independent of the LDS Church. The town was profoundly, militantly "Gentile," or non-Mormon, such that it became known as the "Gentile Capital of Utah." One visitor described Corinne as "a thorn in the flesh of Mormonism." Mary Ann's residence there suggests that she had rejected her mother's faith. How she supported herself in Corinne is not spelled out in the extant records; the 1870 Federal Census listed her, living with her two-year-old son Isaac R., "keeping house." Her surname, Robinson, suggested that she had married, but her husband was not present. He may have worked for the newly built railroad that was the economic mainstay of the town. But Mary Ann's "married" name may also have been a way of disguising her lack of a socially and legally sanctioned male partner. Mary Ann may have been a mistress or a prostitute, using her sexuality to keep body and soul together. It's hard to say how much Jane knew of Mary Ann's life, but sometime in the latter part of 1870 or in early 1871, Mary Ann came to stay with her. Jane's daughter was pregnant again. Perhaps she hoped to give this child a better chance at surviving infancy by leaning on her mother's care. Tragically, Jane lost both her daughter and her baby grandson in April of 1871. Mary Ann died in childbirth or shortly thereafter: county records listed her cause of death as "child bed." A week later, the newborn Henry died of "lung disease." Henry was listed as the son of Mary Ann; a blank was left where the father's name should have gone. The Eighth Ward Relief Society stepped in to help Jane pay the funeral expenses, contributing $3 for the baby's grave clothing and $20 for two coffins and funeral expenses. Mother and baby were buried in the same grave.[14]

Less than a year after losing her marriage, and with it, her ability to claim a normative LDS femininity, Jane had now lost a daughter and two grandsons. It is easy to imagine that Jane's grief was crosscut with shame: her marriage had dissolved; her daughter had left the church and borne the children of unknown men. The respectability that Jane had so carefully cultivated seemed to be slipping from her grasp. And still, the deaths kept coming. On May 17, 1872, Jane's second-oldest son, Silas, died of consumption, now known as tuberculosis, in her home. The death records noted that he was attended by Doctors Crane and Wesley, but it's doubtful that the doctors' treatment had much effect. Historian Tera W. Hunter writes that until the 1880s, "consumption was largely believed to be a disease that was inherited or one that spontaneously erupted as a result of a weak physical constitution." In the American South, tuberculosis became thoroughly associated with black bodies and was characterized as a "Negro disease."[15] While Southerners recognized that white people also contracted tuberculosis, it was both possible and socially advantageous for white people to frame the disease as one that was spread by black people and that victimized white people. Such a framing was much more difficult in the Salt Lake Valley, where black people made up a much smaller percentage of the population. Still, Southern converts to the LDS Church likely brought with them ideas about the association between "consumption" and blackness that may have been manifested as a reluctance to interact with African Americans in Salt Lake, even when those African Americans were members of the same congregation. Fears of contamination, based on a characterization of black women as unhygienic vectors of disease, may have kept some white Saints from employing Jane as a domestic servant or as a laundress. Silas's death in Jane's house could only have exacerbated those fears.[16]

Perhaps to combat a sense that she was rapidly losing people, Jane began gathering friends and family around her. Days after Silas's death, Jane deeded a portion of her Eighth Ward home site to her daughter Miriam, drawing Miriam, her husband Joseph, and their three children close. Within a few years, Jane's friends Samuel and Amanda Chambers, and Amanda's brother Ned Leggroan and his wife Susan, also moved closer, becoming Jane's neighbors. Although the Chambers and the Leggroans would later move away, perhaps for the time being Jane gained some comfort from having family and friends nearby. She may also have seen transactions like the gift of property to her daughter as a way of both meeting a need and creating some security for herself. By deeding her property to her daughter, Jane created a financial tie between herself and her daughter's entire family. Now that Isaac was gone, perhaps Jane felt she needed to ensure her future through the strategic construction and maintenance of social, economic, and familial relationships.[17]

But Jane's efforts to solidify these connections were continually thwarted by human frailty. Miriam never recovered from giving birth to her fourth child, Nettie, in October 1873. Jane surely nursed her daughter, and cared for her granddaughter, as weakness and infection lingered and ultimately took them both. Nettie died in June 1874; Miriam followed about six months later. Three of Jane's four oldest children had now died within four years of each other. Grief could easily have overwhelmed Jane, combining with shame and self-doubt to undermine any sense of herself as a faithful Latter-day Saint woman. She had lost so much of what attested to her status as a member of the church: her marriage had dissolved, several of her children had fallen away from the church, and so many of them had died. What did that say about her as a wife and a mother, the highest callings available to women in the LDS Church? Despite the tragedies she endured, Jane remained faithful. Perhaps she reassured herself by remembering the "something more" she had found in Charles Wesley Wandell's preaching, and the promises of still greater treasures in Hyrum Smith's 1844 patriarchal blessing. Perhaps she bolstered her commitment by remembering Joseph Smith, the charismatic first prophet of the church, who had treated her like family. Perhaps she thought about how the white women in the Relief Society supported her through her troubles, and felt an obligation to respond in kind. Relief Society minutes from the time documented her periodic donations, usually in cash, but sometimes in goods like rags, soap, or pumpkins.[18]

Jane also remarried. Frank Perkins, her second husband, was an African American man from Missouri. Frank's wife Esther had died in 1865; Jane's son, Sylvester, had married Frank's daughter, Mary Ann, around the same time. Frank and Jane had almost certainly known each other since the Perkins family arrived in the Salt Lake Valley in the late 1840s. Their children had grown up together. Joining their families might bring advantages to both: Frank's income would bring Jane additional financial security; Jane's domestic skills would make Frank's home life more pleasant. There is no official documentation of this union, but scholars have noted that because Mormons saw marriage as a religious ceremony, "the legislature made no provision for the civil recording of marriages nor did it pass any other regulatory measures." Consequently, scores of marriages were not officially recorded. One clue that Jane and Frank had married was that she began appearing as "Jane Elizabeth Manning Perkins" in legal documents and in notes on Relief Society meetings. The transition to her new name was uneven; from August of 1874 through the end of 1875,

Jane appeared in local church records as both "Sister Jane Perkins" and "Jane E. James." Another clue to Jane and Frank's marriage was that in 1875, Jane and Frank went to the Endowment House in Salt Lake City to do baptisms for the dead. If church leaders had not seen their relationship as legitimate, neither Jane nor Frank would have been considered worthy to participate in these rituals. Thus, although no official record of their union existed, circumstantial evidence demonstrates that the marriage was recognized by the church and the community.[19]

The Endowment House was on the same block as the slowly growing LDS temple in the center of Salt Lake City. The unassuming two-story adobe building had been built and dedicated in the 1850s to provide a space for the performance of endowments, sealings, and baptisms for the dead while the Saints worked to build temples. The baptistery, where Jane and Frank spent their time that day in 1875, was a one-story addition on the northwest side, extending from the Endowment House to the wall that enclosed Temple Square.[20]

The ritual of proxy baptism for the dead set Mormons apart from their contemporaries. First discussed publicly by Joseph Smith in 1840, the practice is based on the Latter-day Saints' interpretation of a passage in Paul's letter to the Corinthians that seems to refer to baptism for the dead as a regularly performed ritual. Latter-day Saints believe that this ritual allows the dead to accept the LDS gospel in the afterlife, the first step to joining their families in eternity.[21]

Jane and Frank went to the Endowment House on a sunny Friday in early September. Brigham Young had directed that time be set aside for black Latter-day Saints to go to the Endowment House to perform baptisms for the dead. Young instructed the temple workers that these rituals were "to be entered in a Book by themselves; the book to be headed '*Record* of *Baptisms for the Dead* of the (*Seed of Cain*') or (of the People of African Descent)." Jane and Frank were joined by Samuel and Amanda Chambers, Susan and Ned Leggroan, Frank's daughter Mary Ann Perkins James, and another woman, Annis Bell Lucas Evans. Jane and the others entered the Endowment House that day through the main entrance, on the east side of a small northern extension of the Endowment House. The cool, soft light of the reception room that they entered provided a welcome respite from the bright sunlight of that September day. The building's adobe walls, two feet thick, helped keep the Endowment House cool in the summer, and the white paint that coated the walls and ceiling reflected the light that entered through two windows, making the room seem light and airy. After checking in, the group walked down a small set of stairs into the initiatory room. Jane and the others could not see most of the room; it was divided by canvas partitions so that the door from the reception room led into a kind of hallway, with the wall on the left made of canvas and the wall on the right made of adobe (Figure 6.1). Had Jane had the opportunity to explore this room, she would have found more canvas partitions dividing it into smaller spaces that were used for washings

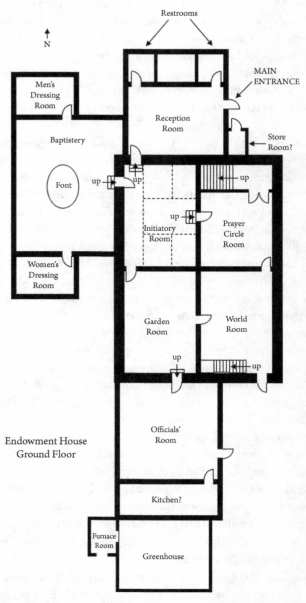

Figure 6.1 The Salt Lake Endowment House served as a space where Latter-day Saints could perform temple rituals while the temple was still under construction. This diagram shows the spaces on the first floor of the Endowment House that Jane saw as well as those she did not see because they were obscured by canvas partitions (indicated by the dotted lines) or because they were behind closed doors. Diagram by the author (not drawn to scale), following Lisle G. Brown, "'Temple Pro Tempore': The Salt Lake City Endowment House," *Journal of Mormon History* 34, no. 4 (Fall 2008): 33.

and anointings, rituals in which black Saints were no longer permitted to participate. But Jane and those with her had little time to contemplate what might be on the other side of the canvas wall along which they walked; in a few steps they had reached the door into the baptistery. They turned right and went down two steps into the room where they would spend most of their time that day.[22]

Like the rest of the Endowment House, the baptistery was painted white. The baptismal font stood in the middle of the large room, which likely had benches along the walls where Jane and others sat when they were not actively being baptized for their dead. There was almost certainly a desk as well, where a temple worker sat to record the rituals. Extant sources do not describe the font in detail, but scholar Lisle G. Brown suggested that it was oval, with a base anchored in the ground and the basin entirely above the floor, following the design of the baptismal font in the Nauvoo Temple. If Brown was correct, those participating in baptisms had to climb a ladder or small staircase to enter the font. Jane and the other women went to the women's dressing room through a door on the south wall of the baptistery, while the men used the dressing room on the north.[23] When they emerged, everyone was dressed in pure white. Five men, all of them white priesthood holders, stood ready to officiate and assist in the baptismal ritual. For each baptism, one priesthood holder would perform the baptism, standing with the baptismal candidate in the font, intoning the words of the ceremony, and immersing the candidate in the water. Two priesthood holders would witness the baptism, ensuring that the ritual was performed completely and correctly. And two priesthood holders would confirm the person who was baptized, laying hands on the newly baptized person's head and praying that she or he would receive the gift of the Holy Ghost.

As each person in the group entered the font, Jane and others who were still dry waited and watched. Men were baptized for men; women for women. Samuel went first, then Amanda; next Annis, and then Frank. Finally, it was Jane's turn. She conferred with the elder who would be baptizing her; she would be baptized for Susan Brown, perhaps a friend she knew growing up in Wilton, Connecticut. Frank had been baptized for Morris Brown, possibly Susan's father.[24] Standing in the font with Jane, the priest took her right wrist with his left hand. Jane held on to his left wrist with her left hand and took a deep breath. The priest raised his right hand "to the square," the position prescribed by the church for this ritual (Figure 1.2). His upper arm extended straight out to his right, his elbow level with his shoulder. His lower arm extended directly upward, parallel to his upright body, the tips of his fingers pointing upward to heaven. "Jane Elizabeth Manning Perkins," he intoned, "having been commissioned of Jesus Christ, I baptize you for and in behalf of Susan Brown in the name of the Father, and of the Son, and of the Holy Ghost. Amen." He lowered his right hand to Jane's back, guiding her under the water, as two other priesthood holders watched to make sure she was completely immersed. As she underwent this baptism for her friend, perhaps Jane thought back to her own baptism in Connecticut. She had performed this same ritual with Charles Wesley Wandell over three decades earlier. He had used nearly identical words. It had been the beginning—one of them—of the odyssey that had led her to this font, in Utah, more than thirty years later.

The water was cold. The font was most likely fed by water from City Creek, piped directly into the Endowment House. The creek, in turn, was fed by natural springs in the mountains northeast of the city, augmented by melting snow. Construction had begun on a municipal water system, which would pipe the water from City Creek all over Salt Lake, but for now, creek water was likely carried to the font through wood stave pipes.[25] The elder raised Jane from the water. She opened her eyes and exhaled as the water streamed down her face. Jane climbed out of the baptismal font and, as Susan Leggroan was baptized for her relatives, Jane dried off. She may even have changed into a second set of white clothing. Then she took a seat in the baptistery. By this time Jane's daughter-in-law, Mary Ann Perkins James, might have been the one being baptized. The two elders who were not performing or witnessing the baptisms placed their hands on Jane's head and prayed that she, as a proxy for Susan Brown, would receive the gift of the Holy Ghost, completing the ritual of baptism and confirmation.

In all, the group of eight people was baptized for forty-six friends and relatives. Those for whom biographical information was recorded were all deceased: many of them had died within the previous decade. For the most part, the people in the Endowment House that day had probably not been in contact with the people for whom they were baptized since the ritual participants had moved to Utah, and perhaps long before that. The rituals they performed that day were a way to renew long-dormant emotional relationships, the first step in creating spiritual kinship networks that would endure through eternity.

Given the gravity of this ritual, it is curious that the only people Jane added to the list of those to be baptized were Susan and Morris Brown. Why not add others, like the father who died when she was a girl, or other relatives left behind in the east? We can only speculate. It is possible that one of Jane's brothers had been baptized for their father back in Nauvoo, when Joseph Smith first taught the doctrine of baptism for the dead, so that although the record of this ritual did not survive, Jane knew it had been accomplished. She may have felt more secure submitting the names of Morris and Susan Brown than those of her relatives because the Browns had died while Jane was still in Connecticut. If she believed the extended family members she left behind in Connecticut might still be alive, they would not have been appropriate candidates for proxy baptism. Jane would later perform proxy baptisms for several of her relatives, but at this time she chose not to do so.

In April 1876, Relief Society records listed Jane Perkins as the donor of two bars of soap, worth a total of twenty cents.[26] It is the last record I have found in which Jane used Frank's surname. At some point after that, her marriage to Frank Perkins ended. Subsequently, Jane appeared in records consistently as Jane James, reverting to her earlier married name for good. Just as there was no official record of the marriage, no record of a divorce appears to exist. It may be that the couple decided to separate without divorcing; it could be that a legal divorce seemed an unnecessarily expensive or troublesome way to end a marriage that had lasted less than two years. Jane and Frank do not appear to have merged their finances at any point, so there was no need of a legal division of property; and they had no children together, so there was no question of custody or child support. Jane had initiated divorce proceedings in 1870 when her marriage to Isaac fell apart. She may have worried that requesting a second divorce would affect her reputation. Of course, it may also be that the couple obtained a legal divorce, but the record of it simply has not been found or did not survive. One thing seems certain: the marriage had ended.

On July 6, 1876, Jane went to the Eighth Ward Relief Society meeting. She was one of several women who shared their thoughts with the group that day. "Jane James did not know as she could add to what had been said," the Society's secretary noted in the minutes, adding that Jane "desired to do right." It's easy to imagine this statement as a resolution to do better: to somehow keep her family together, to stay on the straight and narrow, to be a better woman and a better Latter-day Saint. It might sound to our ears like a reflection of the shame and embarrassment Jane felt in the wake of another failed marriage, a sense of guilt for whatever part she played in the dissolution of that relationship. Those feelings might have been compounded by a sense that she had failed as a mother: so many of her children had died, and those who still lived were not upstanding members of the church. Where had she gone wrong? She desired to do right. Then again, this statement has a formulaic ring to it. In 1871, Jane had said in the June 1 Relief Society meeting that she "wished to do her duty[,] &c." The statement was so ordinary that the Relief Society secretary did not even bother recording the bulk of it. A mere "&c." stood in for Jane's statement. "Wish[ing] to do her duty" and "desir[ing] to do right" might have easily been two ways of saying the same thing.[27]

At some point in 1876, Jane's mother died in Iowa. It is difficult to know how well Jane kept in touch with her mother and siblings. Her literacy was limited, as theirs may also have been: Jane claimed to be able to read and write, but the only evidence that survives shows other people reading to and writing for her. Jane's brother Isaac could write at least enough to sign his name; perhaps he was the one who wrote to inform Jane of Philes's death.[28] Jane's reaction to her mother's death did not leave a perceptible trace in the historical record. Relief Society minutes did not record her speaking of her grief or speculating about whether her

mother and her dead children were together in the afterlife. Jane did not bring her
mother's death to the Salt Lake community's attention by placing an obituary in
the newspaper. No legal record suggested that Philes's death had a financial impact on Jane's life. In many ways, Philes's death merely finalized her physical absence from Jane's life. Jane had not seen her mother in thirty years, and with the
exception of Sylvester, none of Jane's children had any memories of their grandmother. For Jane and her family, life went on as usual after Philes's death, though
this loss may have increased, in some small way, Jane's growing sense of urgency
about solidifying the eternal connections between her family members.

In 1877, workers finally finished the St. George Temple. Located in southern
Utah, the St. George Temple was the first to be completed in the Saints' adopted
land. It had been the focus of considerable fundraising: Jane and Frank had each
given fifty cents toward its construction back in 1874. Brigham Young went
south in April to dedicate the temple, the only one completed in his lifetime.
Jane did not: the trip would have been expensive and disruptive. Like most Salt
Lake Saints, she heard about the dedication afterward, whether from the pulpit
or in casual conversation. The ceremony was covered extensively in the Salt Lake
papers. Latter-day Saints flocked to St. George to complete temple work for their
loved ones, even though the Endowment House remained mostly open in Salt
Lake for several more years. We do not know when, or how, Jane learned that
she would not set foot inside the finished building for which she had given hard-
earned money.[29] Perhaps this was apparent to her by the time she went to the
Endowment House to do baptisms for her dead in 1875, given the restrictions
that were placed on her activity even there.

   With the completion of the St. George Temple, the temple restrictions that
were the corollary to the priesthood ban for black men came into full force. Black
people—people Mormons believed were descended from Cain—were permitted
to perform baptisms for the dead, as Jane, Frank Perkins, and others had done
in the Salt Lake Endowment House. But they were not allowed to participate
in any other temple rituals. Temple rituals both presume and make available
certain kinds of access to the LDS priesthood: according to scholar Jonathan
Stapley, the temple liturgy created a "material heaven on earth," a network
of people sealed to one another in what they referred to as the "priesthood."
Religious studies scholar Kathleen Flake, similarly, interprets sealing rituals
as a way in which participants were endowed with divine power.[30] In Brigham
Young's logic, the priesthood restriction righted the primordial wrong of Abel's
murder by requiring the descendants of the murderer, Cain, to wait until the
descendants of his victim had all received their spiritual blessings. Thus the
priesthood, and the divine power available through endowments and sealings,
were to be withheld from black people indefinitely.

Brigham Young had articulated this restriction nearly a quarter-century earlier, in 1852, but the church leadership was still working out its ramifications. Their understanding that the divine power of the priesthood flowed along family lines resulted in increasingly far-reaching decisions, revoking the priesthood of white men who married black women, withdrawing blessings from white women who married black men, and otherwise attempting to channel priesthood power away from people of African descent.[31] For Jane and her family, these restrictions had very real consequences: the Jameses, like other African American Mormons, were reliant on white men to fill the priesthood roles that husbands, fathers, and sons normally played in LDS families. Every time a family member needed a blessing—whether a newborn baby, who would usually be welcomed into the community with a father's blessing, or an ill family member, who needed a healing blessing—an outsider had to enter the family circle. Most importantly, Jane believed that without temple endowments and sealings, her family would not be together after death, and they would not be able to attain the highest degrees of glory in the afterlife. As she watched her children and her grandchildren succumb to disease, Jane could not turn to Mormonism's comforting promise that families are eternal. Her family, Brigham Young taught, was cursed.

At the end of August 1877, Brigham Young died. He had been ill for about a week with "cholera morbus," a vague diagnosis. His nephew and attending physician later asserted that Young's death was due to a burst appendix, but the symptoms he exhibited could have been caused by a wide variety of maladies.[32] On Saturday, September 1, Young's body lay in state in the Salt Lake City Tabernacle, with mourners filing through the building to view him one last time. Perhaps Jane joined the crowd, pressing forward to say a few last words to the man she had known for more than three decades—the man in whose household she had been neither "family" nor "hired help," the man who, more than any other, had consolidated the exclusion of her and her family from the holy community of the Latter-day Saints even as he had depended on their labor to sustain his polygamous family on earth. Perhaps she joined the congregation the next day at the burial service, which filled the tabernacle to capacity and attracted another two thousand people who stood outside the building. Perhaps she walked with the procession to the family cemetery, just to the northeast of the Endowment House. Or perhaps she could not bring herself to pay her respects to the man who did not respect her, and she stayed home.

Is There No Blessing for Me?

(*ca. 1880–1894*)

The belief that she would not reach the highest degrees of glory in the after-life seems to have bothered Jane more and more as she got older. She was a faithful member of the church. She paid her tithes, donated to causes the church promoted, and participated actively in the Relief Society. Latter-day Saints believed that they could only reach the celestial realm in the company of their families, bound to one another for eternity by temple sealings, able to make the journey to glory because they had received their endowments in the temple. Jane's children were dying, and many of them had a tenuous relationship with the church at best, though she continued to try to bring them back into the fold. Likewise, despite her best efforts, Jane was not able to sustain a marriage. And the temple rituals, which would have transformed her earthly kin into her eternal family, were just beyond Jane's grasp.

Isaac James, Jane's first husband, was long gone. He appeared in the 1880 census in Portland, Oregon, a lodger described as divorced and mulatto. Frank Perkins, her second husband, was still nearby. He worked as a servant for a family that lived about three blocks north of Jane's home.[1] Although the two households belonged to different wards, Jane couldn't have avoided Frank even if she had wanted to. Whether or not they ran in the same social circles, Jane and Frank remained connected through the marriage of their children Sylvester and Mary Ann. Any family function involving the grandchildren would have brought them together. There is no evidence to indicate how Jane or Frank experienced such encounters. Perhaps they were friendly reunions, tinged with wistfulness, regret for what might have been. Perhaps Jane and Frank transitioned seam-lessly back to their previous relationship as parents-in-law. Or perhaps their meetings were filled with tension, setting everyone's teeth on edge.

Jane was described in the 1880 census as "married," a designation she almost certainly supplied to the census taker herself, despite the fact that her marriage to Frank Perkins had dissolved and that she had divorced Isaac James years earlier. It is, of course, possible that this description was technically accurate, that Jane was still married to Frank, even though the census taker checked the "single" box next to Frank's name in the same census, and even though Jane had returned to using "James" as her surname. It seems more likely, though, that Jane described herself as married because she viewed her marital status as a crucial marker of social and religious position. Latter-day Saint women of Jane's age were expected to be married. "Single" or "divorced" would have seemed to Jane to be markers of failure. Moreover, "married" supplied a respectable explanation for the presence in her home of the grandchildren she was raising: Malvina and Jessie, ten-year-old and five-month-old granddaughters.[2] (Malvina was Ellen Madora's daughter; it is unclear who Jessie's parents were.) Jane may have been ambivalent about describing herself as married: as early as 1884, an entry for Jane in a Salt Lake City directory designated her a widow, even though Frank Perkins lived until 1888. Like "married," "widow" was a respectable status in the Mormon church and helped Jane fit into the social structure at a time when her ability to conform to community expectations felt uncertain.

Married, single, widowed, divorced: although these labels shaped Jane's standing in her community, she knew they mattered much less than the assurance of her eternal status that she would gain through the performance of temple rituals. In a letter dated December 27, 1884, Jane wrote to the church President John Taylor, "Dear Brother, I called at your house last Thursday to have conversation with you concerning my future salvation." If Jane was not mixing up her dates, she had either visited Taylor on Christmas day or a week before Christmas. In Jane's account, the conversation seems to have been rushed. "I did not explain my feelings or wishes to you," she wrote. Then she went on, as if responding to what Taylor had said that day: "I realize my race & color & can't expect my Endowments as others who are white. My race was handed down through the flood & God promised Abraham that in his seed all the nations of the earth should be blest & as this is the fullness of all dispensations is there no blessing for me?"[3]

In this deft act of scriptural interpretation, Jane turned the LDS belief that African Americans' dark skin was a physical marker of a divine curse on its ear. She claimed instead the blessings to which "all nations" were entitled through Abraham. Jane's use of scripture may have been a way to parry Taylor's own use of biblical texts to support his decision not to let Jane participate in the rituals she longed to experience.

Jane's discussion with Taylor had been going on for almost two years, if not longer. On March 20, 1883, she went to the president's office with another woman whose identity was recorded only as "Sister Ellis." The office journal summarized the meeting:

The question was could Sister James who had long been a faithful member of the Church, but was a negress receive her endowments. President Taylor talked the matter over with her, but gave her no hope that at present such ordinances could be performed in behalf of the negro race, but promised to consider it. He quoted the scripture that Ethiopia should stretch out her hands to God, but did not think the time had yet come for that race to receive the benefits of the House of the Lord.

While Taylor, as president of the church, had the final word on the interpretation of scripture and the performance of temple rituals, Jane may have been less inclined than others to consider that the end of the conversation. After all, she had worked for both of Taylor's predecessors. She knew that they were human, just like everyone else in the church. And she knew that interpretations could change: she had seen it happen.[4]

Jane also knew better than to put all her eggs in one basket. In addition to petitioning the president of the church, she turned to her stake president, the man charged with leading the congregations in Salt Lake. She received a temple recommend—essentially, a pass to enter the temple—from the president of her stake, Angus M. Cannon, in June 1888. "Mrs. Jane James," Cannon had written in a letter accompanying the recommend, "I enclose you your recommend properly signed, which will entitle you to enter the Temple to be baptized and confirmed for your dead kindred." The letter suggests that Jane had been seeking more than this permission from Cannon. "You must be content with this privilege," Cannon went on, "awaiting further instructions from the Lord to his servants."[5]

That fall, Jane made her way to Logan to do baptisms for the dead. Some eighty miles north of Salt Lake City, nestled in Cache Valley, Logan was the site of the second temple that the Saints completed in the West. No documentation exists to tell us how Jane traveled to and from Logan, who might have accompanied her, nor how long her trip lasted. Perhaps the most convenient mode of transport would have been the railway. Jane could have boarded a train to Ogden at the train depot in Salt Lake, a few blocks north and west of her home. Disembarking thirty-six miles later, she might have lingered in the station for a while before boarding a 4:40 p.m. train to Logan. The train hugged the Wasatch mountains as it made its way north, finally climbing upward and over the summit to drop down into Cache Valley and arrive in Logan shortly after 7:00 p.m. The train was the fastest and most comfortable way to get between Salt Lake and Logan, but it was expensive. Jane may have found another way to Logan: perhaps Sylvester was headed there for business, or perhaps she was able to ride with friends. Traveling by horse-drawn cart or carriage was slower and less comfortable, but the route was very similar. Jane stayed at least a couple of nights in or near Logan. There were hotels in the area, but it seems unlikely that black people would be welcomed as guests in these establishments, unless Jane was traveling as the employee of a white person. She was a bit old to be working as a domestic servant, but there is a chance that Jane seized an opportunity to visit Logan in exchange for helping a white acquaintance for a few days. Otherwise, Jane probably stayed with friends or acquaintances in the area. Logan was an overwhelmingly white place: the 1880 Census counted no black people in the entire settlement. If Jane enjoyed the hospitality of someone she knew, it was almost certainly someone white.[6]

On Tuesday, October 16, Jane went to the baptistery in the Logan Temple. The temple was a striking stone affair, with creamy white paint that made it stand out against the mountains in the distance (Figure 7.1). Rising five stories, with arched windows, crenellated walls, and a cupola at each end, the building's design recalled both European castles and New England chapels. Unlike the Salt Lake Endowment House, where the baptistery was an addition to the main building, in the Logan Temple the baptistery was at the very center of the building. In the imposing font, which rested on the backs of twelve stone oxen, Jane was baptized six times: for her mother, Philes Manning; her sister, Angeline Manning; her daughter, Mary Anne James; her maternal grandmother, Philes Abbett; her maternal aunt, Dorcas Abbett; and her cousin, Dorcas's daughter, Harriet Abbett. Mary Ann had been baptized before, and Jane's mother and sister almost certainly had as well. Jane may have thought these relatives needed rebaptism because they had left the church.[7] Jane could not be baptized for her male relatives; a male proxy had to perform that ritual labor. But Jane did not pursue the task of finding and hiring such a proxy, or at least the existing records do not show that she did so. Jane's attentions to the eternal welfare of her female relatives may have reflected a lingering sense of the importance of the women in her family.

As Jane tried to knit her family together in eternity, her earthly family seemed to be unraveling. In October 1885, Jane's oldest son Sylvester was cut off from the church by a Bishop's Court for "unchristianlike behavior." This description covered a wide range of infractions, from refusing to follow the counsel of an ecclesiastical leader to sexual misconduct to breach of contract. For Latter-day Saints, bishops' courts could be a supplement to civil and criminal legal proceedings, but they could also be a substitute for these venues, providing a religious solution for conflicts between church members and ecclesiastical punishments to atone for religious sins. In an 1883 speech, church president John Taylor rhetorically asked his audience, "What are laws for? What are Bishops' Courts and High Councils for?" Taylor answered his own questions: "That when men transgress the laws of God, they shall be tried according to the laws of the Church, and if found guilty, and are worthy of such action, they shall be cast out; that

Figure 7.1 The Logan Temple, pictured here, was completed in 1884. In 1888, Jane received permission to do baptisms for some of her dead relatives there. It was one of only two times she would enter a temple for ritual purposes. Used by permission, Utah State Historical Society.

the pure and the righteous may be sustained, and the wicked and corrupt, the ungodly and impure, be dealt with according to the laws of God. This is necessary in order to maintain purity throughout the Church, and to cast off iniquity therefrom." For the church, cutting off Sylvester was a way to preserve the purity of the institution. But for Jane, it was heartbreaking. As a woman, Jane was supposed to be able to depend on the men in her life, but her marriages had failed. Now her oldest son, the one who had achieved the greatest material success and who appeared to have the most respectable family life, had been excommunicated.[8]

As Sylvester was cast out of the church, Jane's daughter Ellen Madora spun out of control. In 1870, Ellen lived at home with Jane. Eighteen years old and unmarried, she was described in the census that year as "keeping house." Ellen's daughter Malvina was already one year old. By the following census, Ellen had left Malvina in Jane's care and was living in Eureka, Nevada. Eureka was a mining town founded in the mid-1860s that reached its peak population in 1878. Historian Amy Tanner Thiriot identified a "courtesan," listed in the 1880 census as "Mrs. Nellie Kidd," as Jane's daughter Ellen Madora. Not many twenty-seven-year-old black women that year could claim to have been born in Utah to parents born in New Jersey and Connecticut, as "Mrs. Nellie Kidd" did. In fact, Ellen Madora may have been the only person in the world who fit that profile at that time. In 1879, the San Francisco *Daily Evening Bulletin* reported that "Nellie Kidd, convicted of keeping a house of ill-fame, was fined $50" by the San Francisco Criminal Court at the end of June. Ellen may have moved to Nevada because it offered a more hospitable place to ply her trade.[9]

By 1886, Ellen was back in Salt Lake. There, she went by her given name; a pseudonym was useless in her hometown. But she apparently persuaded her mother to help her get ahead: in 1886, Jane transferred the deed to her home to Ellen, who then mortgaged the property. Perhaps Ellen was paying off personal debts, or perhaps she had convinced her mother that some seed money would allow her to start a respectable business with which she could support herself, her daughter Malvina, and even Jane. But by 1888 Ellen could not make the payments on the loan. She transferred the mortgage back to Jane and soon returned to California and her pseudonym. Malvina went with her, relieving Jane of the financial burden of caring for her granddaughter. Jane shifted her attention to other granddaughters: Estela, Josephine, and Emmeline Williams, the daughters of Jane's late daughter Miriam. The girls' father had lost the land Jane had gifted to their mother. Now that the girls had become young women, Jane could bypass their father and transfer property directly to them, which she did in January 1890.[10]

A few months later, Isaac James returned to Salt Lake. There is no way to know whether Jane expected him; although he might have written to Jane or others, nothing survives in the historical record to indicate that he had notified anyone of his arrival. Jane was about seventy years old now, and Isaac a few years older than that. His body was broken down from decades of manual labor. When he arrived in the city, he found an urban space far more developed than it had been when he left more than a decade earlier. His children were grown; his daughters had died or left the region; most of his sons had died as well. Sylvester, whom Isaac had adopted over forty years ago, and Jesse, Isaac's youngest son, were the only boys still living.

Jane may still have been working as a laundress in 1890, taking in washing to make ends meet and pay off the mortgage on her property. She took Isaac in, though her reasons for doing so are not clear. Perhaps she hoped that her first marriage might be saved; perhaps she expected that Isaac would pay rent; perhaps she felt it was her Christian duty to put a roof over his head. Isaac was received by rebaptism in the Eighth Ward in July 1890.[11] The church gave Isaac a clean slate through this ritual, but no ritual was available to wipe the slate clean of all the unhappiness Jane and Isaac had caused one another. Whether two decades apart had allowed them to forgive one another, we have no way to tell. It is possible that Jane and Isaac remarried; no marriage record exists, and since Jane had been using Isaac's surname since her separation from Frank Perkins, no name change provides a clue.

On August 7, Jane spoke up in her Relief Society meeting: "Sister James felt the Spirit of the Lord was with us," the acting secretary of the group recorded. "Knew the Lord had blessed her since childhood. Bore a strong testimony, prayed she so might live as to receive salvation in Kingdom of God." Was Jane experiencing Isaac's return as a blessing? His renewed presence in her life may have been a comfort: her children were grown and had moved out of her house. Isaac might have provided some welcome company in a home that had once been crowded with their children and grandchildren. But Isaac's return may also have been a trial. When the couple had divorced two decades earlier, Judge Elias Smith had written that "it was fully and satisfactorily made to appear that [Jane and Isaac] could not live together in peace and union" and that "their welfare and happiness required that they should be separated from each other." There was no guarantee that their feelings had softened toward each other in the twenty years they spent apart. Jane's comments at her Relief Society meeting may have indicated some uncertainty about whether she had it in her to live with Isaac so "as to receive salvation."[12]

Isaac's presence could also have strained Jane's finances; he may have been too feeble to work, and therefore unable to contribute to the household economy. On June 18, 1891, the annual Old Folks' Day celebration took Salt Lake's aged citizens by railroad to Springville, a small settlement south of Provo. "The morning was delightful," the *Deseret Evening News* reported. "A few white clouds gave to the deep blue of the sky a lovelier hue, and the air was clear and bracing while the sunbeams chased away the faintest traces of cold."[13] Among the nearly six hundred "old folks" seventy years old or older, on the fourteen railway cars, the paper reported "there were the lame, the halt, the blind and the deaf, but very few, however, who were not in possession of all their faculties, and two or three persons of color." Jane was one of those two or three, but Isaac was not. While not conclusive, Isaac's absence may suggest that physical infirmity kept him housebound.

In November 1891, perhaps a year and a half after his return to Salt Lake, Isaac died. He had been ill for six weeks, but his death record lists no cause other than "old age." Jane held Isaac's funeral in her home. Even this decision might have been a strategy to claim her status as a married—now widowed—woman. Reporting Isaac's death, the *Deseret Evening News* opined, "'Brother Isaac,' as he was familiarly called, will be well and kindly remembered by the old settlers of Utah." Strikingly, though, the paper did not mention Jane, averring that Isaac died "at his residence" and that his funeral would take place "from his late residence." Jane's invisibility in Isaac's death notice might have suited her just fine: to insist that the residence was hers, not his, would only have raised questions about their relationship. Instead, by hosting Isaac's funeral at her house—"his late residence"—Jane reinforced the appearance that they were married, even if it was an illusion. From Jane's house, the funeral procession headed northeast, past the nearly finished temple to the Salt Lake City Cemetery. Isaac was interred there, next to his four children and several grandchildren.[14]

Isaac's death was still fresh in the minds of Jane and her children when Christmas came. In Salt Lake, the *Deseret News* carried reports of dinners and advertisements of holiday sales at local retail establishments. Stories of Christmas far and near tugged on the heartstrings, cementing the connections between Christmas, family, and gift-giving that were crystallizing throughout the nation. The *Salt Lake Herald* reported that it "was an ideal Christmas, crisp and white, and the merrymaking was general and of an innocent order. . . . Family gatherings formed the main feature of the day, and in many homes near friends were drawn together about the dinner table decked with the traditional turkey and other toothsome things. Business was entirely suspended, and all the work that was done consisted in charity or amusements. Christmas trees peeped from every parlor, and the faces of the children beamed with delight. Sleighing was never better in Salt Lake and the biting air added zest to the pleasure."[15] It seems most likely that Jane spent the day with Sylvester, his wife Mary Ann, and their children. Jane's granddaughters Estela, Josephine, and Emmeline Williams— Miriam's daughters—might also have joined them. Since Isaac had died little more than a month earlier, the gathering may have been more subdued than usual. Sylvester and Mary Ann's youngest, Nettie, was almost fifteen years old, too grown up to distract the gathering with childish antics. Esther Jane, their older daughter, was married with a child of her own. Perhaps she and her husband Henry brought little Hyrum to Sylvester and Mary Ann's, but perhaps they stayed home. It was cold, after all, and their son was only a toddler.

Jane's youngest son Jesse might also have joined the family for Christmas if his labor was not needed at the hotel where he worked, but this seems unlikely given the *Salt Lake Herald's* report that "the hotels all had excellent spreads, the menus far exceeding anything of the previous years, and plenty of guests to relish the bounty." Jane might have thrown another celebration a few days later when Jesse had time off from work. For several years, Jane had received a Christmas basket full of food from the Eighth Ward Relief Society. Usually, baskets arrived a day or two before Christmas, but this year's basket was delivered on December 29, just in time to celebrate the New Year. The Relief Society records do not list the contents of the thirty-two baskets the group distributed in 1891, but Jane's 1889 basket was typical. That year she received chicken, sugar, raisins, candy, currants, rice, butter, crackers, and cake. This mix of staples, meat, and sweets strongly suggests that the Relief Society conceived of these baskets not as a way to meet practical needs, but rather as a way to supply the holiday cheer expected at Christmas.[16]

By the following Christmas, Jane would no longer be alone in her home: her brother Isaac Manning moved to Salt Lake in 1892 and took up residence in Jane's house. An 1892 Salt Lake directory listed Isaac as a carpenter, suggesting that he continued to work despite his advanced age. Isaac, along with most of Jane's family, had stayed behind in Iowa when Jane moved to Utah with her husband and son. His wife had died in 1891; as far as Isaac knew, Jane was the only family he had left.[17]

Like many followers of Joseph Smith, Isaac Manning had not been convinced by Brigham Young's claims to leadership of the church in the tumultuous period following Smith's death. Instead, he eventually joined what became known as the Reorganized Church of Jesus Christ of Latter Day Saints (the RLDS Church), a movement led by Joseph Smith's direct descendants, centered in the Midwest. The RLDS Church interpreted Smith's teachings and legacy differently than did the LDS Church in Utah, and in the 1860s, they began ordaining black men to the RLDS priesthood. When Isaac moved in with Jane, he might have brought the priesthood with him. We do not know how Jane thought about the RLDS Church. But she was undoubtedly glad to see her brother rebaptized in the LDS Church in March 1892.[18] Jane and Isaac had been among the first of their family to join the Mormon movement in Connecticut; now, they were united in faith once again.

In October 1889 Jane requested and received a second patriarchal blessing. John Smith, the Presiding Patriarch of the church at the time, was the son of Hyrum Smith, who had pronounced Jane's first patriarchal blessing. The blessing given by the son was more positive than the conditional blessing given by the father; John Smith's blessing reassured Jane that despite her frustrations in life, things would turn out well in the end. "Let thy heart be comforted, look always upon the bright side for better days await thee," Smith told Jane. "Thou shalt complete thy mission, and receive thine inheritance among the Saints, and thy name shall be handed down to posterity in honorable remembrance." Jane needed this reassurance: although she had been permitted to perform baptisms for her dead, she had not received her endowment or been sealed to her family members. She had been requesting these privileges for years by the time John Smith laid his hands on her head; she must have been tired of fighting for the blessings white

Saints took for granted. The patriarchal blessing assured her that her struggle was not in vain: "The Lord has heard thy petitions," Smith comforted Jane. "He knowest the secrets of thy heart, He has witnessed thy trials, and although thy life has been somewhat checkered His hand has been over thee for good and thou shalt verily receive thy reward."[19]

Smith's reference to Jane's "checkered" past was a clue to how Jane's white co-religionists viewed her history. Unlike white Saints, Jane had to overcome prejudice that painted her as lazy, ignorant, and immoral. Latter-day Saints used stories from the Bible, the Book of Mormon, and other LDS scriptures to justify their discrimination against black people. But Hyrum Smith had promised that God could remove the curse of Cain and "stamp upon [her] his own Image." And Hyrum Smith's son went further: "For thy kindness many shall bless thee in thine old age and as a Mother in Israel thou shalt be known among the people," he promised.[20] "Mother in Israel" was the highest honorific that could be bestowed on a Mormon woman. The title was reserved for the most respected women in the community, some of whom Jane turned to for help in requesting temple rituals. To be told that she, too, would be known as a mother in Israel, despite her "checkered" past and her restricted access to the temple, must have been comforting to Jane.

Smith's blessing may have encouraged Jane to believe that her struggle for her temple privileges would ultimately succeed. In February 1890 she wrote a letter to Joseph F. Smith, the nephew of church founder Joseph Smith, who had become a member of the Quorum of the Twelve Apostles: "Can I also be adopted in Brother Joseph Smith's the prophet's family? I think you are somewhat acquainted with me—I lived in the prophet's family with Emma and others, about a year—and Emma said Joseph told her to tell me I could be adopted in their family. She asked me if I should like to. I did not understand the law of adoption then—but understanding it now, can that be accomplished and when?" This request reiterated one she had made in her 1884 letter to John Taylor, one she would make several more times during the years that remained to her. Jane enlisted the help of her sisters in the Relief Society to press her case. Zina D. H. Young, a plural wife of the now-deceased Brigham Young and the president of the Relief Society, forwarded Jane's request to Joseph F. Smith in 1894, writing, "Jane E. James says, Sister Emma Smith asked her if she would like to be adopted into Joseph Smith's family as a child, & not understanding her meaning [Jane] said no." This narrative—of an offer that Jane turned down out of ignorance—remained consistent in Jane's telling across the roughly two-decade period in which it shows up in the evidence. In her autobiography, dictated sometime between 1902 and her death in 1908, Jane again repeated the story and lamented her decision: "I did not comprehend," she said.[21]

In the early 1840s, around the time Jane said Emma offered her adoption into Joseph Smith's family, the prophet introduced the idea of "sealing" family members together into an "eternal family unit." This idea included the sealing of husbands and wives, as well as children to parents, though Joseph Smith never performed the ritual of sealing children to parents. In time, as scholar Jonathan Stapley wrote, "Kinship, priesthood, and salvation became synonymous." This understanding of adoption sealing, linking familial relationships with salvation, explains why Jane was so intent on being sealed: without that ritual, she would be " 'single & alone' in the eternities."[22]

Adoption sealings could only be performed in consecrated temples, so once the Saints left Illinois they ceased performing adoptions for nearly thirty years. The dedication of the sealing rooms in the St. George Temple made adoptions possible once more, and thousands of Saints were sealed to parents. Those with biological parents who were faithful Latter-day Saints were sealed to them; those with unbelieving parents were allowed to select a believing father of their choice. Perhaps unsurprisingly, church leaders—and especially founder Joseph Smith—were popular choices.[23] Thus, Jane's request to be adopted into Joseph Smith's family was far from unusual.

Unlike most people who sought to be adopted by Joseph Smith, Jane bolstered her request with stories, likely in an effort to overcome the resistance that an interracial adoption might meet. In Jane's eyes, this ritual would not create a wholly different relationship between her and Joseph: "He used to be just like I was his child," she said in a 1905 interview. She reinforced this view of Joseph Smith as a kindly, generous, paternal figure in other accounts as well. The sealing Jane longed for would fulfill the potential Jane had sensed in her relationship with the prophet. Jane's other sealing requests were similarly aspirational: she requested that her brother Isaac Manning and her husband (probably Isaac James) be sealed to Joseph Smith as children, but she also requested that she be sealed in marriage by proxy to the deceased Q. Walker Lewis, one of the few early black priesthood holders. Lewis's ecclesiastical credentials suggested a level of worthiness that far outshone that of Isaac James or Frank Perkins. In these sealing requests, Jane attempted to create a heavenly family that more closely conformed to her understanding of LDS ideals than her earthly family did.[24]

The white men who led the LDS Church had other opinions of the ideal composition of earthly and eternal families. They balked at the idea of giving Joseph Smith a black daughter in eternity. Worn down by Jane's persistent requests, they created a new ritual as a compromise between her wish and their reservations. The ceremony, performed in May 1894, appears to have been based on a revelation that Joseph Smith received in which God instructed the Latter-day Saints to practice plural marriage. The revelation commanded men and women to be sealed in order for their marriages to last beyond death and into the resurrection. According to the revelation, those who did not comply, as Jane James was unable to do, were destined to be "appointed angels in heaven, which angels are ministering servants, to minister for those who are worthy of a far more, and an exceeding, and an eternal weight of glory." The revelation continued, "For these angels did not abide my law; therefore they cannot be enlarged, but remain separately and singly, without exaltation, in their saved condition, to all eternity; and from henceforth are not gods, but are angels of God forever and ever." In creating a ceremony for Jane, the Quorum of the Twelve Apostles drew on this description of "angels [that] are ministering servants," developing a category that would satisfy Jane's desire for a connection to Joseph Smith while preserving their sense that she was not entitled to the same blessings as white Saints.[25]

And so, on May 18, 1894, Zina D. H. Young, Joseph F. Smith, John R. Winder, and two witnesses went to a sealing room in the Salt Lake Temple. Jane was not with them; she was not allowed in that part of the temple. Instead, Young stood as a proxy for Jane. Joseph F. Smith, similarly, represented his uncle Joseph Smith. Winder began by asking a question of Young: "Jane Elizabeth Manning, do you wish to be attached as a Servitor for eternity to the Prophet Joseph Smith, and in this capacity be connected with his family, and be obedient to him in all things in the Lord, as a faithful Servitor?" Jane probably had not been told ahead of time what questions would be asked in the ceremony. She may not even have known exactly how the connection between her and Joseph Smith would be framed. So when Young responded "yes" to this question, her answer was not based on Jane's expressed wishes, but on Young's understanding of Jane's best interests. After Joseph F. Smith affirmed, on his uncle's behalf, that he "wish[ed] to receive Jane Elizabeth Manning as a Servitor to [him]self and family," Winder declared: "By the authority given me of the Lord, I pronounce you, Jane Elizabeth Manning, a Servitor to the Prophet Joseph Smith, . . . and to his household, for all eternity, through your faithfulness in the New and Everlasting Covenant, in the name of the Father, and of the Son, and of the Holy Ghost. Amen." With that pronouncement, made in a temple room she could not enter, in front of people who acted on her behalf, Jane's status changed. She would no longer be alone for eternity; instead, she would serve Joseph Smith's family, just as she had done in Nauvoo.[26]

The ceremony was an unsatisfactory compromise for both Jane and the church leaders who authorized it. Jane had requested adoption as a child of Joseph Smith, a sealing she said had been offered to her; the Council of the Twelve Apostles gave her "attachment" as a "Servitor," a connection that made her part of the household, but not quite family. The use of the verb *attach* rather than *seal* indicates the Council's ambivalence: they discussed this ceremony as a sealing, like the sealing of parents to children and wives to husbands, but they did not use the language of *sealing* in the ceremony itself, as they would have in other kinds of sealing ceremonies. And the ritual was never performed again, an indication that church leaders did not find it to be an effective means of structuring eternal relationships. For her part, Jane saw the ceremony as progress, but not enough. The minutes of a 1902 meeting of the Council of the Twelve Apostles recorded that "Aunt Jane was not satisfied with this [ceremony], and as a mark of her dissatisfaction she applied again after this for sealing blessings, but of course in vain."[27]

The day after the ceremony, Jane attended a Retrenchment Society meeting. The Retrenchment Society had been formed in 1869 to support LDS women and girls in their efforts to live modestly and faithfully. Jane regularly attended Retrenchment Society meetings, which were scheduled every other week and could attract up to two hundred women. At this particular meeting Jane asked that her 1844 patriarchal blessing be read to the group. The president of the Retrenchment Society granted Jane's unusual request, and the assistant secretary of the group, Lydia D. Alder, read the blessing aloud. Jane watched and listened as Alder read the words Jane had meditated on for half a century. "Behold I say unto you, Jane," Alder read, repeating the words Hyrum Smith had intoned in 1844,

> if you will keep the commandments of God you shall be blessed Spiritually and Temporally, and shall have a place and a name in the midst of the people of Zion, even a place and where to lay your Head. And you shall have food, and Raiment, and habitations to dwell in, and shall be blessed in your avocations, that is, in the labor of your hands. And you shall have a knowledge of the Mysteries as God shall reveal them, even the Mysteries of his Kingdom, manifested in his wisdom unto your capacity, according to your accessions in knowledge, in obedience to his requisitions, you having a promise through the Father of the New World coming down in the lineage of Canaan, the Son of Ham, which promise the fullness thereof is not yet revealed. The same is sealed up with the sacred records hereafter to be revealed. Now, therefore, I say unto you, Jane, it is through obedience to the Gospel that you are Blessed, and it is through a continuation in obedience to the Commandments of God, even unto the end of your days, that you may be saved. Shun the path of vice; turn away from wickedness; be fervent unto prayer without ceasing; and your name shall be handed down to posterity, from generation to generation. Therefore, let your Heart be comforted, for he that changeth times and seasons, and placed a mark upon your forehead, can take it off and stamp upon you his own Image. Now, therefore, look and live; and remember the Redemption and the Resurrection of the just; and it shall be well with you. These Blessings and promises I seal upon your Head. Behold, I say unto you, Jane, if thou doest well thou shalt be accepted; if thou doest not well, Sin lieth at the Door. These Blessings and promises I seal upon your Head. Even so, Amen.

Jane's reasons for requesting that her patriarchal blessing be read to the gathered group cannot be fully known, but the convergence of this request with the performance of the master–servant sealing ceremony is striking. Jane was concentrating the sacred resources available to her, gathering the temple ceremony and the patriarchal blessing together in time, balancing the ceremony that was shielded from the world's eyes, and even from her own eyes, with the blessing that could be read out for everyone to hear. Attached to Joseph Smith as a servant, she claimed again the blessing of Hyrum Smith, his brother, that she would "have a knowledge of the . . . Mysteries of [God's] Kingdom." Excluded from the temple because of the curse of Cain, she made sure everyone heard the patriarch's words that she had "a promise through the Father of the New World coming down in the lineage of Canaan, the Son of Ham" and that God could even "stamp upon [her] his own Image."[28]

The day after the public reading of her patriarchal blessing, Jane's son Jesse died. The city's death records listed paralysis as the "remote" cause of death, and "3° stroke" as the "immediate" cause of death. Jesse had been a porter in a hotel on East Temple Street. In 1880, he was listed as a boarder at the hotel where he worked; he was the only black man living in the building, according to the federal census. But Jesse was apparently paralyzed in July 1893. Jane took him home and cared for him for ten months. Jesse occupied Jane's time, her energy, her thoughts. In a Relief Society meeting that fall, Jane addressed the group. "Sis. James then spoke for a short time and related a dream she had had regarding her son," the secretary reported, somewhat cryptically. Jane had long thought of her dreams as a conduit for divine communications. Near the end of her life, she recalled that before she had left Connecticut as a young woman, she saw Joseph Smith in a dream and understood that he was a prophet. That dream allowed her to recognize Smith in the flesh immediately when she arrived in Nauvoo. Jane found the dream she narrated to her Relief Society sisters similarly noteworthy. The group's secretary did not indicate which son it concerned. Jane had given birth to at least four boys, only two of whom were still alive in 1893. The dream may have reassured Jane about Silas's state in the afterlife, or about the salvation of her stillborn son Isaac. It seems more probable, though, that it dealt with Jesse, who was, at the time, occupying Jane's home and likely taking up more than his usual amount of real estate in Jane's mind. Whether the dream contained warning or reassurance, the secretary's notes did not say.[29]

A couple of days later Jane went to a Retrenchment Society meeting. The memberships of the Retrenchment Society and the Relief Society overlapped, so it is likely that at least some of the women attending the second meeting had heard Jane's account of her dream at the Relief Society meeting earlier that week. Jane again addressed the group and spoke of her son: "Sister Jane James, said many encouraging things but felt that she could not express her feelings," wrote the group's secretary. "Said she hoped light would yet reach her people and prayed that her son, might be faithful and go to them, as the Prophet Joseph had predicted. She then spoke in tongues, Sister Paul giving the interpretation." Although Jane's reference to Joseph Smith might indicate that Jane was speaking here about Sylvester, the only son the prophet had met, Jane's understanding of Smith's prophetic powers meant that his ability to speak about the future included predictions about those not yet born. Jane may have been holding on to this prophecy as a kind of assurance that Jesse would recover from his illness: that he would not only return to physical health, but that he would also overcome whatever was keeping him away from the church. Later that month, Jesse was received into the Eighth Ward by rebaptism, perhaps setting his own and his mother's minds at ease concerning his eternal fate and strengthening her hope that he might experience some measure of physical healing.[30]

Nevertheless, Jesse's health continued to flag. As the winter wore on, he declined; spring brought no relief. It is easy to imagine Jane's worry, her constant prayers. No records exist to document the help she sought or received from church leaders, but it seems likely that Jane used all of the healing resources Latter-day Saints could muster, that she regularly anointed Jesse with consecrated oil, that his uncle Isaac called down blessings on him, and that Jane's ecclesiastical leaders—her bishop and other priesthood holders in her ward—visited to pray over and lay hands on and bless this ailing son. Jesse finally died on May 20, 1894. There was no attending physician.[31]

That Was Faith

(*ca. 1892–1908*)

In November 1894, Jane went to the Salt Lake Temple to be baptized for her niece, Mary Stebbins.[1] This is the only recorded instance of Jane's physical presence in the Salt Lake Temple, a building that had been consecrated less than two years earlier. The temple had been under construction for the better part of Jane's life. Jane's home, for most of the last two decades of construction, was only a few blocks from the temple site. It is possible that Jane attended one or more of the dedication services, but we have no evidence to confirm that she did. On that late fall day in 1894 Jane entered the building through an annex, where her temple recommend was checked by a clerk, and proceeded to the baptistery, on the lowest level of the building. Just like the baptismal font in the Logan Temple, the font Jane found in the Salt Lake Temple rested on the backs of twelve oxen sculpted from stone (Figure 8.1). Given the deaths of so many of her relatives, it is curious that Jane chose to be baptized only for her sister's daughter Mary. We do not know when news of Mary's death reached Jane, but it is safe to assume that Jane's decision to seek a temple recommend was prompted, at least in part, by this news.

If Jane had a strategy in doing work for her dead kin, it is difficult to discern. Some people, especially those who lived near a temple, performed a steady stream of baptisms for the dead. Others, including many who lived further from a temple or for whom temple ordinances were otherwise more challenging to obtain, performed such baptisms in spurts, for as many people as they could each time they went to the temple. Samuel and Amanda Chambers's baptisms for their dead in 1875 are a good example of this pattern: each was baptized for several people in a row. Unlike the Chamberses, Jane was baptized for her dead in dribs and drabs: one in 1875, a handful in 1888, one in 1894. This pattern may have been due in part to the flow of information; it certainly took time for news of her relatives' deaths to reach Jane, and she could not seek baptism for them while they remained alive. But there may have been something else going on as well.

Figure 8.1 When Jane was baptized for her niece Mary Stebbins in 1894, she was immersed in this font. Like the font in the Logan Temple (and like most fonts in LDS temples worldwide), this font is supported on the backs of twelve sculpted oxen representing the twelve tribes of Israel. Baptismal Font, Mormon Temple, Salt Lake City, Utah, 1911–1912, LOT 3275, Prints and Photographs Division, Library of Congress, LC-DIG-ds-11734.

Perhaps Jane used baptisms for the dead as a rationale for entering the temples, for seeing the insides of the buildings that Latter-day Saints held so sacred. Each temple recommend was, in this sense, a ticket stamped "Admit One," purchased with the need to baptize a dead relative. Perhaps Jane conserved the names of her dead, spreading them out so as to make the most of these rare opportunities to enter the consecrated buildings. Her decision to go to the Logan Temple in 1888, even though the Salt Lake Endowment House remained open until the following year, might support this interpretation. Alternatively, since Jane lived so close to the Salt Lake Temple, perhaps she anticipated that once construction was complete, it would be easy to obtain a temple recommend. She might have imagined that she would be able to go to the temple frequently and do one or two baptisms for her dead each time. But she may have found that it was more difficult than she expected to persuade ecclesiastical leaders to approve her visits to the temple; or other factors, such as a lack of time or increasingly serious health issues, may simply have made it more difficult to go to the temple or complete the baptismal ritual.

Health concerns began to appear more regularly in Jane's life as she aged. In 1892, when she was about seventy years old, she stated in a Relief Society meeting that she "felt in better health. Desired to keep all the commandments of her heavenly Father."[2] The following year, the Relief Society secretary recorded that "Jane James said she knew the Spirit of God was here, she also came in early days, said she desired to help herself, she was feeling better than she had been, for which she was thankful, was glad she had obeyed the Gospel, hoped she would always be faithful, desired the sisters to pray for her that her sight might be better." Jane combined prayer requests like this with more tangible ritual action. In 1896, Jane spoke up in a Retrenchment Society meeting, telling her sisters that, as the society secretary reported, "she had been terribly afflicted in her head, and she took her consecrated oil and anointed herself and she was healed. Felt that *that* was faith, and praised the Lord for her blessings." In performing this healing ritual on herself, Jane reached back to an earlier understanding of Mormonism that enthusiastically embraced charismatic experiences, and especially healing, as a sign of faith. When Jane first joined the church, the practice of faith healing was widespread. However, as the century wore on, women's roles in healing diminished as men's priesthood authority expanded. In 1903, church leaders stated definitively that "the practice [of administering to the sick should] be confined to the elders," or Melchizedek priesthood holders, articulating clearly a policy that had emerged in the late nineteenth century. Jane's editorial comment in her Retrenchment Society remarks suggested a certain skepticism about the importance of the ecclesiastical priesthood to the practice of healing.[3]

Despite her increasing physical fragility, Jane remained active in the community. She regularly attended and participated in Relief and Retrenchment Society meetings. She also participated in special events sponsored by these groups and others. In 1896, for example, she joined another Old Folks' Day excursion, this time to Ogden. Her brother Isaac joined in the fun. The *Broad Ax*, an African American newspaper published in Salt Lake, reported:

> It filled our heart with joy and delight to see the following members of our race mingling with the old folks as brothers and sisters: There was Isaac Manning, Esq., who is 81 years old; he lived with Joseph Smith, and he helped to build the Temple at Nauvoo, and he has been a member of the Church for fifty-five years. His sister, Mrs. Jane James, has been a faithful member of the Church for a great many years.

The editor identified three other African American men who joined the excursion; if any other women were there, they remained unnamed. The *Broad Ax* adorned its subjects with the trappings of respectability: Isaac received the honorific "Esq." and Jane got the title of "Mrs." The statement about Isaac's lengthy church membership obscured the many years Isaac had spent away from the

LDS Church, turning the focus instead to his connection to Joseph Smith. Had the editor of the *Broad Ax* asked, Jane probably could have told him exactly how many years she had been a member of the church, but the vague "a great many years" was sufficient.[4]

Perhaps the merriment of the Old Folks' Day excursions distracted Jane from the many sorrows that attended her later years. At the end of February 1897, Jane's youngest daughter Vilate died. Jane hadn't seen her in years. As a young woman, Vilate left Utah for California, where she married William A. Warner. Together, the couple became Methodist missionaries in Liberia. Vilate's work as a missionary in Africa adds depth to Jane's 1893 statement in the Retrenchment Society meeting that "she hoped light would yet reach her people and prayed that her son, might be faithful and go to them, as the Prophet Joseph had predicted." Perhaps not coincidentally, Vilate and her husband had been sent home from Liberia in 1893 on sick leave. Of all of Jane's children, Vilate seems to have been the most conventionally religious. Jane may have wondered why her other children didn't follow similarly respectable paths, perhaps serving a mission for the LDS Church rather than for a rival denomination.[5]

We have few possible clues to Jane's thinking about the religious differences that separated her from Vilate. One was Jane's hope that her son might become a missionary for the LDS Church, as it was expressed in her recollection of Smith's prediction. Another was the fact that Jane never performed a proxy baptism for Vilate after her death. Jane did perform proxy baptisms for her mother and her sister Angeline, both of whom she knew had been baptized. But both Philes and Angeline had left the LDS Church, which Jane may have believed nullified their LDS baptisms. Vilate's decision to join the Methodist church, in contrast, did not appear to raise similar concerns for Jane. The last proxy baptism that Jane performed was for Mary Stebbins in 1894; she may have felt physically unable to perform that ritual any longer at her advanced age. (By 1897, she was at least seventy-five years old, and by some estimates as old as eighty-six.) But if she was unable to go through the baptismal ritual anymore, Jane could surely have found someone else to do so on her daughter's behalf. She did not.

In July 1897, the LDS Church celebrated the fiftieth anniversary of the first Mormons' arrival in the Salt Lake Valley. The festivities were elaborate: parades and fireworks, speeches and solemn resolutions marked the day. Along with other Pioneers of 1847, Jane marched in the parade that wound its way through the city.[6] The Pioneers also assembled to have their portrait taken (Figure 8.2). Jane was there, a lone black face in a sea of white. Her diminutive figure almost vanished amid the mass of white bodies surrounding her. There were other black people who could have been in the photo; Jane's son Sylvester was a notable example. But Jane was the only one who decided to join the group that day. On the

Figure 8.2 In 1897, Latter-day Saints marked the fiftieth anniversary of their arrival in the Salt Lake Valley with a Jubilee. The surviving Pioneers of 1847 gathered for a photograph and Jane planted herself in the center of the group, a tiny black face amid a sea of white faces. She can be found about seven rows from the front, almost directly in front of the light post that stands behind the group. "Pioneers of 1847 at the Utah Pioneer Jubilee, Salt Lake City, Utah, July 24th 1897," Prints and Photographs Division, Library of Congress, LC-USZ62-63677.

outs with the church since his excommunication in 1885, Sylvester may not have felt welcome among the group that had led the religiously motivated migration to the Salt Lake Valley fifty years earlier.

That afternoon, the pioneers convened to adopt a series of resolutions intended to express their gratitude for the work of the Jubilee celebration's organizers. The resolutions dwelt on the mortality of their group: "We have met and renewed old acquaintance, have called the roll and found that but little more than one-fourth of our original members stand on this side of eternity," the first resolution noted. The third resolution was even more direct: "Resolved, that in our pleasures of the grand Jubilee one with another we have not forgotten that silent majority of our noble band who, worn out and weary, have passed from us to the great beyond, to enjoy and receive the reward that awaited them. Many of us are now nearly ready to follow; and another fifty years will make the labors of the next Jubilee commission a light one in caring for the remaining remnants of our band."[7] After adopting the proposed slate of six resolutions, the group then voted to create "a permanent Pioneer organization" and elected officers for that group.

The Jubilee Commission's focus on "taking care of" the pioneers, and the pioneers' complementary awareness of their imminent deaths, highlight both the value that Mormons ascribed to the pioneer generation's memories and their sense of those memories' fragility. As the pioneers themselves noted, nearly three quarters of their original number had already died. Jane was thus part of a shrinking group of people who had lived during Joseph Smith's time. The group that had known Joseph Smith personally was even smaller. In the late nineteenth century, the LDS Church was trying to transform itself from a radical, fringe group into an accepted part of the American mainstream. To accomplish this goal, Latter-day Saints actively built their church's new identity by collectively constructing usable memories of their founder. Celebrations like the Jubilee were one medium through which to negotiate the church's historical legacy and its future position on the national stage. Another was the collection and preservation of the memories of those who had known and interacted with the prophet.[8]

Therefore, as the LDS Church celebrated the fifty-year anniversary of its arrival in the Salt Lake Valley, and as it approached the centennial of Joseph Smith's 1805 birth, Jane's memories were valuable not just to her and her family, but to the entire institution. Jane also had more personal reasons to make her memories a part of the public record: she wanted her temple endowment and sealings. At least three versions of Jane's life story circulated in print during her lifetime. Jane's autobiography, which she dictated to Elizabeth J. D. Roundy, was the fullest version of this story. Jane also gave an interview to the *Young Woman's Journal* in 1905 for a feature celebrating Joseph Smith's birth; and Elvira Stevens Barney published a version of Jane's account in a letter to the editor of the *Deseret News* in 1899, correcting an article that had been published previously in the Salt Lake *Herald*. The central position Smith occupied in Jane's memory was evident from the disproportionate attention she gave him in her life story. In her autobiography of approximately 2,800 words, about 1,100— nearly 40 percent—concerned Jane's experience in Nauvoo, where she lived with and worked for Joseph Smith and his family. Jane was probably eighty years old or more when she dictated that autobiography, yet she spent almost half of her words on a period of about eight months.[9]

Like many women who remembered Joseph Smith, Jane lingered over his physical appearance: "Oh, he was the finest man I ever saw on earth," she reminisced in her 1905 interview in the *Young Woman's Journal*. Jane was not alone in idealizing Smith's body. Another woman interviewed for the same feature recalled that "the Prophet was a handsome man,—splendid looking, a large man, tall and fair and his hair was light. He had a very nice complexion, his eyes were blue, and his hair a golden brown and very pretty." Other women and men made similar comments. Taken together, these physical descriptions of Joseph Smith attested to Smith's manhood and established his whiteness, both important tasks for a church struggling to gain acceptance in the American nation. Throughout the church's short history, detractors had characterized Mormons as lacking in both whiteness and manliness. In an 1860 report to the United States Senate, for example, Doctor Roberts Bartholow—who had accompanied US forces during the Utah War in 1857–1858—wrote that the Latter-day Saints' bodies were characterized by "an expression compounded of sensuality, cunning, suspicion, and smirking self-conceit. The yellow, sunken, cadaverous visage; the greenish-colored eyes; the thick, protuberant lips; the low forehead; the light, yellowish hair; and the lank, angular person, constitute an appearance so characteristic of the new race, the production of polygamy, as to distinguish them at a glance." Bartholow also noted that polygamous practice that produced this "new race" also had specific consequences for male Mormons' ability to be proper men, because it resulted "genital weakness of the boys and young men" of the group. Bartholow's report, and myriad other representations of the Mormons as racially suspect and insufficiently masculine, raised questions about Mormons' standing as "real" Americans. By the early twentieth century, the LDS Church's suspension of polygamy had prompted the US government and media outlets to change their tune, advocating the inclusion of Mormons as the equals of other white Americans. But the shift in public opinion happened slowly. The reminiscences of Joseph Smith that the *Young Woman's Journal* printed in 1905 and 1906 demonstrated that Mormons did not yet feel their "struggle for whiteness" had reached a successful conclusion.[10]

Latter-day Saints also sought to model their behavior on that of their founder, and to that end they collected and passed down stories about Smith's words and deeds. In this context, Jane's memories were especially important. In February 1896, for example, the Retrenchment Society's secretary reported that "Sister Jane James said she had lived in the Prophet's family: could not express what a great man he was." Later that year, Jane told the women of the Retrenchment Society that she "felt to rejoice that she had the privilege of seeing the prophet Joseph." In 1898, Jane expanded on this theme. "Sister Jane James praised the Lord that she had seen the Prophet Joseph Smith and that he had blest her," wrote the secretary. "Spoke also of the kindness shown to her by Sister Emma Smith, wife of the Prophet Joseph Smith." According to Jane, Joseph Smith treated her as if she was a member of the family. "He'd always smile, always just like he did to his children. He used to be just like I was his child," she recalled in the *Young Woman's Journal*. That familial affection was all the more striking because of the racial difference between Jane and Smith. In Jane's telling, Smith did not see racial difference as an obstacle to kinship. She insisted, repeatedly, that Joseph Smith had offered to adopt her as a child.[11]

This story and the others that Jane told about Joseph Smith, all of which portrayed Smith as a benevolent, paternalistic figure willing to welcome a black woman into his family, was at odds with the emerging official depiction of Smith, in which he was the source of the priesthood and temple restrictions that church leaders worked out over the course of the nineteenth century. Starting in the late 1870s, church officials began to revisit the story of Elijah Abel, an African American man who had been ordained during Joseph Smith's lifetime. In 1879, a church patriarch asserted that when he served as a president of the church leadership body known as the Seventy, "the Prophet [Joseph Smith] directed that Abel be dropped because of his 'lineage.'" Other prominent church leaders corroborated this recollection. Joseph F. Smith, the nephew of the founding prophet, disputed these stories, but he was in the minority and he eventually reversed his position. Smith stated in 1908—by which time he had become the president of the church—that Abel's "ordination was declared null and void by the Prophet [Joseph Smith] himself."[12] Jane's presence may have helped bolster Smith's reluctance to change his position: his reversal occurred four months after her death. Still, despite the apparent support of the church president, Jane's alternative perspective—a memory of a racially progressive prophet, willing to create family relationships that breached the color barrier—remained marginalized.

Jane's eyesight grew weaker as she aged. She began noticing a decline in her vision as early as 1893: in a Relief Society meeting, she requested her sisters' prayer "that her sight might be better." A decade or more later, dictating her autobiography, Jane described herself as "nearly blind" and claimed that the loss of her sight was "the greatest trial I have ever been called upon to bear." Still, she said, "I hope my eyesight will be spared to me poor as it is, that I may be able to go to meeting, and to the temple to do more work for my dead." Despite her failing eyesight, Jane continued to participate in her community, attending women's meetings, going on Old Folks' Day outings, and receiving visitors. She continued to take in washing to support herself, and she remained meticulous in her personal appearance and her housekeeping. Her great-granddaughter Henrietta, who was born in 1895, remembered going to Jane's home as a girl. "They had a red velvet couch," Henrietta recalled, "and she had curtains with tassels. . . . The blinds were kept closed so the sun didn't fade the curtains. . . . Oh, they had beautiful lamps all flowered and all that, homemade shades. Oh, yes, they had beautiful lamps, oil lamps."[13]

Another of Jane's visitors was Elizabeth Jefford Drake Roundy. A convert from England, Roundy had joined the church at the end of 1851 and emigrated to the United States in 1857. She spent two years in Philadelphia, then made the trek to the Salt Lake Valley in 1859. Like Jane, Roundy had lived through two failed marriages—though unlike Jane, she had married a third time, this time becoming a plural wife. Roundy was a key figure in rallying the Saints around the memory of Joseph Smith. A small collection of her papers archived at the LDS Church History Library includes a four-page poem dedicated to Joseph Smith that she composed in 1897. The work established the prophet's spiritual precedents by reviewing the stories of the biblical patriarchs Abraham, Joseph, Moses, and Aaron. Roundy used Jesus's ministry and resurrection as a bridge of sorts into the present day, and then began her narration of Joseph Smith's life and work. She placed Hyrum Smith alongside Joseph as worthy of the Saints' praise and respect: "Of all the world's heroes, there is none can compare/With Joseph, and Hyrum, our Prophets and Seer," she wrote. "Then all Hail! to our Prophet, and Patriarch dear,/" she continued later in the same stanza, referring to Joseph and Hyrum by their respective ecclesiastical titles, "Their memory is sacred, their names we revere/We'll honor their virtues while on earth we remain." But the main focus of Roundy's adoration was Joseph Smith, and the last stanzas of the poem centered on him. Directing the reader's attention to images of Joseph and Hyrum, she wrote,

> These pictures to us may look noble,
> Each lineament placed in line,
> Alas! 'tis but the canvas,
> 'Tis not the soul sublime
> That shone through Joseph's features,
> Lit up with kingly grace,
> So full of loving kindness,
> To all the human race.

The poem concluded with a stanza resolving: "Then all honor, the birth of our heroes,/In memory they shall ever be green,/Each year we'll embellish with laurels,/Garland roses, and lilies between." Roundy enacted this determination to "honor the birth of [her] heroes" and urged others to join her. In his 1901 biographical account, LDS Church historian Andrew Jenson noted that "In 1874 Sister Elizabeth took the lead in arranging the first celebration in honor of the Prophet Joseph Smith's birthday. . . . Since that time Sister Roundy has been persevering in her efforts to have the Prophet's birthday anniversary remembered among the Saints; and after twenty-seven years' persistent effort and waiting she had lived to see it universally honored amongst the Saints." One of Joseph Smith's plural wives wrote to Roundy in 1909, thanking Roundy for her persistence in honoring Joseph Smith's birthday. "I love you dear sister for your integrity to the Prophet and the lone ones he left; you have spent your last dollar again & again in honor of the anniversary of the birthdays as the years glide on & on, but your warfare is nearly over when oh, the joyful greeting beyond will be envied by hundreds who have not supported you with kind words & acts," she wrote. Roundy's commemorative work included collecting the memories of Latter-day Saints who had known Joseph Smith, a project that aligned easily with Jane's effort to solidify her position in the LDS community by speaking about her association with the prophet. A note at the top of Jane's autobiography said that it was "written from her verbal statement and by her request," but it was surely also by Roundy's request, given her desire to commemorate Joseph Smith. Roundy also collected statements from other Saints who had known and interacted with Smith, including Isaac Manning, suggesting that her primary interest was not in Jane herself, but rather in the Prophet.[14]

Jane had earned the respect of her community. She and her brother Isaac had reserved seats in the tabernacle, the iconic auditorium near the temple where the church held its semiannual church-wide conferences and other major events. According to one account, "Jane made cushions for the seats, and the old couple and their friends had exclusive right to the seats." A woman who moved to Salt Lake City as a girl in 1901 recalled "each Sunday. . . seeing two Negroes sitting on the stand and of being told they both had been servants in the home of the Prophet Joseph Smith. They were very old and their skin looked like parchment, but they appeared to be strong and well. Jane Manning James and her brother Isaac were given the seats of honor." Latter-day Saints expressed their respect for Jane in the way they addressed her also: according to her obituary in the *Deseret Evening News*, Jane was "familiarly known as 'Aunt Jane.'" Earlier documents corroborate this honorific nickname: a June 1905 article in the *Salt Lake Herald* also referred to James as "Aunt Jane" and James's reminiscences of Joseph Smith in the *Young Woman's Journal* in 1905 were headed "'Aunt' Jane James."[15]

The appellation "aunt" was also applied to other respected older women in the Latter-day Saints' community. Zina D. H. Young and Bathsheba W. Smith, for example, both received this honorific in the October 1901 issue of the *Young Woman's Journal*. Both were prominent LDS women, well known for their work in the Relief Society and other organizations. An editorial describing Zina Young's funeral referred to her exclusively as "Aunt Zina," and a poetic tribute to the recently deceased women's leader was entitled simply "Aunt Zina." One of the speakers at Young's funeral remarked that she "was more than a friend, she was 'Aunt Zina' to all Israel." Young's status as a "mother in Israel," alluded to in the speaker's phrasing, was echoed in a profile of Bathsheba W. Smith that appeared in the same issue of the *Young Woman's Journal*. "One has but to look into the kind gentle features of Aunt Bathsheba to realize that he is face to face with a mother in Israel," the article began. The status of "mother in Israel" recognized women's outstanding piety and moral authority in the community. It was applied sparingly. In her 1889 patriarchal blessing, Jane had also been promised that she would be known as a "mother in Israel," but Latter-day Saints did not apply this label to Jane during her lifetime the way they did to Zina Young and Bathsheba Smith. In combination with the appellation "mother in Israel," references to Young and Smith as "Aunt" were a way of honoring their spiritual standing and according them the measure of respect that the community felt they were due.[16]

The term "aunt" implies affection and familial connection, but by definition it erases sexuality: a woman becomes an aunt not through her own sexual activity, but through that of her parents, who give birth to her and at least one sibling; and her sibling, who gives birth to a child, thereby making her an aunt.[17] Jane had no meaningful relationships with any of her nieces or nephews, most—possibly all—of whom were dead by the time Jane reached old age, so as a biological classification, "aunt" was an ill-fitting way to categorize Jane. Her sexuality was very much a part of her self-presentation: she repeatedly emphasized her role as a mother and grandmother. But Jane's sexuality was a problematic part of her identity as a Mormon, because her sexual activity did not follow LDS norms. The term "aunt," while it erased Jane's success in fulfilling the LDS ideal of motherhood, also obscured her failures to live up to the LDS ideal of marriage. It highlighted Jane's femininity, but allowed a focus on her nurturing qualities while de-emphasizing her maternity and her on-again, off-again status as a wife.

However, the title of "Aunt" also bore racial connotations. As scholars Patricia J. Sotirin and Laura L. Ellingson note, the title of "Aunt" was traditionally given to the mammy to mark her superiority to other servants while not granting the authority that the title "Mistress" entailed. The same was true in Connecticut when Jane grew up there. In his history of African American Connecticut, Frank Stone wrote that "slaves were called by their first names with 'Aunt' or 'Uncle' preceding if they were older, well liked, and respected in the dominant white community." Sotirin and Ellingson's point is apt in Jane's case: with the exception of *The Broad Ax*, an African American newspaper, print publications almost never referred to Jane as "Mrs. Isaac James," or even as "Mrs. Jane James." Instead, if Jane received a title, it was "Sister Jane James" or "Aunt Jane." Sometimes the condescension was even more bold, as in a *Salt Lake Herald* article covering the 1906 Old Folks' Day excursion. The author of this article consistently referred to white women using their surnames, preceded by "Miss" or "Mrs.," as in "Miss C. R. Savage drew a picture of Mrs. Margaret Hart." Jane, on the other hand, appeared as "Aunty" or "Auntie Jane" (the author's spelling was inconsistent), with no surname: "'Aunty Jane' wore a spotless white waist, little poke bonnet and white apron." Quotation marks set off the moniker, heightening the distancing effect that the difference in title created. Sotirin and Ellingson write that the title of "aunt" can connect a woman to the family while keeping her at arm's length. "Servants—slaves or economically disadvantaged women, particularly immigrants and minorities—historically have been designated 'aunt.'" Like sealing Jane to Joseph Smith as a servant, then, referring to her as "Aunt Jane" connected her to the community while also relegating her to a subservient role.[18]

As the Latter-day Saints entered their second half-century in the Salt Lake Valley, Jane could depend on the attentions of her brother Isaac Manning, her son Sylvester, and her grandchildren. In Jane's last years her grand-daughter Josephine, one of Miriam's daughters, checked on her each morning. Josephine's proximity and Isaac's company may have been the reasons Jane was able to remain in her home, rather than moving in with her son or one of her granddaughters. Jane's ability to stay put, taking in other relatives from time to time but maintaining her control over her property, was unusual. It marked her as an exception among American widows in the early twentieth century, very few of whom avoided having to move in with children or take up residence as a boarder in the home of someone unrelated.[19]

Jane's campaign for temple privileges continued unabated. In August of 1903, Jane wrote to church President Joseph F. Smith. "Dear Brother," she wrote, "I take this opportunity of writing to ask you if I can get my endowments and also finish the work I have begun for my dead. And Dear Brother I would like to see and talk with you about it, will you please write to me and tell me how soon, when and where I shall come and I will be there by doing so you will be conferring a great favor." Jane signed herself "Your sister in the Gospel," claiming a spiritual kinship with the church's leader and adding, "I have enclosed a stamped Envelope for reply."[20]

Jane had claimed the same relationship of spiritual fraternity to Joseph F. Smith over a decade earlier in a letter requesting her temple privileges. In that 1890 letter, though, she had reminded Smith in a postscript, "I am Coloured." Jane's racial identity was never in question: her ecclesiastical leaders knew well that she was black. But the theological meaning of blackness was not as clear. Talking with Elvira Stevens Barney in 1899, Jane made a remarkable claim: "I am white with the exception of the color of my skin." Barney's response seems to be a non sequitur: "I then said to her," wrote Barney, " 'I have known you since 1846. There were a half a dozen of your colored people that I saw at the meeting under the Bowery, west of the Temple.' 'Yes,' " replied Jane, " 'there were eleven of us in all. . . . In Nauvoo all dressed in beautiful pure white.' " Although Barney did not provide enough context to fully understand Jane's remark that she was "white with the exception of the color of [her] skin," Jane's comment that she and her family "dressed in beautiful pure white" seems to refer to temple clothing and suggests that whiteness, for Jane, might have been a way of talking about access to temple ceremonies. Jane's statement that she was white was a way of saying that she wanted what whiteness represented—the endowments and sealings she had been requesting for decades.[21] If this interpretation is correct, it helps us understand why Jane felt that she needed to remind Joseph F. Smith that she was "Coloured": that postscript quickly summed up the obstacle she faced in receiving the temple access she so desired.

By 1907, it appeared that Jane could not "go to meeting" any longer. At a June meeting of the Relief Society, Sister Sarah J. Chamberlain "spoke of the spirit of Sister James." And Sister Hunter "said in attending to Sister Jane she bathed her head tenderly and her body, spoke of the satisfaction of our children to us when they do right." Despite the care she received from her community and her family, Jane kept looking for that "satisfaction" from her daughter Ellen Madora. Jane's actions suggest that she wanted Ellen to come home, to become a part of Jane's community again. In 1907, Jane deeded her homesite to Ellen for the second time, again without payment. By that time, Ellen had married a white man and lived in Wyoming. Jane's financial move does not make a lot of sense at first glance: her financial situation was stable, and Ellen had already proven that she was not a reliable property manager. Instead, Jane's decision to transfer her property—her home, her financial security—to Ellen seemed like a gamble to try to bring her daughter home again. If that was Jane's intent, the move failed.[22]

Jane died on a Thursday: April 16, 1908. Her passing made headlines. The *Deseret Evening News* printed her obituary the same day, stating that "up to a few months ago [she] was comparatively hale and hearty. A severe fall caused a marked decline in her physical condition and gradually she grew weaker until the end came." The *Salt Lake Herald* ran the story the next day. An account of her funeral appeared five days later in the *Deseret News*. It referred to her as "Aunt Jane," and described her as "the aged colored woman." Joseph F. Smith spoke at her funeral. "The house was crowded," the *Deseret News* reported, "many in the congregation being of her own race." Perhaps Smith reminisced for the audience about knowing Jane when he was a child, when she did the laundry for his uncle's family. "I think you are somewhat acquainted with me," she had written to him. "I lived in the prophet's family with Emma and others, about a year." Perhaps he spoke about the way she wouldn't take no for an answer, kept importuning him and other church leaders for her endowments and for sealings. Perhaps he told the congregation about how she was now with his uncle, church founder Joseph Smith, in glory, serving him and his family for eternity. One prominent church member who may have been in the audience that day later wrote that Smith "declared that she would in the resurrection attain the longings of her soul and become a white and beautiful person."[23]

The funeral was held in the Eighth Ward meeting house four days after Jane's death. She had spent a lot of time there. It was where she went to worship every week, where she took the sacrament and where she sang, and prayed, and spoke about her faith. Now it was full of flowers. The bishop of her ward, Oscar F. Hunter, presided. As a young man, Bishop Hunter had helped build the railroad in Utah. His wife, Mindwell Chipman, was the daughter of one of the Pioneers of 1847. She served as president of the Eighth Ward Relief Society for many years, so she was well aware of Jane James. Jane attended Relief Society meetings regularly. She contributed her "widow's mite"—ten cents here, a quarter there—and she received baskets of food from the society. From time to time, she spoke in tongues at Relief Society meetings. Bishop Hunter would die in 1931, and his funeral would also be held in the Eighth Ward meeting house. Speakers would remember his "fatherly ways" and recall the righteousness of his ancestors.[24]

Now, he sat in front of the congregation and listened as President Joseph F. Smith spoke. Elizabeth J. D. Roundy read Jane's sketch of her life. The ward choir sang. Who could recall the righteousness of Jane's ancestors? Joseph F. Smith might have met Philes Manning in Nauvoo, but he would have been a boy, about the same age as Jane's son Sylvester. Born in November of 1838, Smith had not yet been baptized, had not reached the Saints' "age of reason," when Jane and her family arrived in Nauvoo. He did not meet Jane's biological father, who had died before she was baptized. Joseph F. Smith might have met Cato Treadwell, Jane's stepfather. But neither Philes Manning nor Cato Treadwell followed Brigham Young west. In Salt Lake, Jane had been baptized for Philes, implying that she had fallen away from the LDS Church. She was not a righteous ancestor, with whom mourners could imagine Jane reuniting in glory.

Jane had outlived her husband Isaac by nearly two decades. Frank Perkins had died years before. Jane had buried most of her children as well: only Sylvester and Ellen Madora were alive at the time of her funeral. Sylvester was almost certainly there, though he had been excommunicated nearly a quarter-century before. Ellen Madora had also left the church. She lived in Wyoming; we do not know if she made it back to Salt Lake City for the funeral. Jane's brother Isaac Manning was surely in the congregation. If Isaac or Sylvester spoke at Jane's service, their words were not recorded. Some of those in the crowd were her grandchildren, her great-grandchildren, her in-laws. Some were friends. Some were Latter-day Saints; others had helped start other churches in the city, churches that were more welcoming to people with dark skin. A sea of black faces stared up at the pulpit as the leader who would refuse ordination to black men eulogized "the aged colored woman." It was late April and the ground had thawed. How many people followed Jane's body to the city cemetery? No grave-side service was recorded. There was no stone to mark the grave. The news of the funeral, two paragraphs, appeared on the second page of the *Deseret Evening News*, below a story about a wealthy drunkard and above a notice that property owners in certain areas of the city would be required to plant trees to beautify the streets.[25]

The Relief Society of the Eighth Ward met on the day Jane died. The women gathered that day noticed Jane's absence; Emma Carter informed the group of

Jane's death and "told of her blessings . . . and of her good deeds." Carter also noted that "there is lots of sickness in the City," apparently attributing Jane's death to the local environment rather than to Jane's advanced age and recent fall, as the *Deseret News* did in the obituary it ran that day. Eighth Ward records do not indicate that the congregation provided monetary assistance for Jane's funeral or burial; Jane's estate covered those expenses.[26]

In the autobiography she dictated to Elizabeth J. D. Roundy, Jane expressed her desire that her brother Isaac Manning retain the use of her home. "I want him to stay there after me," she said, just before concluding her account. Jane's later decision to deed her home to Ellen Madora contradicted this desire. Perhaps Jane had changed her mind; perhaps Isaac had expressed a wish to live elsewhere; perhaps Jane had simply forgotten her earlier words; or perhaps Ellen, short of funds, had pressured her mother into transferring the real estate. A lengthy legal process following Jane's death ultimately undid her 1907 gift of the home to Ellen. Jane's estate, valued at $885 after expenses were deducted, was split between Ellen and Sylvester; Isaac received $100 for his "life estate" in Jane's home and lived with his grand-niece Josephine until his death in 1911.[27]

Epilogue

Jane believed that she would live forever, that she would eventually receive a glorified body, uniquely hers and perfect in all respects. She strived to live her mortal life in a way that would make her worthy of that body, and of the relationships she would enjoy with her prophet Joseph Smith, her savior Jesus Christ, and her family, stretching back to Adam and down through the generations, long past the great-grandchildren she knew in her mortal life. After the leaders of the LDS Church announced a revelation in 1978 opening the priesthood to "all worthy male members" of the church and by extension lifting the temple restriction that had kept Jane from performing endowments and sealings, proxies performed these ceremonies on her behalf, ritually ensuring that she could finally have in death what she had so persistently requested during her life.[1]

Jane wanted to be remembered. Before she died, she spoke frequently—in public and in private—about her relationship with Joseph Smith and about her own religious experiences of seeing visions, dreaming dreams, speaking in tongues, and healing the sick. She made sure her words were written down. After her death, however, Jane quickly faded into obscurity. The Latter-day Saints did not discuss Jane in print for more than half a century after reports on her funeral faded from the pages of local newspapers. But that began to change in the 1960s, and by the turn of the twenty-first century, Jane's story became ubiquitous in productions of LDS history meant for popular consumption. She appeared in venues including LDS Church magazines, children's books, personal and group blogs, historical novels, stage plays, films, monuments, and visual art both fine and mass-produced. In both popular and official LDS discourse Mormons used the story of Jane James to reimagine their church, commonly stereotyped as lily-white, as "always, already" racially diverse and their founder Joseph Smith as racially egalitarian. These reinterpretations of the past, necessitated by changes in the church's racial policies and prompted by the bicentennial of Smith's birth, allowed members of the church to imagine a racially diverse, harmonious future. Like other historical figures, Jane took on symbolic meaning that could be used to reinforce present-day LDS values and to advocate for change.[2]

As important as Jane's story is for modern-day Mormons reckoning with the LDS Church's troubling racial history, however, her experience also contains lessons for those whose interests lie elsewhere—most especially for historians of American religion. The history of Mormonism is most frequently told from the perspective of those in charge—usually white men like Joseph Smith and Brigham Young—and those with whom they worked to create and institutionalize a new faith tradition. Jane gives us the history of Mormonism from below, from the perspective of a person with expansive access, but little power. Looking at Mormonism through Jane's eyes, we can see why the LDS Church appealed to converts. We also begin to see that limits quickly formed around the radical, democratizing impulse present at the beginning of the church. The hierarchy of the church became whiter and more male with every passing year, excluding and subordinating people of color—especially people of African descent—and women. Despite these barriers, Jane's story shows us the variety of religious experience in Mormonism, and demonstrates how a focus on temple rituals and priesthood blinds us to the everyday lived religion of thousands of nineteenth-century Mormons, regardless of race.

As we have seen, Jane had very limited access to the sacred spaces and ceremonies of the LDS temple. The first time Jane performed a baptism for the dead, it was recorded in a separate book, set aside to keep track of the souls of black bodies. And baptisms for the dead were the only ceremonies Jane ever attended in LDS temples. Jane's husbands and sons were also excluded from the LDS priesthood, so Jane and her family could not enjoy its day-to-day blessings. Any time that priestly ministrations were needed in Jane's family, outsiders had to be summoned to provide them. Nevertheless, Jane developed a rich spiritual life that centered on charismatic experiences of visions, healings, and tongues. She found a measure of religious community in the Relief Society and Retrenchment Society. Those groups accepted and recorded her testimonies. They valued her experiences of speaking in tongues. And they provided a venue in which she could live up to LDS ideals of femininity. While they were not free of racial prejudice, the Relief Society and Retrenchment Society were spaces in which Jane found respect and support despite the racial difference that separated her from most of the other women in these groups.

Jane's life was shaped by her intersecting identities as an African American, as a woman, and as a Mormon. Her experience of Mormonism was very different from that of George Parker Dykes, or Patty Sessions, or even Isaac James. Jane's Mormonism, though, was no less "correct," no less Mormon, than the faiths of these people; instead, Jane's experience helps us begin to see the ways in which both whiteness and blackness shaped ways of being Mormon. It opens our eyes to the possibility that there were, and are, a multitude of ways of being Mormon—of practicing any religious tradition, in fact—ways that can be seen in the historical record if we attend to how religion intersects with race and gender.

And although her contributions were largely invisible to those without "eyes to see," Jane's interventions as a faithful African American woman shaped Mormon history in crucial ways. She performed labor that allowed Joseph and Emma Smith to run a bustling home in Nauvoo that welcomed strangers and celebrated friends and family, strengthening the prophet's reputation. She and her family made plural marriage more manageable in the early days of the practice in Winter Quarters by helping the wives of George Parker Dykes when he was away with the Mormon Battalion. And she persistently requested blessings from church leaders who, in response, wrestled with the theological meanings of racial difference and created a new ritual in an unsuccessful attempt to satisfy a stalwart member. What can we learn about American religious history if we focus our attention on religious traditions' less powerful members, looking at those traditions through the eyes of adherents whose faiths seem to oppress them? Certainly the specific lessons vary across time, space, and tradition, but Jane's life shows us that asking questions about such people will yield striking insights about the complexities of religious faith and experience, and the relationships between race, gender, and religion.

The image most often used to illustrate accounts of Jane's life is the likeness of an African American woman taken in the studio of Edward Martin in the 1860s (Figure 5.2). But as I noted in chapter 5, historians are not positive that Jane was the woman in that photograph. Martin's photo depicts a woman in isolation, separate from the social, political, and religious contexts that shaped her life. In contrast, two images of the Pioneers of 1847 in which Jane appeared are much more accurate illustrations of Jane's life. In the first (Figure 8.2), taken in 1897 by George Anderson, Jane positioned herself in the center of the group, where she was almost overwhelmed by the sea of white faces surrounding her. She is barely visible among all the other details of the photo. In the second (Figure EP.1), taken in 1905 by C. R. Savage, Jane stood at the edge of the gathering, a part of the group and yet slightly separated at the same time. These photos strike me as apt metaphors for Jane's life among the Latter-day Saints: she positioned herself at the center of LDS life, with intimate access to the founding prophet and personal relationships with many of the most powerful people in the church. But she was also denied access to the most sacred rituals of Mormonism, given the status of a servant rather than a daughter, known as "Aunty Jane" rather than as a mother in Israel.

That distance between Jane and the church's white members lessened significantly in the late twentieth and early twenty-first centuries, as Jane's story became an important component in Latter-day Saints' efforts to come to terms with the church's history of racial prejudice and discrimination. Jane's present status in the LDS Church is demonstrated by two recent retellings of her story in official church events. Twice a year, Latter-day Saints gather for General

Figure EP.1 As they had in 1897, the Pioneers of 1847 gathered for a group photo in 1905. This time Jane was accompanied by her brother Isaac Manning, even though he had not joined the Latter-day Saints' trek to the Salt Lake Valley in 1847. C. R. Savage, "Utah Pioneers of 1847," Princeton University Library.

Conference, a meeting of the entire church held at the Conference Center and broadcast to LDS congregations worldwide. Jane appeared in Apostle M. Russell Ballard's talk during the October 2017 General Conference. Edward Martin's studio portrait of the woman believed to be Jane displayed on an enormous screen while Ballard described Jane as a "pioneer ancestor" and counseled his audience to "eliminate any prejudice, including racism, sexism, and nationalism." The following June, the same photograph was projected on a somewhat smaller screen in the same conference center during the church's official commemoration of the fortieth anniversary of the revelation that ended the priesthood and temple restrictions. Latter-day Saints of African descent narrated Jane's story, holding her up as a black foremother for the millions of nonwhite Mormons worldwide. Another indication of Jane's new currency among Latter-day Saints is the use of artist Elspeth Young's paintings of a black woman in LDS temples and other church buildings. Young explicitly intended one of these paintings to represent Jane, but viewers frequently interpret Young's other images as representations of Jane as well and they celebrate Jane's presence, at long last, inside the temple walls. Images of Jane have also gained prominence in Mormon popular culture: she appears in a coloring book that LDS artist Molly Cannon

Figure EP.2 Matt Page's "Mormon Prayer Candles" draw on Catholic iconography and material culture. The trio of figures Page chose for the candles—LDS founder Joseph Smith (center), his wife Emma Hale Smith (right), and Jane Manning James (left)—is one indication of Jane's elevated status among Latter-day Saints in the twenty-first century. Mormon Prayer Candles, copyright 2018, Matt Page.

Hadfield illustrated for the 175th anniversary of the Relief Society's founding and—perhaps especially telling—alongside Joseph Smith and Emma Smith in the set of three "Mormon prayer candles" created by LDS graphic artist Matt Page (Figure EP.2).[3]

   All of these instances suggest that more than a century after her death, Jane has finally achieved what she worked so hard for during her life: Latter-day Saints of all races now hold Jane in "honorable remembrance," as Patriarch John Smith promised her would happen. As Latter-day Saints tell the story of Jane's life, they no longer blame her for her "checkered past," nor do they burden her with the curses of Cain or Canaan. Instead, they emphasize the same themes to which she constantly returned: her steadfast faith, her personal relationship to Joseph Smith, her extraordinary religious experiences, and her sacrificial motherhood. For Latter-day Saints, Jane has truly become both a mother in Israel and, as she signed her letters to church leaders, "Your sister in the Gospel."

Appendix

PRIMARY SOURCES

This appendix provides five of the key primary sources for understanding Jane's life in the approximate chronological order of their creation. The first two are the patriarchal blessings Jane received in 1844 and 1889; the latter three are the most extensive accounts Jane gave of her life. The transcriptions of these sources retain the originals' spelling, grammar, capitalization, and punctuation. Where necessary, they use typographic cues to mark the idiosyncrasies of texts such as later additions and emendations.

Document 1: Jane's first patriarchal blessing (1844)

Hyrum Smith, Patriarchal Blessing of Jane Manning, March 6, 1844, LDS Church
History Library, Salt Lake City. Reprinted courtesy of Louis Duffy.[1]

A Patriarchal Blessing of Jane Manning Daughter of Isaac and Eliza Manning
Born in the Town of Bridgefield County of Fairfield State of Connecticut.

May 11th 1818.

Behold I say unto you Jane if you will keep the commandments of god you
shall be blessed Spritualy and Temporaly and shall have a place and a name
in the midst of the people of zion even a place and where to lay your Head
and you shall have food and Raiment and habitations to dwell in and shall
be blessed in in your avocations that is in the labour of your hands and you
shall have a knowledge of the Mysteries as god shall reveal them even the
Mysteries of his Kingdom manifested in his wisdom unto your capasity according to your accessions in knowledge in obedience to his requisitions you
having a promise through the Father of the New World coming down in the
lineage of Cainaan the Son of Ham which promise the fullness ther^e of is
not yet revealed, the same is sealed up with the sacred records hereafter to
be revealed, now therefore I say unto you Jane it is through obedience to
the gospel that you are Blessed and it is through a continuation in obedience
to the commandments of god even unto the end of your days that you may
be saved, shun the path of vice, turn away from wickedness be fervent unto
prayer without ceasing and your name shall be handed down to posterity,
from generation to generation, therefore let your Heart be comforted for he
that changeth times and seasons and placed a mark upon your forehead, can
take it off and stamp upon you his own Image, now therefore look and live;
and remember the Redemption and the Resurrection of the just and it shall
be well with you these Blessings and promises I seal upon your Head; Behold
I say unto you Jane if thou doest well thou shalt be accepted, if thou doest
not well Sin lieth at the Door, These Blessings and promises I seal upon your
Head. Even so Amen.

Given by Hyrum Smith Patriarch of the Church of Jesus Christ

March 6th 1844.

Document 2: Jane's second patriarchal blessing (1889)

John Smith, Patriarchal Blessing of Jane Elizabeth James, October 10, 1889, LDS Church History Library, Salt Lake City. Reprinted courtesy of Louis Duffy.

No. 914 Salt Lake City Oct 10th 1889

A Blessing given by John Smith Patriarch upon the head of Jane Elizabeth James, daughter of Isaac and Fillis Manning born in Wilton Fairfield County Connecticut May 11th 1821.

Sister Jane Elizabeth James, as thou hast desired it I place my hands upon thy head to pronounce and Seal a blessing upon thee, And I ask God the Eternal Father for His spirit to indite thy blessing and fill thee with the influence thereof and I Say unto thee be of good faith and of good cheer hold sacred thy covenants for the Lord has heard thy petitions, He knowest the secrets of thy heart, He has witnessed thy trials and although thy life has been somewhat checkered His hand has been over thee for good and thou shalt verily receive thy reward. Thy life has been preserved for a wise purpose, Therefore continue as thou hast in the past to put thy trust in him whose right it is to give and the peacefull influence of the spirit of the Lord shall rest upon thee and give thee peace of mind, strength of body and make thee Equal unto every task and thy days and years shall be prolonged until thou art satisfied Therefore let thy heart be comforted, look always upon the bright side for better days await thee, Thou shalt complete thy mission, and receive thine inheritance among the Saints, and thy name shall be handed down to posterity in honorable remembrance, Therefore suffer not thyself to be bowed down in Spirit, but in the future, as it was in thy youth be cheerfull, in thy deportment and listen to the whisperings of the Spirit, and thou shalt not lack for food raiment or shelter and no one shall be turned from thy door hungry and for thy kindness Many shall bless thee in thine old age and as a Mother in Israel thou shalt be known among the people, Therefore again I say unto thee be comforted for all shall be well with thee both here and hereafter, This with thy former blessings I seal upon thee in the name of Jesus Christ and I seal thee up unto Eternal life to come forth in the morning of the first resurrection

Even so Amen,

Document 3: Jane's conversation with Elvira Stevens Barney (1899)

Elvira Stevens Barney, "Jane Manning James," *Deseret Evening News*, October 4, 1899, page 6.

JANE MANNING JAMES.

———

Dr. Elvira Stevens Barney Interviews a Well Known Colored Woman.

———

To the Editor:

I herewith call your attention to an article in the Herald of October 2nd, in which I found the sketch of the life and virtues of Jane Manning James (colored). I have personally known her for fifty-three years, and I read the article with very much interest, until I reached the last sentence, where it refers to her having "seen the plates that the Book of Mormon were translated from." This caused me to go and see her. The following is what I obtained:

"Jane Elizabeth Manning James, was born May 11, 1821, in Connecticut, Fairfield county, Town of Wilton, and was baptized in New Canaan by Charles Wesley Wandall. We walked from Eckland, Ohio, 1,000 miles afoot, and we were fed by the people as we went along; and had our three meals a day; we waded the rivers, and I arrived at Nauvoo the 22nd of November, 1843. I was bare-footed, and bare-headed, and my feet were sore and bleeding, and were very painful, and my clothing consisted of two pieces, an undergarment, and a dress. We went immediately to the home of the Prophet Joseph Smith, by the direction of Orson Spencer, and remained there till the last of May, 1844."

She said: "It was a custom for Joseph to visit his mother, Lucy Smith, every morning. About Christmas time as he came from her room, I shook hands with him, and then went into her room. She said: 'Good morning, Jane,' and she bade me to bring her a bundle from the bureau drawer; she then told me that I was not permitted to see it uncovered, but could handle it all I wanted to. When she thought I had handled it long enough, I was told to lock it in the bureau drawer, and bring her the key; which I did. She explained to me that it was the instrument, called the Urim and Thumim, that Joseph talked through. She did not say that Joseph used it to translate the Book of Mormon. Neither have I ever said that I saw the plates that the Book of Mormon was translated from. The instrument as near as I can describe it, which I handled, was made of some kind of metal, because it was so very heavy.

"It was firmly attached, one piece upon another. One piece seemed to be about the size of my wrist, (which was good size and not perfectly round).

"The other piece was not so large. These were set upright in a circular base. Lucy Smith also told me that I should live many years after she was dead and gone."

While I was conversing with her she said: "I am white with the exception of the color of my skin." I then said to her: "I have known you since 1846. There were a half a dozen of your colored people that I saw at the meeting under the Bowery, west of the Temple." "Yes, there were eleven of us, in all, including my husband, Isaac James. In Nauvoo all dressed in beautiful pure white; my brother here, and his wife, brother-in-law and sister-in-law, and three children." She and her husband, were many years, in the service of President Brigham Young. For the last twenty years she has supported herself by her own labors.

DR. ELVIRA STEVENS BARNEY.

Document 4: Jane's autobiography, dictated to Elizabeth J. D. Roundy (between 1902 and 1908)

"Jane Manning James Autobiography, Circa 1902," MS 4425, LDS Church History Library, Salt Lake City.[2]

Biography of Jane E. Manning James written from her own verbal statement and by her request, she also wishes it read at her funeral by EJD Roundy

written in the year 1893

When a child only six years old I left my home and went to live with a family of white people their names were Mr, and Mrs, Joseph Fitch, they were aged people and quite wealthy, I was raised by their daughter, when about fourteen years old I joined the Presbyterian Church. yet I did not feel satisfied it seemed to me there was something more that I was looking for. I had belonged to the Church about eighteen months when an Elder of the church of Jesus Christ of Latter-day Saints was travelling through our country preached there, The pastor of the Presbyterian Church forbid me going to hear them as he had heard I had expressed a desire to hear them, but nevertheless I went on a Sunday and was fully convinced that it was the true Gospel he presented and I must embrace it

The following Sunday I was baptized and confirmed a member of the Church of Jesus Christ of Latter-day Saints. About three weeks after while kneeling at prayer the Gift of Tongues came upon me, and frightened the whole family who were in the next room. One year after I was baptized I started for Nauvoo with my Mother Phillis Eliza Manning my brothers Isaac, Lewis and Peter. my Sisters Sarah Stebbings, and Angeline Manning. My brother in Law Anthony Stebbings, Lucinda Manning a sisterinlaw and myself *fall of 1840* [erasure] We started from Wilton Conn, and travelled by Canal to Buffalo N.Y. We were to go to Columbus Ohio before our fares were to be collected, but they insisted on having the money at Buffalo <*and would not take us farther.*> So we left the boat, and started on foot to travel a distance of over eight hundred miles.

We walked until our shoes were worn out, and our feet became sore and cracked open and bled until you could see the whole print of our feet with blood on the ground. We stopped and united in prayer to the Lord, we asked God the Eternal Father to heal our feet and our prayers were answered and our feet were healed forthwith.

When we arrived at Peoria Illinois the authorities threatened to put us in jail to get our free papers we didnt know at first what he meant for we had never been slaves, but he concluded to let us go, so we travelled on until we came to a river and as there was no bridge we walked right into the stream, when we got to the middle the water was up to our necks but we got safely across, and then it became so dark we could hardly see our hands before us, but we could see a light in the distance, so we went toward it and found it was an old Log Cabin here we spent the night; next day we walked for a considerable distance and staid that night in a forest, out in the open air. The frost fell on us so heavy that it was like a light fall of snow. we rose early and started on our way walking through that frost with our bare feet, until the sun rose and melted it away. But we went on our way rejoicing singing hymns and thanking God for his infinite goodness and mercy to us, in blessing us as he had, protecting us from all harm, answering our prayers and healing our feet. In course of time we arrived at La harpe Ill, about thirty miles from Nauvoo

At La harpe we came to a place where there was a very sick child, we administered to it, and the child was healed I found <after> the elders had before this given it up as they did not think it could live,

We have now arrived to our destined haven of rest, the beautiful Nauvoo! here we went through all kinds of hardship, trial, and rebuff, but we at last got to brother Orson Spencer's, he directed us to the Prophet Joseph Smith's Mansion, when we found it, Sister Emma was standing in the door, and she kindly said come in, come in! Brother Joseph said to some White Sisters that was present, Sisters I want you to occupy this room this evening with some brothers and Sisters that have just arrived, Brother Joseph placed the chairs around the room then he went and brought Sister Emma and Dr Bernhisel and introduced them to us, brother Joseph took a chair and sat down by me, and said, You have been the head of this little band havent you? I answered Yes sir! he then said God bless you! Now I would like you to relate your experience in your travels, I related to them all that I have above stated, and a great deal more minutely, as many incidents has passed from my memory since then. Brother Joseph slapped Dr Bernhisel on the knee and said, What do you think of that Dr, isn't that faith, the Dr, said, Well I rather think it is, if it had have been me I fear I should have backed out and returned to my home! he then said God bless you, you are among friends, now and you will be protected. They sat and talked to us a while, gave us words of encouragement and good counsel. We all stayed there one week, by that time all but myself had secured homes, Brother Joseph came in every morning *to* say good morning and ask how we were. During our trip I had lost all my clothes, they were all gone, my trunks were sent by Canal to the care of Charles Wesley Wandel, one large trunk full of clothes of all descriptions mostly new. On the morning that my folks all left to go to work, I looked at myself, clothed in the only two pieces I posessed, I sat down and wept, Brother Joseph came into the room as usual and said good morning, Why not crying, Yes sir the folks have all gone and got themselves homes, and I have got none. He said yes you have, you have a home right here if you want it, you musn't cry, we dry up all tears here. I said I have lost my trunk and all my clothes, he asked how I had lost them? I told them I put them in care of Charles Wesley Wandle and paid him for them and he has lost them. Brother Joseph said dont cry you shall have your trunk and clothes again.

Brother Joseph went out and brought Sister Emma in and said Sister Emma here is a girl that says she has no home, havent you a home for her? Why yes if she wants one, he said she does and then he left us,

Sister Emma said what can you do? I said I can Wash, Iron, Cook, and do housework! Well she said when you are sested you may do the washing, if you would just as soon do that, I said I am not tired, Well she said you may commence your work in the morning. The next morning she brought the clothes down in the basement to wash [ripped] Among the clothes I found brother Josephs Robes. I looked at them and wondered, I had never seen any before, and I pondered over them and thought about them so earnestly that the spirit made manifest to me that they pertained to the new name that is given the saints that the world knows not off. I didnt know when I washed them or when I put them out to dry.

Brother Josephs four wives Emily Partridge Eliza Partridge, Maria and Sarah Lawrence and myself, were sitting discussing Mormonism and Sarah said what would you think if a man had more wives than one? I said that is all right! Maria said Well we are all four Brother Josephs wives! I jumped up and clapped my hands and said that's good, Sarah said she is all right, just listen she believes it all now.

I had to pass through Mother Smiths room to get to mine, she would often stop me and talk to me, she told me all Brother Josephs troubles, and what he had suffered in publishing the Book of Mormon. One morning I met Brother Joseph coming out of his Mothers room he said good morning and shook hands with me. I went in to his Mothers room she said good morning bring me that bundle from my bureau and sit down here I did as she told me, she placed the bundle in my hands and said, handle this and then put in the top drawer of my [erasure] bureau and lock it up, after I had done it she said sit down. Do you remember that I told you about the Urim and Thumim when I told you about the book of Mormon? I answered yes Mam, she then told me I had just handled it, You are not permitted to see it, but you have been permitted to handle it. You will live long after I am dead and gone And you can tell the Latter-day Saints, that you was permitted to handle the Urim and Thumim.

Sister Emma asked me one day if I would like to be adopted to them as their child? I did not answer her, she said I will wait a while and let you consider it; she waited two weeks before she asked me again, when she did I told her No Mam! because I did not understand or know what it meant, they were always good and kind to me but I did not know my own mind I did not comprehend.

Soon after they broke up the Mansion and I went to my mother, there was not much work because of the persecutions, and I saw Brother Joseph and asked him if I should go to Burlington and take my sister Angeline with me? He said yes go and be good girls, and remember your profession of faith in the Everlasting Gospel, and the Lord will bless you. We went and stayed three weeks then returned to Nauvoo. During this time Joseph and Hyrum were killed.

I shall never forget that time of agony and sorrow, I went to live in the family of Brother Brigham Young, I stayed there until he was ready to emigrate to this valley. While I was at Bro, Brighams I married Isaac James, when Bro, Brigham left Nauvoo I went to live at Bro, Calhoons, In the spring of 1846 I left Nauvoo to come to this Great and Glorious Valley. We travelled as far as winter quarters there we stayed until spring, At Keg Creek my son Silas was born. In the spring of 1847 we started again on our way to this Valley We arrived here on the 22nd day of September 1847, without any serious mishaps, the Lords blessing was with us and protected us all the way, the only thing that did occur worth relating was when our cattle stampeded, some of them we never did find. May 1848 My daughter Mary Ann was born, all of my children but two were born here in this valley, their names are Silas, Silvester Mary Ann, Miriam, Ellen Madora, Jessie, Jerry, Boln, Isaac, Vilate, all of them are with their heavenly father except two Sylvester and Ellen Madora, My children were all raised to men and women and all had families except two. My husband Isaac James worked for Brother Brigham, and we got along splendid accumulating Horses, cows, oxen, sheep, and chickens in abundance. I spun all the cloth for my family clothing for a year or two, and we were in a prosperous condition, until the grasshoppers and crickets came along carrying destruction wherever they went, laying our crops to the ground, striping the trees of all their leaves and fruit, bringing poverty and desolation throughout this beautiful Valley. It was not then as it is now, there were no trains running bringing fruits and vegetables from California or any other place. All our importing and exporting was done by the slow process of ox teams.

Oh how I suffered of [erasure] cold and hunger and the keenest of all was to hear my little ones crying for bread, and I had none to give them; but in all the Lord was with us and gave us grace and faith to stand it all. I have seen Bro,

Brigham, Bro's Taylor Woodruff and Snow, Rule this great work and pass on to their reward, and now Brother Joseph F. Smith I hope the Lord will spare him if tis his holy will for Many many years, to guide the Gospel ship to a harbor of safety, and I know they will if the people will only listen and obey the teachings of these good great and holy men. I have lived right here in Salt Lake City for fifty two years, and I have had the privelege of going into the Temple and being baptized for some of my dead

I am now over eighty years old <*Her brother Isaac said she was born in 1813.*> and I am nearly blind which is a great trial to me, it is the greatest trial I have ever been called upon to bear, but I hope my eysight will be spared to me poor as it is, that I may be able to go to meeting, and to the temple to do more work for my dead

I am a widow, my husband Isaac James died in November 1891. I have seen my husband and all of my children but two, Laid away in the silent tomb, But the Lord protects me and takes good care of me, in my helpless condition, And I want to say right here, that my faith in the Gospel of Jesus Christ as taught by the Church of Jesus Christ of Latter-day Saints, is as strong today, nay, it is if possible stronger than it was the day I was first baptized I pay my tithes and offerings, keep the word of wisdom, I go to bed early and rise early, I try in my feeble way to set a good example to all; I have had eighteen grand children eight of them are living also 'seven great grand children I live in my little home with my brother <Isaac who is good to me> we are the last two of my mothers family <I want him to stay there after me>.

This is just a concise <but true> sketch of my life and experience

Yours in truth

Jane Elizabeth James

Jane Elizabeth James called on me to write this. It was her own statement and she declared it was true. The only error, or you may call it evasion, was her reticence pertaining to one of her children. She stated in her brothers presence that all but two were born in the valley, one Silas was born on their way to the valley but the other was born before she was baptized or soon after.

Patriarch John Smith read or heard her history read, he said that when she came to Nauvoo she had a boy five or six years old at any rate he said that he was a good chunk of a boy, and told me to find out about it; I could not get any thing out of Jane but her brother Isaac came to my house one day and he said that the boy was Sylvester, that he was born in Conn, at her Mothers, that he was the child of a white man a preacher, but he could not tell if he was the child of the Presbyterian or a Methodist preacher, that Jane was nearly eighteen or quite that old when the child was born, and her mother kept the child and Jane went back to the Fitch family, and then she heard the Gospel and was baptized, and soon after she got her mother and the whole family to be baptized. Isaac said in a year or two after they all started for Nauvoo as Jane has stated in her sketch

Elizabeth J. D. Roundy

Document 5: Jane's reminiscence in "Joseph Smith, the Prophet" (1905)

Susa Young Gates, compiler and editor, "Joseph Smith, the Prophet," *Young Woman's Journal* 16, no. 12 (December 1905): 551–53.

"AUNT" JANE JAMES,

(Colored Servant in the Prophet's House.)

Yes, indeed, I guess I did know the Prophet Joseph. That lovely hand! He used to put it out to me. Never passed me without shaking hands with me wherever he was. Oh, he was the finest man I ever saw on earth. I did not get much of a chance to talk with him. He'd always smile, always just like he did to his children. He used to be just like I was his child. O yes, my, I used to read in the Bible so much and in the Book of Mormon and Revelations, and now I have to sit and can't see to read, and I think over them things, and I tell you I do wake up in the middle of the night, and I just think about Brother Joseph and Sister Emma and how good they was to me. When I went there I only had two things on me, no shoes nor stockings, wore them all out on the road. I had a trunk full of beautiful clothes, which I had sent around by water, and I was thinking of having them when I got to Nauvoo, and they stole them at St. Louis, and I did not have a rag of them. They was looking for us because I wrote them a letter. There was eight of us, my mother and two sisters and a brother and sister-in-law, and we had two children, one they had to carry all the way there, and we traveled a thousand miles. Sister Emma she come to the door first and she says, "Walk in, come in all of you," and she went up stairs, and down he comes and goes into the sitting room and told the girls that they had there, he wanted to have the room this evening, for we have got company come. I knew it was Brother Joseph because I had seen him in a dream. He went and brought Dr. Bernhisel down and Sister Emma, and introduced him to everyone of us, and said, "Now, I want you to tell me about some of your hard trials. I want to hear of some of those hard trials." And we told him. He slapped his hands.

"Dr. Bernhisel," he said, "what do you think of that?" And he said,

"I think if I had had it to do I should not have come; would not have had faith enough."

I was the head leader. I had been in the Church a year and a little over. That is sixty-nine years ago. [She was at the time about twenty years of age.] So then our folks got places. He kept them a whole week until they got homes, and I was left. He came in every morning to see us and shake hands and know how we all were. One morning, before he came in, I had been up to the landing and found all my clothes were gone. Well, I sat there crying. He came in and looked around.

"Why where's all the folks?"

"Why Brother," I says, "they have all got themselves places; but," I says, "I haint got any place," and I burst out a-crying.

"We won't have tears here," he says.

"But," I says, "I have got no home."

"Well you've got a home here," he says, "Have you seen Sister Emma this morning."

"No, sir," I says.

So he started out and went upstairs and brought Sister Emma down and says, "Here's a girl who says she's got no home. Don't you think she's got a home here?"

And she says, "If she wants to stay here."

And he says, "do you want to stay here?"

"Yes, sir," says I. "Well, now," he says, "Sister Emma you just talk to her and see how she is." He says, "Good morning," and he went.

We had come afoot, a thousand miles. We lay in bushes, and in barns and outdoors, and traveled until there was a frost just like a snow, and we had to walk on that frost. I could not tell you, but I wanted to go to Brother Joseph.

I did not talk much to him, but every time he saw me he would say, "God bless you," and pat me on the shoulder. To Sister Emma, he said, "go and clothe her up, go down to the store and clothe her up." Sister Emma did. She got me clothes by the bolt. I had everything.

The folks that come to me think I ought to talk and tell what Brother Joseph said, but he was hid up (his enemies were seeking his life) and I cannot remember now. I could not begin to tell you what he was, only this way, he was tall, over six feet; he was a fine, big, noble, beautiful man! He had blue eyes and light hair, and very fine white skin.

When he was killed, I liked to a died myself, if it had not been for the teachers, I felt so bad. I could have died, just laid down and died; and I was sick abed, and the teachers told me,

"You don't want to die because he did. He died for us, and now we all want to live and do all the good we can."

Things came to pass what he prophesied about the colored race being freed. Things that he said has come to pass. I did not hear that, but I knew of it.

After I saw him plain, I was certain he was a prophet because I knew it. I was willing to come and gather, and when he came in with Dr. Bernhisel I knew him. Did not have to tell me because I knew him. I knew him when I saw him back in old Connecticut in a vision, saw him plain and knew he was a prophet.

This is the Gospel of Jesus Christ and there will never be any other on earth. It has come to stay.

NOTES

Introduction

1. On African American history, see Lean'tin Bracks, Jessie Carney Smith, and Linda T. Wynn, *The Complete Encyclopedia of African American History*, 3 vols. (Canton, OH: Visible Ink Press, 2015); Henry Louis Gates Jr. and Donald Yacovone, *The African Americans: Many Rivers to Cross* (Carlsbad, CA: SmileyBooks, 2013); Nell Irvin Painter, *Creating Black Americans: African-American History and Its Meanings, 1619 to the Present* (New York: Oxford University Press, 2006); Paul Finkelman, ed., *Encyclopedia of African American History, 1619–1895: From the Colonial Period to the Age of Frederick Douglass* (New York: Oxford University Press, 2006); Manning Marable, ed., *Freedom on My Mind: The Columbia Documentary History of the African American Experience* (New York: Columbia University Press, 2003); James Oliver Horton, *Hard Road to Freedom: The Story of African America* (New Brunswick, NJ: Rutgers University Press, 2001); Robin D. G. Kelley and Earl Lewis, *To Make Our World Anew: A History of African Americans*, 2 vols. (New York: Oxford University Press, 2000); and Charles Melvin Christian, *Black Saga: The African American Experience* (Boston: Houghton Mifflin, 1995). On American women's history, see Joyce Appleby, Eileen K. Cheng, and Joanne L. Goodwin, eds., *Encyclopedia of Women in American History* (New York: Routledge, 2015); Linda K. Kerber and Jane Sherron De Hart, *Women's America: Refocusing the Past*, 6th ed. (New York: Oxford University Press, 2004); Nancy A. Hewitt, ed., *A Companion to American Women's History*, Blackwell Companions to American History (Malden, MA: Blackwell, 2002); Angela Howard and Frances M. Kavenik, eds., *Handbook of American Women's History*, 2nd ed. (Thousand Oaks, CA: Sage Publications, 2000); Wilma Pearl Mankiller, ed., *The Reader's Companion to U.S. Women's History* (Boston: Houghton Mifflin, 1998); Kathryn Cullen-DuPont, *The Encyclopedia of Women's History in America* (New York: Facts on File, 1996); Linda K. Kerber, Alice Kessler-Harris, and Kathryn Kish Sklar, eds., *U.S. History as Women's History: New Feminist Essays*, Gender & American Culture (Chapel Hill: University of North Carolina Press, 1995); Vicki Ruíz and Ellen Carol DuBois, eds., *Unequal Sisters: A Multicultural Reader in U.S. Women's History*, 2nd ed. (New York: Routledge, 1994); Ruth Barnes Moynihan, Cynthia Eagle Russett, and Laurie Crumpacker, eds., *Second to None: A Documentary History of American Women* (Lincoln: University of Nebraska Press, 1993); Teresa L. Amott and Julie A. Matthaei, *Race, Gender, and Work: A Multicultural Economic History of Women in the United States* (Boston: South End Press, 1991); and Carol Berkin and Mary Beth Norton, *Women of America: A History* (Boston: Houghton Mifflin, 1979). On the history of the American West, see William Deverell, ed., *A Companion to the American West*, Blackwell Companions to American History (Malden, MA: Blackwell, 2004); Robert V. Hine and John Mack Faragher, *The American West: A New Interpretive History* (New Haven, CT: Yale University Press, 2000); Clyde A. Milner II, ed., *A New Significance: Re-Envisioning the History of the American West* (New York: Oxford University Press, 1996); Clyde A. Milner

II, Carol A. O'Connor, and Martha A. Sandweiss, eds., *The Oxford History of the American West* (New York: Oxford University Press, 1994); Richard White, *"It's Your Misfortune and None of My Own": A History of the American West*, 1st ed. (Norman: University of Oklahoma Press, 1991); and Patricia Nelson Limerick, *The Legacy of Conquest: The Unbroken Past of the American West* (New York: Norton, 1987). On African Americans in the West, see Quintard Taylor, *In Search of the Racial Frontier: African Americans in the American West, 1528–1990* (New York: Norton, 1998). For volumes focused on women and gender in the American West, see Virginia Scharff, *Twenty Thousand Roads: Women, Movement, and the West* (Berkeley: University of California Press, 2003); John Mack Faragher, *Women and Men on the Overland Trail*, 2nd ed., Yale Nota Bene (New Haven, CT: Yale University Press, 2001); Elizabeth Jameson and Susan H. Armitage, eds., *Writing the Range: Race, Class, and Culture in the Women's West* (Norman: University of Oklahoma Press, 1997); Susan H. Armitage and Elizabeth Jameson, eds., *The Women's West* (Norman: University of Oklahoma Press, 1987); and Sandra L. Myres, *Westering Women and the Frontier Experience, 1800–1915*, Histories of the American Frontier (Albuquerque: University of New Mexico Press, 1982). An important, but isolated, exception occurs in the historiography of African American women in the West. See Ronald G. Coleman, "'Is There No Blessing for Me?': Jane Elizabeth Manning James, a Mormon African American Woman," in *African American Women Confront the West: 1600–2000*, ed. Quintard Taylor and Shirley Ann Wilson Moore (Norman: University of Oklahoma Press, 2003), 144–62. On the tendency to omit Mormonism from the history of the American West, see Jan Shipps, *Sojourner in the Promised Land: Forty Years among the Mormons* (Urbana: University of Illinois Press, 2000), 21. Shipps describes the historiography of the American West as a "doughnut, circling all around the Great Basin, taking into account and telling nearly every western story except the Mormon one."

2. This account of Biddy Mason's life is based on Dolores Hayden, "Biddy Mason's Los Angeles 1856–1891," *California History* 68, no. 3 (1989): 86–99.

3. Biddy Mason is excluded from most of the books cited in note 1, but she does appear in Bracks, Smith, and Wynn, *The Complete Encyclopedia of African American History*, 2: 102–103; Christian, *Black Saga*, 154–55; Appleby, Cheng, and Goodwin, *Encyclopedia of Women in American History*, 265; Deverell, *A Companion to the American West*, 221; Milner, O'Connor, and Sandweiss, *The Oxford History of the American West*, 152; Taylor, *In Search of the Racial Frontier*, 72, 79–80, 90, 206, 207; and Myres, *Westering Women and the Frontier Experience, 1800–1915*, 263. Jane James does not appear in any of these volumes.

4. Although African Americans' surnames might signal independence, they could also encode a history of enslavement. The Moorish Science Temple and the Nation of Islam emerged after Jane's death, but their practice of taking new names to replace "slave names" is revealing. See Judith Weisenfeld, *New World A-Coming: Black Religion and Racial Identity during the Great Migration* (New York: New York University Press, 2016), especially 104–10. On surnames as a mark of male ownership of women, see Hortense J. Spillers, *Black, White, and in Color: Essays on American Literature and Culture* (Chicago: University of Chicago Press, 2003), 230, 232.

5. On how including Jane James changes the stories we tell about Mormon history, see Quincy D. Newell, "What Jane James Saw," in *Directions for Mormon Studies in the Twenty-First Century*, ed. Patrick Q. Mason (Salt Lake City: University of Utah Press, 2016), 135–51.

6. For discussion of the ways Latter-day Saints have represented Jane and the uses to which her representation has been put, see Quincy D. Newell, *Narrating Jane: Telling the Story of an Early African American Mormon Woman*, Leonard J. Arrington Mormon History Lecture 21 (Logan: Utah State University Press, 2016), http://digitalcommons.usu.edu/cgi/viewcontent.cgi?article=1020&context=arrington_lecture.

7. The quotation from Glaude comes from *African American Religion: A Very Short Introduction*, Very Short Introductions 397 (New York: Oxford University Press, 2014), 6. Historian W. Paul Reeve has identified over two hundred black people who joined the LDS Church between 1830 and 1930, the church's first century of existence. For more information, see *A Century of Black Mormons*, www.centuryofblackmormons.org.

Chapter 1

1. On where enslaved Africans were taken by British ships, see James Walvin, *Atlas of Slavery* (New York: Routledge, 2014), 46, 74. On how enslaved Africans arrived in Connecticut, see Frank Andrews Stone, *African American Connecticut: The Black Scene in a New England State; Eighteenth to Twenty-First Century* (Deland, FL: Global Research Center, continuing the Isaac N. Thut World Education Center, 2008). On Jane's family, see Doris Soldner, "The Manning Family of Wilton" 1991, Slaves and Free Blacks in Canaan Parish and New Canaan to 1880, New Canaan Historical Society Library. Jane's grandmother's name and birthplace, and her mother's birthdate, as Jane reported them, are given in Church of Jesus Christ of Latter-day Saints, Logan Temple, "Baptisms for the Dead, 1884–1943," entry 11466, microfilm 0,177,847, LDS Family History Library. The story about Philes and the Grummons comes from David Hermon Van Hoosear, "Annals of Wilton: Negroes of Wilton (Continued)," *Wilton Bulletin*, March 23, 1939. Van Hoosear's story, passed down to him through family lines, is difficult to document: Philes's trail goes cold at Sarah Abbott's marriage, when Philes supposedly went from Ebenezer Abbott's control to that of Uriah Grummon.

2. Daniel Cruson, *The Slaves of Central Fairfield County: The Journey from Slave to Freeman in Nineteenth-Century Connecticut* (Charleston, SC: The History Press, 2007), 14, 16. In 1797, the legislature lowered that age to twenty-one for those born after August 1, 1797.

3. A black man named Robert Manning lived in New Canaan, not far from Wilton. Congregational Church (New Canaan, CT), *Church Records, 1733–1899* (Salt Lake City: Filmed by the Genealogical Society of Utah, 1954), 1: 85. Historian David W. Wills noted that African Americans in antebellum New England moved along kinship networks. Personal communication, November 19, 2017. Van Hoosear, "Annals of Wilton: Negroes of Wilton (Continued)."

4. Most documents that gave a birthdate for Jane stated that she was born on May 11, but they disagreed about the year. See, for example, Hyrum Smith, "Patriarchal Blessing," March 6, 1844, copy in my possession, courtesy of Louis Duffy (reprinted in the Appendix, 140), which gives Jane's birthdate as May 11, 1818; Linda King Newell, "James, Jane E. M.— Miscellaneous Material," Linda King Newell Papers, Marriott Library Special Collections, University of Utah, which gives Jane's birthdate as May 11, 1822, based on Eighth Ward [LDS Church] records; and John Smith, "Patriarchal Blessing," October 10, 1889, copy in my possession, courtesy of Louis Duffy (reprinted in the Appendix, 141), which gives Jane's birthdate as May 11, 1821. Michael A. Cant and Rufus A. Johnstone give the average maternal age at first birth as 19.1 years and mean age at last birth as 38.2 years. Given this information, the births of Jane's first child in the late 1830s and of her last child in the late 1850s suggest that Jane herself was born in the early 1820s. "Reproductive Conflict and the Separation of Reproductive Generations in Humans," *Proceedings of the National Academy of Sciences of the United States of America* 105, no. 14 (2008): 5333; Judith Goldsmith, *Childbirth Wisdom: From the World's Oldest Societies* (Brookline, MA: East West Health Books, 1990), 24–25; Barbara Bush, "African Caribbean Slave Mothers and Children: Traumas of Dislocation and Enslavement across the Atlantic World," *Caribbean Quarterly* 56, no. 1/2 (June 2010): 73–74, 83; Linda Janet Holmes, "African American Midwives in the South," in *The American Way of Birth*, ed. Pamela Eakins, Health, Society, and Policy (Philadelphia: Temple University Press, 1986), 281–82.

5. Bush, "African Caribbean Slave Mothers and Children," 74. It is difficult to ascertain the birth order of the Manning children, but both Sarah and Isaac married before Jane did, suggesting that they were older than she was. Isaac's birth year is consistently given as 1815 in most sources. See, for example, Van Hoosear, "Annals of Wilton: Negroes of Wilton (Continued)." Scholar Joseph Holloway pointed out that "in African naming practices, children are named after parents because it is believed that the parent spirit resides in the children." Joseph E. Holloway, "Names and Naming, African," in *Encyclopedia of African-American Culture and History*, ed. Colin A. Palmer, 2nd ed., vol. 4 (Detroit: Macmillan, 2006), 1574. That may have been Philes and Isaac's motivation in bestowing their names on their

children, or they may have been following an Anglo-American custom of naming children after their parents as a way of honoring the parents. Holloway also says that it is common for individuals to have two names, and for African Americans to "change . . . their names to correspond to major life changes." This may be why Jane's mother appears in the historical record as both "Philes Manning" and "Eliza Mead." Holloway, 1573.

6. Jack Ericson Eblen, "New Estimates of the Vital Rates of the United States Black Population during the Nineteenth Century," in *Studies in American Historical Demography* (New York: Academic Press, 1979), 306, 307, 310; Town Clerk Wilton, CT, "Land Records, 1802–1902, Vol. 4: 1816–1826" (Genealogical Society of Utah, 1949, 1986, 1987), 8: 176, film 6249, Family History Library, Salt Lake City.

7. Philes's baptism is recorded in Wilton (CT) Registrar of Vital Statistics, "Records of Births, Marriages, and Deaths, 1776–1901" (Genealogical Society of Utah, 1986), image 360, film 1435805, Family History Library, Salt Lake City. The literature on the Second Great Awakening is vast. A brief introduction to the movement may be found in Brett E. Carroll, *The Routledge Historical Atlas of Religion in America* (New York: Routledge, 2000), 62–63.

8. Lyman Beecher, *The Autobiography of Lyman Beecher*, ed. Barbara M. Cross (Cambridge, MA: Harvard University Press, 1961), 1: 253, excerpted in Edwin S. Gaustad and Mark A. Noll, eds., *A Documentary History of Religion in America*, 3rd ed., vol. 2: To 1877 (Grand Rapids, MI: William B. Eerdmans Publishing Company, 2003), 300.

9. Sylvia R. Frey and Betty Wood, *Come Shouting to Zion: African American Protestantism in the American South and British Caribbean to 1830* (Chapel Hill: University of North Carolina Press, 1998), 118; Richard J. Boles, "Documents Relating to African American Experiences of White Congregational Churches in Massachusetts, 1773–1832," *New England Quarterly* 86, no. 2 (2013): 315; Robert H. Russell, *Wilton, Connecticut: Three Centuries of People, Places, and Progress* (Wilton, CT: Wilton Historical Society, 2004), 183–84, 191.

10. The date of Isaac's death is given in Van Hoosear, "Annals of Wilton: Negroes of Wilton (Continued)." The makeup of the household in 1830 is reported in Charles Isaacs, "United States Federal Census, Town of Wilton, Fairfield County, Connecticut" (US National Archives and Records Administration, 1830), 223, microfilm 2,799, Family History Library, Salt Lake City.

11. Jane Manning James, "Jane Manning James Autobiography" (Salt Lake City, ca. 1902), 1r, MS 4425, Church of Jesus Christ of Latter-day Saints Church History Library (hereafter LDS Church History Library), reprinted in the Appendix, 144–48. Henceforth, all citations of this document will refer to the version printed in the Appendix. On the Fitch family, see Charles Melbourne Selleck, *Norwalk* (The author, 1896), 196–98, 207, 215–16. Robert and Rose Manning's church membership is attested in Congregational Church (New Canaan, CT), *Church Records, 1733–1899*. That Jane was the only black person in the Fitch household is shown in Isaacs, "United States Federal Census, Town of Wilton, Fairfield County, Connecticut." On indentured labor, see Erica Armstrong Dunbar, *A Fragile Freedom: African American Women and Emancipation in the Antebellum City* (New Haven, CT: Yale University Press, 2008), 27–28, 36–37.

12. Gayle T. Tate, *Unknown Tongues: Black Women's Political Activism in the Antebellum Era, 1830–1860*, Black American and Diasporic Studies (East Lansing: Michigan State University Press, 2003), 111; Daniel E. Sutherland, *Americans and Their Servants: Domestic Service in the United States from 1800 to 1920* (Baton Rouge: Louisiana State University Press, 1981), 48.

13. Cruson, *The Slaves of Central Fairfield County*, 17; Samuel St. John, *Historical Address, Delivered in the Congregational Church of New Canaan, Conn., July 4th, 1876* (Stamford, CT: Wm. W. Gillespie & Co., 1876), 38–39, http://books.google.com/books?id=1PA_AAAAY AAJ&pg=PA18&dq=%22canaan+parish%22&hl=en&sa=X&ei=XgRmVJSMFtO0yATZl4LI Aw&ved=0CCgQ6AEwAg#v=onepage&q=%22canaan%20parish%22&f=false. Although St. John did not specify in this passage the racial identities of the men punished for theft, his mention of the whipping post and the men whipped for petty theft occurred within his discussion of slavery in New Canaan, strongly implying that the whipping post was used primarily for the punishment of enslaved people and that the men he recalled were enslaved.

14. Charles Isaacs, "United States Federal Census, Town of New Canaan, Fairfield County, Connecticut" (US National Archives and Records Administration, 1830), microfilm 2,799, Family History Library, Salt Lake City; Stone, *African American Connecticut*, 72, 76. The ratio of black women to black men was also lopsided in larger northeastern cities like Philadelphia and New York at the time. See Dunbar, *A Fragile Freedom*, 5.

15. Selleck gave Joseph Fitch's birthdate as October 21, 1758. *Norwalk*, 197. New Canaan Congregational Church records, however, showed that he was baptized on December 2, 1753, and listed his age at death as seventy-nine in 1833, also putting his birth in 1753. "New Canaan, Connecticut Congregational Church Records Vol. 1A, 1806–1853" 1: 24, Connecticut State Library, Hartford, CT; and "New Canaan, Connecticut Congregational Church Records Vol. 1A, 1806–1853," 52. This is more consistent with Fitch's gravestone, which said Fitch "died April 1, 1833, in the 80th year of his age." "Joseph Fitch, Sr (1753–1833)—Find A Grave Memorial," FindaGrave, https://www.findagrave.com/memorial/50807048/joseph-fitch#. Hannah Fitch's birth year is in "New Canaan, Connecticut Congregational Church Records Vol. 1A, 1806–1853," 72. Jane's statement that the Fitches' daughter raised her is in James, "Autobiography," Appendix, 144.

16. "New Canaan, Connecticut Congregational Church Records Vol. 1A, 1806–1853," 52.

17. Gary Laderman, "Locating the Dead: A Cultural History of Death in the Antebellum, Anglo-Protestant Communities of the Northeast," *Journal of the American Academy of Religion* 63, no. 1 (1995): 32–33.

18. FindaGrave says the Fitches were buried on family land on Brushy Ridge. "Joseph Fitch, Sr (1753–1833)—Find A Grave Memorial." The details of the funeral procession are taken from Laderman, "Locating the Dead," 34–35.

19. Thavolia Glymph, *Out of the House of Bondage: The Transformation of the Plantation Household* (New York: Cambridge University Press, 2008), 18–31; Albert J. Raboteau, *Slave Religion: The "Invisible Institution" in the Antebellum South* (New York: Oxford University Press, 1978), 80–86, 275–88.

20. Congregational Church (New Canaan, CT), *Church Records, 1733–1899*, 1: 116, 162.

21. Linda King Newell gives 1839 as Sylvester's birth year. "James, Jane E. M.—Miscellaneous Material." John Smith's recollection that Sylvester was five or six years old in 1843 would put his birth slightly earlier, in 1837 or 1838. On this and Isaac's statement about Sylvester's father, see James, "Autobiography," Appendix, 149. On Sylvester's appearance and Henrietta Bankhead's memory that Sylvester's father was French Canadian, see Florence Lawrence, Henrietta Leggroan Bankhead interview, transcript, November 22, 1977, 9, 24, Helen Zeese Papanikolas papers, box 2, folder 3, Marriott Library Special Collections, University of Utah.

22. James, "Autobiography," Appendix, 144; Van Hoosear, "Annals of Wilton: Negroes of Wilton (Continued)"; Tera W. Hunter, *Bound in Wedlock: Slave and Free Black Marriage in the Nineteenth Century* (Cambridge, MA: The Belknap Press of Harvard University Press, 2017), 214–15; Harriet Jacobs, "Incidents in the Life of a Slave Girl," in *The Classic Slave Narratives*, ed. Henry Louis Gates Jr. (New York: Penguin Books, 1987), 333–515.

23. Jacobs, "Incidents," 478, 479; Ann Taves, "Spiritual Purity and Sexual Shame: Religious Themes in the Writings of Harriet Jacobs," *Church History* 56, no. 1 (March 1987): 64, quoting Harriet Jacobs to Amy Kirby Post, Cornwall, Orange Co., NY, after December 27, 1852, and before February 14, 1853, printed in Harriet A. Jacobs et al., *The Harriet Jacobs Family Papers* (Chapel Hill: University of North Carolina Press, 2008), 191.

24. Sharon P. Johnson, "Cultural Blindness and Ambiguity: Reading (for) and Writing about Rape," *French Cultural Studies* 27, no. 2 (May 2016): 119; Hazel V. Carby, *Reconstructing Womanhood: The Emergence of the Afro-American Woman Novelist* (New York: Oxford University Press, 1987), 39. I originally found this quotation in Wilma King, "'Prematurely Knowing of Evil Things': The Sexual Abuse of African American Girls and Young Women in Slavery and Freedom," *Journal of African American History* 99, no. 3 (Summer 2014): 173. Andrea G. Radke-Moss, "Silent Memories of Missouri: Mormon Women and Men and Sexual Assault in Group Memory and Religious Identity," in *Mormon Women's History: Beyond Biography*, ed. Rachel Cope et al. (Vancouver: Fairleigh Dickinson University Press, 2017), 67.

25. King, "Prematurely Knowing of Evil Things," 186; Hannah Rosen, *Terror in the Heart of Freedom: Citizenship, Sexual Violence, and the Meaning of Race in the Postemancipation South*, Gender and American Culture (Chapel Hill: University of North Carolina Press, 2009), 227; Radke-Moss, "Silent Memories of Missouri," 69.

26. On the stereotype of black women as victims of white men's sexual aggression, see Mary Vermillion, "Reembodying the Self: Representations of Rape in *Incidents in the Life of a Slave Girl* and *I Know Why the Caged Bird Sings*," *Biography: An Interdisciplinary Quarterly* 15, no. 3 (Summer 1992): 244–45. Historian Jean Fagan Yellin reported Foster's question in a comment on Janell Hobson's original publication of "The Rape of Harriet Tubman" on the *MS.* blog. Hobson discussed the question in a postscript to the article, published as Janell Hobson, "The Rape of Harriet Tubman," *Meridians: Feminism, Race, Transnationalism* 12, no. 2 (2014): 166. Andrea Radke-Moss demonstrates that memories of the rape of prominent Mormon women, most notably Eliza R. Snow, also transformed these women into role models for women who experienced sexual violence and other trauma. See "Silent Memories of Missouri," 74–75.

27. James, "Autobiography," Appendix, 149. Sylvester's death certificate supports Isaac's recollection: his birthplace in that document is listed as "Wiltown, Conn." Henry Leggroan provided this information. For someone who had probably never visited Connecticut, his phonetic memory of Sylvester's place of origin is relatively accurate. "Sylvester James Death Record," http://archives.state.ut.us/cgi-bin/indexesresults.cgi?RUNWH AT=IDXFILES&KEYPATH=IDX208420074928. On childbirth and nursing practices, see Annabel Desgrées-du-Loû and Hermann Brou, "Resumption of Sexual Relations Following Childbirth: Norms, Practices and Reproductive Health Issues in Abidjan, Côte d'Ivoire," *Reproductive Health Matters* 13, no. 25 (May 2005): 155; Rebecca Sundhagen, "Breastfeeding and Child Spacing," in *Childbirth across Cultures: Ideas and Practices of Pregnancy, Childbirth and the Postpartum*, Science across Cultures: The History of Non-Western Science 5 (New York: Springer, 2009), 29; Bush, "African Caribbean Slave Mothers and Children," 72. On the inhabitants of the Manning home in 1840, see Aaron B. Dikeman, "United States Federal Census, Town of Wilton, Fairfield County, Connecticut" (US National Archives and Records Administration, 1840), microfilm 3,018, Family History Library, Salt Lake City.

28. Sydney E. Ahlstrom, *A Religious History of the American People* (New Haven, CT: Yale University Press, 1972), 456–57; George M. Marsden, *The Evangelical Mind and the New School Presbyterian Experience: A Case Study of Thought and Theology in Nineteenth-Century America*, Yale Publications in American Studies 20 (New Haven, CT: Yale University Press, 1970), 10. For Jane's claim that she joined the Presbyterian Church, see James, "Autobiography," Appendix, 144.

29. The record that Jane was "propounded the usual time" is in Rev. Theophilus Smith, "Pastoral Book" (New Canaan Congregational Church, July 5, 1838), New Canaan Historical Society Library; the definition of what this phrase meant to members of the New Canaan Congregational Church can be found in "Record of a congregational vote, December 4, 1772," Congregational Church (New Canaan, CT), *Church Records, 1733–1899*, 1: 58. Jane's admission to full communion was recorded in Smith, "Pastoral Book"; it was also noted in Congregational Church (New Canaan, CT), *Church Records, 1733–1899*, 1: 116. The requirement that prospective members stand in the aisle of the sanctuary is in "Record of a congregational vote, January 1795," Congregational Church (New Canaan, CT), 1: 75. The New Canaan Congregational Church's confession of faith is in "Record of a congregational vote, Monday, October 24, 1831," Congregational Church (New Canaan, CT), 1: 4–6 (separately numbered page sequence).

30. Smith's conclusion is found in "Record of a congregational vote, Monday, October 24, 1831," Congregational Church (New Canaan, CT), *Church Records, 1733–1899*, 1: 6 (separately numbered page sequence). Attendance on the day Jane joined is noted in "Attendance records for 1841," Congregational Church (New Canaan, CT), 1: 11 (separately numbered page sequence). That the black church members were segregated in a gallery is based on Boles, "Documents Relating to African American Experiences of White Congregational Churches

in Massachusetts, 1773–1832," 315. Jane's baptism record is recorded in Congregational Church (New Canaan, CT), *Church Records, 1733–1899*, 1: 162.

31. Fitch's death date comes from "Hannah Sperry Fitch (1760–1841)—Find A Grave," Find A Grave, https://www.findagrave.com/memorial/50806977/hannah-fitch. Jane's quotation comes from James, "Autobiography," Appendix, 144.

32. Marjorie Newton, *Hero or Traitor: A Biographical Study of Charles Wesley Wandell*, John Whitmer Historical Association Monograph Series (Independence, MO: Independence Press, 1992), 16.

33. Jane's recollection is found in James, "Autobiography," Appendix, 144. The church to which Jane belonged went through several name changes during its early history. By the time Jane joined in the early 1840s, it was called the "Church of Jesus Christ of Latter Day Saints"; in 1851, the segment of the church based in Utah incorporated under the name "Church of Jesus Christ of Latter-day Saints," the same name it uses today. For ease of reading, I use the latter name throughout this book. I use the terms "Latter-day Saint," "LDS," "Mormon," and occasionally just "Saint" interchangeably in reference to members of this church. On the pattern of LDS conversions, see Steven C. Harper, "Infallible Proofs, Both Human and Divine: The Persuasiveness of Mormonism for Early Converts," *Religion and American Culture: A Journal of Interpretation* 10, no. 1 (2000): 99–118; on the rationality of Jane's conversion to Mormonism, see Quincy D. Newell, "'Is There No Blessing for Me?' Jane James's Construction of Space in Latter-Day Saint History and Practice," in *New Perspectives in Mormon Studies: Creating and Crossing Boundaries*, ed. Quincy D. Newell and Eric F. Mason (Norman: University of Oklahoma Press, 2013), 44–45.

34. On Mormon millenarianism, see Grant Underwood, *The Millenarian World of Early Mormonism* (Urbana: University of Illinois Press, 1993), especially 24–41. I appreciate the prodding of one anonymous manuscript reviewer to think more about why Jane opted to join the Mormons, and the question that Delia P. Creveling asked me that helped me think through this issue.

35. The baptismal formula is given in *Doctrine and Covenants* (hereafter *D&C*) 20: 73. Historians believe that at least parts of this section date to as early as 1829. *The Doctrine and Covenants of the Church of Jesus Christ of Latter-Day Saints* (Salt Lake City: Church of Jesus Christ of Latter-day Saints, 1981), 20: 73.

36. Smith, "Pastoral Book."

Chapter 2

1. James, "Autobiography," Appendix, 144.
2. Orson Pratt, *A Series of Pamphlets on the Doctrines of the Gospel* (Salt Lake City: Juvenile Instructor Office, 1884), 100, quoted in Lee Copeland, "Speaking in Tongues in the Restoration Churches," *Dialogue: A Journal of Mormon Thought* 24, no. 1 (Spring 1991): 21.
3. Copeland, 18, 21, 23; *Painesville Telegraph* quotation on 18.
4. George H. Williams and Edith Waldvogel, "A History of Speaking in Tongues and Related Gifts," in *The Charismatic Movement*, ed. Michael P. Hamilton (Grand Rapids, MI: William B. Eerdmans Publishing Company, 1975), 83–89; Haskett's *Shakerism Unmasked* (1828) is quoted on 83. Bushnell's remarks come from Horace Bushnell, *Nature and the Supernatural as Together Constituting the One System of God*, 5th ed. (New York: Charles Scribner, 1861), 478–79. Perhaps the most well-known instance of glossolalia in early Mormonism was that associated with the dedication of the Kirtland Temple in 1836. See Richard L. Bushman, *Joseph Smith: Rough Stone Rolling* (New York: Knopf, 2005), 315–19.
5. Carroll, *The Routledge Historical Atlas of Religion in America*, 62–63.
6. J. S. Roth, "Died," *The Saints' Herald*, January 4, 1890. Jane's sister Angeline was baptized at about the same time as Jane, also by Charles Wandell; her brother Isaac was baptized by Albert Merrill. Isaac's obituary and the account published by Elizabeth J. D. Roundy both suggested that Isaac was baptized in 1835. But Albert Merrill did not convert until 1841. Albert Merrill, Albert Merrill family record, circa 1845–1917, LDS Church History Library, Salt Lake City. An article in the *Broad Ax*, an African American newspaper published in Salt

Lake, stated that Isaac had "been a member of the Church for fifty-five years," placing his baptism in 1841. "Old Folks' Day," *Broad Ax*, July 25, 1896. Wandell's letter was published in *Times and Seasons*, August 15, 1843.

7. Elizabeth Stordeur Pryor, *Colored Travelers: Mobility and the Fight for Citizenship before the Civil War*, John Hope Franklin Series in African American History and Culture (Chapel Hill: The University of North Carolina Press, 2016), especially 44–102.

8. Jane's trunk is described in "LOST," *Nauvoo Neighbor*, December 6, 1843; that the hide was likely from a pinto horse is based on Mark Staker, personal communication, December 13, 2017. The quotations describing the contents of the trunk come from James, "Autobiography," Appendix, 145; and Susa Young Gates, ed., "Joseph Smith, the Prophet," *Young Woman's Journal* 16, no. 12 (December 1905): 552, reprinted in Appendix, 150. Henceforth, all citations of this document will refer to the version printed in the Appendix.

9. The sale of the Manning family property is attested in a deed recorded January 15, 1844, in Town Clerk, Wilton, CT, "Land Records, 1802–1902, Vol. 9: 1843–1851" (Genealogical Society of Utah, 1949, 1986, 1987), film 6252, Family History Library, Salt Lake City. Margaret Blair Young and Darius Gray rely on unpublished research by Connell O'Donovan to assert that Lucinda Tonquin was married to Isaac Lewis Manning. Margaret Blair Young and Darius Gray, *The Last Mile of the Way*, revised and expanded ed., vol. 3, Standing on the Promises (Provo: Zarahemla Books, 2013), 10. Jane enumerated her traveling companions differently each time she discussed her journey from Connecticut to Nauvoo. See James, "Autobiography," Appendix, 144 and James in Gates, ed., "Joseph Smith, the Prophet," Appendix, 150. See also Elvira Stevens Barney, "Jane Manning James: Dr. Elvira Stevens Barney Interviews a Well Known Colored Woman," *Deseret Evening News*, October 4, 1899, reprinted in the Appendix, 143. Citations of this document hereafter will refer to the version reprinted in the Appendix. I base the suggestion that Mary A. Stebbins was part of the group on Jane's claim in her 1905 interview that "we had two children" and the appearance in the 1850 census of Muscatine, Iowa of a nine-year-old Mary Stebbins living with Eliza Manning and her children and grandchildren. That makes Mary the right age to be the second child, alongside Sylvester; or Jane might have been counting her brother Peter as the second child. (He would have been about twelve years old if the 1850 census, which gives his age as nineteen years, is correct.) Jane may have excluded Sylvester from her headcount altogether. The same census also shows eight-year-old Connecticut-born Julia A. Rapirlee in the same household. Julia's relation to the rest of the household members is unclear, but she may have been Angeline's daughter. Geo[rge] Reeder, "United States Federal Census, Muscatine, Muscatine County, Iowa" (US National Archives and Records Administration, 1850), 366, microfilm 442962, Family History Library, Salt Lake City. Van Hoosear says that Cato Treadwell and Phyllis Manning went to Nauvoo with "a large brood of Manning and perhaps Treadwell children and grandchildren." "Annals of Wilton: Negroes of Wilton (Continued)." He also claims that Henry and Lucinda Tonquin "went off with the Mormons." "Annals of Wilton: Negroes of Wilton (Concluded)," *Wilton Bulletin*, March 30, 1939. Jane's remark that the group "started from Wilton" is in James, "Autobiography," Appendix, 144.

10. Mary Louise King, *Portrait of New Canaan: The History of a Connecticut Town* (Chester, PA: New Canaan Historical Society; printed by John Spencer, Inc., 1981), 141–42. In 1842, the *Nimrod* set a record for the route, getting from New York City to Wilson Point (one of several points of land that reached south toward Long Island from Norwalk) in two hours and 55 minutes. King, 178. On boat travel between Norwalk and New York City, see also Samuel Richards Weed, *Norwalk after Two Hundred & Fifty Years: An Account of the Celebration of the 250th Anniversary of the Charter of the Town* (South Norwalk, CT: C. A. Freeman, 1902), 244–53, https://archive.org/details/norwalkaftertwoh00weed.

11. "INDEPENDENT OPPOSITION LINE TO ALBANY," *New York Herald*, September 1, 1843; A. K. Sandoval-Strausz, *Hotel: An American History* (New Haven, CT: Yale University Press, 2007), 286; Graham Russell Hodges, *David Ruggles: Radical Black Abolitionist and the Underground Railroad in New York City*, John Hope Franklin Series in African American History and Culture (Chapel Hill: University of North Carolina Press, 2010), 108–9, 165.

12. Robert J. Vandewater, *The Tourist, or Pocket Manual for Travellers on the Hudson River, the Western and Northern Canals and Railroads; the Stage Routes to Niagara Falls; and down Lake Ontario and the St. Lawrence to Montreal and Quebec. Comprising Also the Routes to Lebanon, Ballston, and Saratoga Springs, with Many New and Interesting Details*, 9th edition (New York: Harper Brothers, 1841), 33, 36, 38–39; Horatio Gates Spafford, *A Pocket Guide for the Tourist and Traveller along the Line of the Canals and the Interior Commerce of the State of New York* (New York: T. and J. Swords, 1824), 18.

13. John S. Dinger, *The Nauvoo City and High Council Minutes* (Salt Lake City: Signature Books, 2011), 477n78, 480; *The New-York State Guide; Containing an Alphabetical List of Counties, Towns, Cities, Villages, Post-Offices, &c. with the Census of 1840; Canals and Railroads, Lakes and Rivers; Steamboat Routes, Canal Routes, Stage Routes, and Tables of Distances; with Railroad, Steamboat and Canal Arrangements, &c. &c. Compiled from Authentic Sources* (Albany, NY: J. Disturnell, 1843), 91; Sally Randall to "Dear friends," Nauvoo, October 6, 1843, "Letters, 1843–1852," MS 3821, LDS Church History Library.

14. Jane's recollection of being barred from traveling by boat from Buffalo is from James, "Autobiography," Appendix, 144. The suggestion that some members of Jane's group may have turned back is based on the fact that although an early historian of Wilton reported that Jane's stepfather Cato Treadwell started out with this group, for example, no evidence indicated that he actually arrived in Nauvoo. Van Hoosear, "Annals of Wilton: Negroes of Wilton (Continued)." By 1849, Treadwell had returned to Connecticut. He died in March of that year in Trumbull, Connecticut, not quite twenty miles northeast of Wilton. Trumbull (CT) Registrar of Vital Statistics, "Records of Births, Marriages, and Deaths, v. 1–2, 1848–1906" (filmed by the Genealogical Society of Utah, 1987), image 8, LDS Family History Library, https://www.familysearch.org/search/film/007734303?cat=53373. That Jane arranged for Wandell to take her trunk is based on "LOST."

15. Robin W. Winks, *The Blacks in Canada: A History*, 2nd ed. (Montreal: McGill-Queen's University Press, 1997), 169, 144, 172, 145–48. An Isaac Lewis Manning is named as the father of a child, John Lewis, born on January 11, 1878, in London East division of Middlesex County, Ontario. "Ontario Births, 1869–1912" 351, entry 01737, Archives of Ontario, Toronto; microfilm 1,845,217, LDS Family History Library, Salt Lake City. No racial classification is listed for anyone in the family. A man named Peter Manning, born in the United States and of "African" ethnicity, is listed in the 1871 Canada Census living in London, Ontario. Canada Census, 1871, database, *FamilySearch*, citing National Archives of Canada, Ottawa, Ontario. Joseph Smith III also wrote about meeting both men in London, Ontario. *The Memoirs of President Joseph Smith III (1832–1914): The Second Prophet of the Church*, ed. Mary Audentia Smith Anderson (Independence, MO: Price Publishing Company, 2001), 26.

16. Winks, *The Blacks in Canada*, 144–45; William H. Smith, *Smith's Canadian Gazetteer* (Toronto: H. & W. Rowsell, 1846), 4–5, https://archive.org/details/smithscanadianga00smit. On the developing importance of this border in the late eighteenth and early nineteenth centuries, see Gregory Wigmore, "Before the Railroad: From Slavery to Freedom in the Canadian-American Borderland," *Journal of American History* 98, no. 2 (2011): 437–54.

17. Kenneth L. Kusmer, *A Ghetto Takes Shape: Black Cleveland, 1870–1930*, Blacks in the New World (Urbana: University of Illinois Press, 1976), 6–7.

18. John Calvin Smith, *The Western Tourist, and Emigrant's Guide, with a Compendious Gazetteer of the States of Ohio, Michigan, Indiana, Illinois, and Missouri, and the Territories of Wisconsin, and Iowa* (New York: J. H. Colton, 1839), 36–37; Kusmer, *A Ghetto Takes Shape*, 6–7, 10; *The Narrative of William W. Brown, A Fugitive Slave* (Reading, MA, 1969; first published 1848), quoted in Kusmer, 6–7; J. Spencer Fluhman, *"A Peculiar People": Anti-Mormonism and the Making of Religion in Nineteenth-Century America* (Chapel Hill: University of North Carolina Press, 2012), 94.

19. Dinger, *The Nauvoo City and High Council Minutes*, 480; Barney, "Jane Manning James," Appendix, 142.

20. On shoemaking in New Canaan, and specifically the Benedict family, see King, *Portrait of New Canaan*, 139. Jane's recollections about the injuries her group suffered to their feet

may be found in James, "Autobiography," Appendix, 144; and Barney, "Jane Manning James," Appendix, 142.

21. James German, "Economy," in *Themes in Religion and American Culture*, ed. Philip Goff and Paul Harvey (Chapel Hill: University of North Carolina Press, 2004), 271.

22. On Illinois' black code, see Elmer Gertz, "The Black Laws of Illinois," *Journal of the Illinois State Historical Society (1908–1984)* 56, no. 3 (1963): 463. Jane's recollection of the threat of jail in Peoria is in James, "Autobiography," Appendix, 144–45. Van Hoosear wrote that Philes was emancipated in 1811. Unfortunately, his research was written up after his death and presented without documentation. "Annals of Wilton: Negroes of Wilton (Continued)." Margaret Blair Young and Darius Gray suggest that Anthony Stebbins was a fugitive slave, based on Mary Frost Adams's 1906 recollection of a "colored man" named Anthony being fined for selling alcohol on the Sabbath to purchase his child, enslaved in the South. See "Joseph Smith, the Prophet," *Young Woman's Journal* 17, no. 12 (December 1906): 538. Young and Gray corroborate Adams's account by reference to B. H. Roberts, *History of the Church* 5: 57, but this reference indicates that two individuals were fined $10.25 for selling whisky at the 1842 Fourth of July celebration (not for selling liquor on the Sabbath). Moreover, Anthony Stebbins had not arrived in Nauvoo at the time the fine was levied. Adams recalled that the man "had been able to purchase the liberty of himself and wife and now wished to bring his little child to their new home." This order of operations in the purchase of freedom (purchasing the wife before the child) would have been unusual, and if Anthony Stebbins was indeed the person Adams described, these details imply that he had a wife other than Jane's sister Sarah. Margaret Blair Young and Darius Gray, *One More River to Cross*, 1st ed., Standing on the Promises 1 (Salt Lake City: Bookcraft, 2000), 205. On free papers as an instrument of racialized surveillance, see Pryor, *Colored Travelers*, 109–14.

23. James, "Autobiography," Appendix, 144–45.

24. *D&C*, 107: 8, 14; Editor, "Who May Rebuke Disease?" *Deseret Evening News*, April 8, 1901, 4, quoted in Jonathan A. Stapley and Kristine Wright, "Female Ritual Healing in Mormonism," *Journal of Mormon History* 37, no. 1 (Winter 2011): 45; James, "Autobiography," Appendix, 145.

25. Sally Randall, letters to "Dear Friends," Nauvoo, October 6, 1843, and November 12 [1843] in Randall, "Letters, 1843–1852"; Susan Easton Black, "How Large Was the Population of Nauvoo?" *BYU Studies* 35, no. 2 (April 1, 1995): 93.

26. Joseph Smith's *History*, 3: 375, entry for June 11, 1839, quoted in Robert Bruce Flanders, *Nauvoo: Kingdom on the Mississippi* (Urbana: University of Illinois Press, 1975), 38; Joseph Smith's *History*, 4: 177–78, quoting Joseph Smith to John C. Bennett, quoted in Flanders, *Nauvoo*, 51; Samuel Morris Brown, *In Heaven as It Is on Earth: Joseph Smith and the Early Mormon Conquest of Death* (New York: Oxford University Press, 2012), 19–20; Jared Farmer, *On Zion's Mount: Mormons, Indians, and the American Landscape* (Cambridge, MA: Harvard University Press, 2008), 44.

27. Samuel Mosheim Smucker, *The Religious, Social and Political History of the Mormons, Or Latter-Day Saints, from Their Origin to the Present Time* (Hurst & Company, 1881), 155, quoted in Flanders, *Nauvoo*, 115; Gustive O. Larson, *Prelude to the Kingdom: Mormon Desert Conquest, a Chapter in American Cooperative Experience* (Francestown, NH: M. Jones Co., 1947), 48, https//catalog.hathitrust.org/Record/001269091, identifies the minister and gives the date of his visit. Flanders, *Nauvoo*, 145; Sally Randall to "Dear friends," Nauvoo, October 6, 1843, "Letters, 1843–1852"; James, "Autobiography," Appendix, 145; A. P. Rockwood, "Book of Assessment, First Ward, 1843" (Nauvoo, Ill., January 1844), MS 16800, box 4, folder 13, LDS Church History Library; Daniel Hendrix, "Book of Assessment, Second Ward, 1843" (Nauvoo, Ill., February 1844), MS 16800, box 4, folder 14, LDS Church History Library; Jonathan H. Hale, "Book of Assessment, Third Ward, 1843" (Nauvoo, Ill., January 1844), MS 16800, box 4, folder 15, LDS Church History Library; Henry G. Sherwood, "Book of Assessment, Fourth Ward, 1843" (Nauvoo, Ill., January 1844), MS 16800, box 4, folder 16, LDS Church History Library; A.P. Rockwood, "Book of Assessment, First Ward, 1844" (Nauvoo, Ill., October 1844), MS 16800, box 4, folder 18, LDS Church History Library;

Jonathan H. Hale, "Book of Assessment, Third Ward, 1844" (Nauvoo, Ill., February 1845), MS 16800, box 4, folder 19, LDS Church History Library.

28. "Bond to Elijah Able, 8 December 1839," Joseph Smith Papers, http://www.josephsmithpapers.org/paperSummary/bond-to-elijah-able-8-december-1839?p=#!/paperSummary/bond-to-elijah-able-8-december-1839&p=2; William Kesler Jackson, *Elijah Abel: The Life and Times of a Black Priesthood Holder* (Springville, UT: CFI, an imprint of Cedar Fort, Inc., 2013); "Nauvoo 4th Ward Census," 1842, folder 4, 3, Nauvoo Stake ward census, LDS Church History Library, places Isaac James in Nauvoo by early 1842.

29. James, "Autobiography," Appendix, 145; Matthew L. Harris and Newell G. Bringhurst, eds., *The Mormon Church and Blacks: A Documentary History* (Urbana: University of Illinois Press, 2015), 18; Bushman, *Joseph Smith*, 289.

30. James in Gates, ed., "Joseph Smith, the Prophet," Appendix, 150.

31. James, "Autobiography," Appendix, 145; James in Gates, ed., "Joseph Smith, the Prophet," Appendix, 152.

Chapter 3

1. James, "Autobiography," Appendix, 145–46.

2. James, "Autobiography," Appendix, 146.

3. Richard H. Gassan, "Tourists and the City: New York's First Tourist Era, 1820–1840," *Winterthur Portfolio* 44, no. 2/3 (2010): 228–30; Sandoval-Strausz, *Hotel*, 56. By my count, there were at least five young women living with the Smiths at the time of Jane's arrival: Eliza and Emily Partridge, Maria and Sarah Lawrence, and Maria Jane Johnston. On the Partridge and Lawrence sisters, see Bushman, *Joseph Smith*, 494. On Johnston, see Linda King Newell and Valeen Tippetts Avery, *Mormon Enigma: Emma Hale Smith*, 2nd ed. (Urbana: University of Illinois Press, 1994), 160–61. George H. Brimhall had a reminiscence by Maria Jane Johnston Woodward typed up in April 1902 and sent it to Joseph F. Smith (then president of the LDS Church). See "George H. Brimhall to Joseph F. Smith" April 21, 1902, MS 1325, box 20, folder 1, images 15–24, Joseph F. Smith Papers, 1854–1918, LDS Church History Library.

4. Flanders, *Nauvoo*, 175–76; Historic American Buildings Survey, "Mansion House, Main & Water Streets, Nauvoo, Hancock County, IL" (US Department of the Interior, Office of National Parks, Buildings, and Reservations, Branch of Plans and Design, 1934), sheet 2 of 5, Historic American Buildings Survey (Library of Congress), Library of Congress Prints and Photographs Division, Washington, DC, http://www.loc.gov/pictures/item/il0131.sheet.00002a. I am grateful to David Bolton, Co-Team Lead of the Community of Christ Joseph Smith Historic Site, Nauvoo, for pointing me to this resource. That Emma worked alongside Jane is based on Sutherland, *Americans and Their Servants*, 94. Newell and Avery write that when the Smiths moved into the Mansion House in 1843, "Eliza R. Snow, Eliza and Emily Partridge, two young sisters named Sarah and Maria Lawrence, several of the Walker children, including Lucy, William, and Lorin, and Lucy Mack Smith probably moved with them." By the time Jane arrived in the Smith household, Eliza R. Snow had moved elsewhere. *Mormon Enigma*, 132, 136, 12–13.

5. On Smith's leadership of the Nauvoo Legion, see Bushman, *Joseph Smith*, 413. Details about the Christmas Day party come from Newell and Avery, *Mormon Enigma*, 165; but see also Bushman, *Joseph Smith*, 499; and Terryl Givens, *People of Paradox: A History of Mormon Culture* (New York: Oxford University Press, 2007), 129 for mentions of the same party. For subsequent parties given by the Smiths that winter, see Bushman, *Joseph Smith*, 499.

6. James, "Autobiography," Appendix, 146. For more on the development of the endowment and other temple ceremonies, see David J. Buerger, "The Development of the Mormon Temple Endowment Ceremony," *Dialogue: A Journal of Mormon Thought* 20 (Winter 1987): 33–76. For the LDS Church's explanation of the history and purpose of temple garments, see Church of Jesus Christ of Latter-day Saints Newsroom, "Temple Garments," www.mormonnewsroom.org, September 16, 2014, http://www.mormonnewsroom.org/article/temple-garments. For a scholarly analysis of the garments as material objects,

1164   NOTES TO PAGES 43–50

see Colleen McDannell, *Material Christianity: Religion and Popular Culture in America* (New Haven, CT: Yale University Press, 1995), 198–221.

7. Maria J[ane Johnston] Woodward, quoted in "Joseph Smith, the Prophet," *Young Woman's Journal* 17, no. 12 (December 1906): 544. Woodward used her married name when she recorded her memories, but at the time she lived in the Smith household, she was known by her natal surname, Johnston.

8. Maria Jane Johnston Woodward reminiscence, April 1902, in "Brimhall to Smith," MS 1325, box 20, folder 1, image 23.

9. Buerger, "The Development of the Mormon Temple Endowment Ceremony," 47.

10. James, "Autobiography," Appendix, 146; Lucy Mack Smith, "Lucy Mack Smith, History, 1844–1845," Joseph Smith Papers, 5: 7–8, http://www.josephsmithpapers.org/paper-summary/lucy-mack-smith-history-1844-1845.

11. Jane recounts this episode in James, "Autobiography," Appendix, 146–47. In her conversation with Elvira Stevens Barney, she said it occurred "about Christmas time." Barney, "Jane Manning James," Appendix, 142.

12. On the use of "Urim and Thummim" as a general category of stones, see Richard E. Turley Jr., Robin S. Jensen, and Mark Ashurst-McGee, "Joseph the Seer," *Ensign*, October 2015, https://www.lds.org/ensign/2015/10/joseph-the-seer?lang=eng. For a detailed discussion of Smith's various seer stones, his use of them, and their subsequent chains of custody, see Michael Hubbard MacKay and Nicholas J. Frederick, *Joseph Smith's Seer Stones* (Provo and Salt Lake City: Religious Studies Center, Brigham Young University, in cooperation with Deseret Book Company, 2016), 29–43, 45–57, and 65–85. For Jane's conversation with Elvira Stevens Barney, see Barney, "Jane Manning James," Appendix, 143. For Jane's quotation of Lucy Mack Smith, see James, "Autobiography," Appendix, 147.

13. James, "Autobiography," Appendix, 146; Leonard J. Arrington and Davis Bitton, *The Mormon Experience: A History of the Latter-Day Saints* (New York: Knopf, 1979), 69–70; Sarah Barringer Gordon, *The Mormon Question: Polygamy and Constitutional Conflict in Nineteenth-Century America*, Studies in Legal History (Chapel Hill: University of North Carolina Press, 2002), 28; Fluhman, *A Peculiar People*, 97–125.

14. Hunter, *Bound in Wedlock*, especially 32–33; James, "Autobiography," Appendix, 146.

15. James, "Autobiography," Appendix, 146; Todd Compton, *In Sacred Loneliness: The Plural Wives of Joseph Smith* (Salt Lake City: Signature Books, 1997), 6; Newell and Avery, *Mormon Enigma*, 145, 160–62; Bushman, *Joseph Smith*, 496–99.

16. James, "Autobiography," Appendix, 146.

17. James, "Autobiography," Appendix, 146; Newell and Avery, *Mormon Enigma*, 138.

18. Smith, III, *Memoirs of President Joseph Smith III*, 26.

19. James, "Autobiography," Appendix, 145, 147; James in Gates, ed., "Joseph Smith, the Prophet," Appendix, 150.

20. Samuel M. Brown, "Early Mormon Adoption Theology and the Mechanics of Salvation," *Journal of Mormon History* 37, no. 3 (Summer 2011): 18. Jesus's statement is in Matthew 16:19; see also Matthew 18:18. Gordon Irving, "The Law of Adoption: One Phase of the Development of the Mormon Concept of Salvation, 1830–1900," *Brigham Young University Studies* 14 (Spring 1974): 295. For a comprehensive discussion of the development of adoption sealings in Mormonism, see Irving's complete article.

21. For suggestions that Smith was proposing marriage, see, for example, Joseph Stuart, "Holy Races: Race in the Formation of Mormonism and the Nation of Islam" (master's thesis, University of Virginia, 2014), 55–56; Max Perry Mueller, *Race and the Making of the Mormon People* (Chapel Hill: University of North Carolina Press, 2017), 144–45. On the timing of Joseph Smith's plural marriages, see Compton, *In Sacred Loneliness*, 2–3.

22. For the teaching about "Fathers and Mothers in Israel," see Joseph Smith Sr., patriarchal blessing on Jesse Walker Johnstun, February 5, 1839, in H. Michael Marquardt, ed., *Early Patriarchal Blessings of the Church of Jesus Christ of Latter-Day Saints* (Salt Lake City: Smith-Pettit Foundation, 2007), 187, quoted in Brown, "Early Mormon Adoption Theology," 22. On the concern about fatherlessness and the creation of "sacerdotal families," see Brown, 4–6, 22–24.

23. Smith, "1844 Patriarchal Blessing." This document is reprinted in the Appendix, 140, and hereafter, citations of this item will refer to the version printed in the Appendix. Gordon Shepherd, Gary Shepherd, and Natalie Shepherd, "Gender Differences in the Early Patriarchal Blessings of the LDS Church, 1834–1845," *John Whitmer Historical Association Journal* 30 (2010): 44; Brown, "Early Mormon Adoption Theology," 22. For the first scholarly analysis of this patriarchal blessing of which I am aware, see Mueller, *Race and the Making of the Mormon People*, especially 146–49.

24. Irene M. Bates, "Patriarchal Blessings and the Routinization of Charisma," *Dialogue: A Journal of Mormon Thought* 26, no. 3 (Fall 1993): 26–27; Marquardt, *Early Patriarchal Blessings*, x.

25. An unsigned item in the local paper notified the community of the change in the Mansion House's management. "Untitled," *Nauvoo Neighbor*, January 24, 1844; Flanders, *Nauvoo*, 177; Bushman, *Joseph Smith*, 503. For Jane's assessment of the availability of work in Nauvoo, see James, "Autobiography," Appendix, 147.

26. The *Expositor*'s mission was printed in the *Nauvoo Expositor*, June 7, 1844, quoted in Bushman, *Joseph Smith*, 539. For a thorough description of this episode and a detailed analysis of the legal issues involved, see Dallin H. Oaks, "The Suppression of the *Nauvoo Expositor*," *Utah Law Review* 9 (Winter 1965): 862–903. On the *Nauvoo Expositor* and Smith's response, see Bushman, *Joseph Smith*, 539–41. On this time period in Nauvoo, see Arrington and Bitton, *The Mormon Experience*, 65–82.

27. Gertz, "The Black Laws of Illinois," 463–64.

28. H. Smith, Patriarchal Blessing (1844), Appendix, 140.

29. H. Smith, Patriarchal Blessing (1844), Appendix, 140.

30. Armand L. Mauss, *All Abraham's Children: Changing Mormon Conceptions of Race and Lineage* (Urbana: University of Illinois Press, 2003), 17–24.

31. H. Smith, Patriarchal Blessing (1844), Appendix, 140.

32. H. Smith, Patriarchal Blessing (1844), Appendix, 140. Max Perry Mueller notes that Smith's warning is a nearly verbatim quotation of Moses 5:23, which is in turn a slight alteration of Genesis 4:7. Mueller, *Race and the Making of the Mormon People*, 148.

33. On the use of the conditional in patriarchal blessings, see Shepherd, Shepherd, and Shepherd, "Gender Differences in the Early Patriarchal Blessings of the LDS Church, 1834–1845," 61. On stereotypes of black women, see Tera W. Hunter, *To 'Joy My Freedom: Southern Black Women's Lives and Labors after the Civil War* (Cambridge, MA: Harvard University Press, 1997), 197; Brenda E. Stevenson, *Life in Black and White: Family and Community in the Slave South* (New York: Oxford University Press, 1996), 237, 243.

34. On compensation or the lack thereof for patriarchal blessings, see Bates, "Patriarchal Blessings," 26–27. For Jane's interaction with Joseph Smith, see James, "Autobiography," Appendix, 147. On Burlington, see Robert H. Goodwin, "Among the Poorest of Saints: Mormon Migration to and through Burlington, Iowa, 1846–1887," *Mormon Historical Studies* 4, no. 2 (Fall 2003): 97–99. On the size of Nauvoo, see Black, "How Large Was the Population of Nauvoo," 93. On early Iowa black laws, see Robert R. Dykstra, "White Men, Black Laws," *The Annals of Iowa* 46, no. 6 (Fall 1982): 403–40.

35. James, "Autobiography," Appendix, 147.

36. Flanders's assessment of the Mormons' reaction to Smith's death is in Flanders, *Nauvoo*, 310. The quotation from Ford is from Governor Thomas Ford to Nauvoo, July 22, 1844, quoted in Flanders, 311, quoting B. H. Roberts, *A Comprehensive History of the Church of Jesus Christ of Latter-Day Saints Century I* (Salt Lake City: Deseret News Press, 1930), 2: 303. Jane's remark that she "liked to a died" is in James in Gates, ed., "Joseph Smith, the Prophet," Appendix, 151.

Chapter 4

1. James in Gates, ed., "Joseph Smith, the Prophet," Appendix, 151–52.

2. Bushman, *Joseph Smith*, 510–11; John G. Turner, *Brigham Young: Pioneer Prophet* (Cambridge, MA: The Belknap Press of Harvard University Press, 2012), 111–12.

3. Jane said that she married Isaac while she was working for Brigham Young in Nauvoo. James, "Autobiography," Appendix, 147. Assuming that the couple's first son was conceived

after their marriage, and that Jane carried that child to term, then the wedding must have taken place by the beginning of September, 1845.

4. On Isaac James's biographical details, see "Camp of Israel Schedules and Reports: Spring 1847 Emigration Camp, First 100, Second 50, Returns, 1847 June," June 1847, MS 14290, box 1, folder 36, image 2, LDS Church History Library; George F. Fort, "United States Federal Census, Upper Freehold Township, Monmouth County, New Jersey" (US National Archives and Records Administration, 1840), microfilm 16,518, Family History Library, Salt Lake City; "Record of Deaths in Salt Lake City" (Salt Lake City, Salt Lake, Utah, Management and Archives), 40, entry 1633, film 4,139,830, Family History Library, Salt Lake City. On Mormonism in New Jersey's Pine Barrens, see Stephen J. Fleming, "'Sweeping Everything before It': Early Mormonism in the Pine Barrens of New Jersey," BYU Studies 40, no. 1 (2001): 72–104. The quotation about Joseph Smith's visit to the Pine Barrens is from Fleming, 73.

5. Erastus Snow, "Erastus Snow Journals, 1835–1851; 1856–1857," box 1, folder 2, 92–95, 102–3, MS 1329, LDS Church History Library.

6. Graham Russell Hodges, Slavery and Freedom in the Rural North: African Americans in Monmouth County, New Jersey, 1665–1865 (Madison, WI: Madison House, 1997), 166, 178; "Nauvoo 4th Ward Census," LR 3102 27 folder 4, image 3.

7. Ronald Walker, "Young 'Tony' Ivins" (Juanita Brooks Lecture Series, St. George, UT, March 15, 2000), https://library.dixie.edu/special_collections/juanita_brooks_lectures/2000.html.

8. On Mormon marriage during this time period, see Kathleen Flake, "The Development of Early Latter-Day Saint Marriage Rites, 1831–53," Journal of Mormon History 41, no. 1 (2015): 77–102, especially 86–88, 89–90, and 94. Jane's request for sealing to another African American man is in Jane E. James to Apostle Joseph F. Smith, February 7, 1890, Joseph F. Smith Papers, LDS Church History Library, transcribed in Henry J. Wolfinger, "A Test of Faith: Jane Elizabeth James and the Origins of the Utah Black Community," in Social Accommodation in Utah, ed. Clark S. Knowlton, American West Center Occasional Papers (Salt Lake City: University of Utah, 1975), 149.

9. W. Paul Reeve, Religion of a Different Color: Race and the Mormon Struggle for Whiteness (New York: Oxford University Press, 2015), 195.

10. On Young's departure, see Turner, Brigham Young: Pioneer Prophet, 140, 145. Historian William G. Hartley's description of the exodus is clear and well documented. See William G. Hartley, "The Pioneer Trek," Ensign, June 1997, https://www.lds.org/ensign/1997/06/the-pioneer-trek-nauvoo-to-winter-quarters?lang=eng. The quotation from Patty Sessions's diary is found in Patty Bartlett Sessions and Donna Toland Smart, Mormon Midwife: The 1846–1888 Diaries of Patty Bartlett Sessions (Logan: Utah State University Press, 1997), 49.

11. Sessions and Smart, Mormon Midwife, 53. On the Mt. Pisgah settlement, see Leland H. Gentry, "The Mormon Way Stations: Garden Grove and Mt. Pisgah," BYU Studies 21, no. 4 (Fall 1981): 453–59.

12. Sessions and Smart, Mormon Midwife, 54–55.

13. George Parker Dykes, Fort Leavenworth, to Brigham Young, Council Bluff, August 17, 1846, "Brigham Young Office Files, 1832–1878," CR 1234 1, box 20, folder 18, LDS Church History Library; George Parker Dykes, Santa Fe, to Mrs. Dykes, Council Bluffs, October 11, 1846, "George Parker Dykes to Diantha, Alcina, and Cynthia Dykes, 1846 July–September," MS 2070, box 1, folder 12, image 27, LDS Church History Library. Dykes's letters were addressed to "Mrs. Geo. P. Dykes," a title that applied to all three of his wives, Dorcas, Cynthia, and Alcina. At the end of his letters he often included the line "To D. C. A. Dykes," clearly indicating that the "Dear Wife" address that opened the letter was intended for all three. The phrase "come ye blessed of my Father" comes from Matthew 25:34 and refers to the separation of the sheep from the goats in the final judgment.

14. My account of McCary's activities relies on Angela Pulley Hudson, Real Native Genius: How an Ex-Slave and a White Mormon Became Famous Indians (Chapel Hill: The University of North Carolina Press, 2015), especially 69–92.

15. Hudson, *Real Native Genius*, 79; Arrington and Bitton, *The Mormon Experience*, 89; Turner, *Brigham Young: Pioneer Prophet*, 162.

16. Hudson, *Real Native Genius*, 80, quoting Whipple, "Autobiography and Journal of Nelson W. Whipple," 31.

17. Hudson, *Real Native Genius*, 86–87; Thomas Bullock, meeting minutes, March 26, 1847, Church Historian's Office, "General Church Minutes, 1839–1877," CR 100 318, box 1, folder 52, LDS Church History Library. I am grateful to Paul Reeve for generously sharing a transcription of these minutes with me.

18. On the McCarys' movements, see William W. Major, Elk horn, to Brigham Young, June 16, 1847, "Brigham Young Office Files, 1832–1878" CR 1234 1, box 21, folder 8. I thank Paul Reeve for sharing this source with me. See also Hudson, *Real Native Genius*, 90. Nelson Whipple's findings are written up in Whipple, "History of Nelson Wheeler Whipple," 37, quoted in Hudson, 89.

19. Hudson, *Real Native Genius*, 90–91.

20. "Daniel Spencer's 100, Schedules, circa 1847 February," February 1847, MS 14290, box 1, folder 16, image 13, Camp of Israel schedules and reports 1845–1849, LDS Church History Library; Daniel Spencer, "Daniel Spencer Letter, Salt Lake City, Utah to Brother Grove," October 5, 1848, MS 6235, LDS Church History Library; "Camp of Israel Schedules and Reports: Spring 1847 Emigration Camp, First 100, Second 50, Travel Report, 1847 September," September 1847, item 1, MS 14290, box 2, folder 2, LDS Church History Library.

21. Isaac C. Haight, "Isaac C. Haight Journal, 1842 June–1850 April," 72, MS 867 folder 1, LDS Church History Library; Patty Sessions recorded the detail of the white flag in her diary. Sessions and Smart, *Mormon Midwife*, 86 and 88. On liberty poles and associated symbols, see Arthur M. Schlesinger, "Liberty Tree: A Genealogy," *New England Quarterly* 25, no. 4 (December 1952): 435–58 (quotation is from 453); Simon P. Newman, *Parades and the Politics of the Street: Festive Culture in the Early American Republic* (Philadelphia: University of Pennsylvania Press, 2010), 25, 130; Yvonne Korshak, "The Liberty Cap as a Revolutionary Symbol in America and France," *Smithsonian Studies in American Art* 1, no. 2 (Autumn 1987): 53–57.

22. Haight, "Haight Journal," images 72–80. James, "Autobiography," Appendix, 147. Although Isaac Haight's journal does not mention a cattle stampede, he did note on July 19 that "Captain Grant's cattle brouke [*sic*] out of his way last night. Went to hunt them but did not find them." Haight, image 51.

23. Haight, "Haight Journal," images 79–80.

24. On this point, see Farmer, *On Zion's Mount*, 19–35.

25. Leonard J. Arrington, *Great Basin Kingdom: Economic History of the Latter-Day Saints, 1830–1900* (Lincoln: University of Nebraska Press, 1958), 45; Haight, "Haight Journal," images 80–81; J.B. Ireland, "City Wall around Great Salt Lake City Constructed by the Utah Pioneers around 1853 and 1854 [Map]," ed. Nicholas G. Morgan, LDS Church History Library; WPA Biographical Sketches, Utah State Historical Society, n.d., quoted in Wolfinger, "A Test of Faith," 159n13.

26. William G. Hartley, "Mormons, Crickets, and Gulls: A New Look at an Old Story," *Utah Historical Quarterly* 38 (1970): 226–27; Farmer, *On Zion's Mount*, 45, quoting William Clayton, *The Latter-day Saints' Emigrants' Guide* (St. Louis: Republican Steam Power Press and Chambers & Knapp, 1848), 20; Spencer, "Spencer to Grove."

27. Sessions and Smart, *Mormon Midwife*, 112; Jacobs, "Incidents," 405.

28. Jane's comments are in James, "Autobiography," Appendix, 147. For Hartley's documentation of Mormons' encounters with crickets and grasshoppers in the 1840s and 1850s, see Hartley, "Mormons, Crickets, and Gulls," 236–37. For quotations from Steele and Haight, see Steele, "Extracts from the Journal of John Steele," *Utah Historical Quarterly* 6 (January 1933): 21–22 and Haight, "Biographical Sketch and Diary of Isaac Chauncey Haight, 1813–1862" (typescript, Brigham Young University), 49, quoted in Hartley, 227–28. Patty Sessions's comment comes from Sessions and Smart, *Mormon Midwife*, 113.

29. On efforts to drive away or kill the crickets, see Hartley, "Mormons, Crickets, and Gulls," 229–32. The letter to Brigham Young is found in Pauline Udall Smith, *Captain Jefferson Hunt of the Mormon Battalion* (Salt Lake City, 1958), 136–37, quoted in Hartley, 230.

30. Snow, "Erastus Snow Journals," box 1, folder 4, 97, entry for Thursday, August 8, 1847. The practice of rebaptism for newly arrived emigrants continued for years afterward. Elias Smith recorded in his journal on Sunday, May 9, 1852: "In the evening [wife] Lucy and I were rebaptized by Elder Jace A. Weiler as it is the order of the church for all who come here to be rebaptized before having their names recorded in the Church records." Elias Smith journals 1836–1888; Journal, 1851 May–1854 October, MS 1319, box 1, folder 3, image 54, LDS Church History Library.

Chapter 5

1. John G. Turner documents Isaac's employment by Brigham Young in *Brigham Young: Pioneer Prophet*, 218. In 1855, Young lived with his senior wife, Mary Ann Angell Young, in a home known as the Beehive House. But with nearly fifty wives by that date, and scores of children, he could not house all of his family there. A building known as the Lion House was under construction, next door to the Beehive House; twenty of Young's wives would move into that building the following year. Turner, 236. Jane and her family are listed as "Help" in "A List of President Brigham Young's Family Residing in the 18th Ward.," March 19, 1855, Brigham Young office files; Miscellaneous Files, 1832–1878; Family information, circa 1853–1858, LDS Church History Library.

2. M. Skolnick et al., "Mormon Demographic History I: Nuptiality and Fertility of Once-Married Couples," *Population Studies* 32, no. 1 (March 1978): 16, 17.

3. Amy G. Richter, ed., *At Home in Nineteenth-Century America: A Documentary History* (New York: New York University Press, 2015), 52; Jan Shipps, *Mormonism: The Story of a New Religious Tradition* (Urbana: University of Illinois Press, 1985), 109–29.

4. Augusta Adams Cobb Young to Brigham Young, undated (about September 1, 1852), box 66, folder 9, Brigham Young Papers, LDS Church History Library, quoted in Turner, *Brigham Young: Pioneer Prophet*, 192. I thank John G. Turner for sharing this source with me. On the growing number of Southern converts in Salt Lake, see W. Paul Reeve, Christopher B. Rich Jr., and LaJean Carruth, *"Enough to Cause the Angels in Heaven to Blush": Race, Servitude, and Priesthood at the 1852 Utah Legislature*, forthcoming, chapter 2.

5. "An Act to establish a Territorial Government for Utah," September 9, 1850, *Statutes at Large*, 31st Congress, 1st Session, 453, on The Library of Congress, "A Century of Lawmaking for a New Nation: US Congressional Documents and Debates, 1774–1875," *American Memory*, https://memory.loc.gov/cgi-bin/ampage?collId=llsl&fileName=009/llsl009.db&recNum=480.

6. Reeve, Rich Jr., and Carruth, *Enough to Cause the Angels in Heaven to Blush*, Introduction; Christopher B. Rich, "The True Policy for Utah: Servitude, Slavery, and 'An Act in Relation to Service,'" *Utah Historical Quarterly* 80, no. 1 (Winter 2012): 54–74.

7. Brigham Young's speech is given in Reeve, Rich Jr., and Carruth, *Enough to Cause the Angels in Heaven to Blush*; see also Rich, "The True Policy for Utah," 65. Noah's curse is in Genesis 9:25.

8. James, "Autobiography," Appendix, 146; Richard S. Van Wagoner, *Mormon Polygamy: A History*, 2d ed. (Salt Lake City: Signature Books, 1989), 82–114; Kathryn M. Daynes, *More Wives than One: Transformation of the Mormon Marriage System, 1840–1910* (Urbana: University of Illinois Press, 2001), 188–214, especially 207. On the effects of polygamy on families and individual women, see Christine Talbot, "The Church Family in Nineteenth-Century America: Mormonism and the Public/Private Divide," *Journal of Mormon History* 37, no. 4 (Fall 2011): 208–57; Daynes, *More Wives than One*, 67–87; Paula Kelly Harline, *The Polygamous Wives Writing Club: From the Diaries of Mormon Pioneer Women* (New York: Oxford University Press, 2014), 11–58.

9. On Brigham Young's plural wives, see Jeffery Ogden Johnson, "Determining and Defining 'Wife': The Brigham Young Households," *Dialogue: A Journal of Mormon Thought* 20, no.

3 (Fall 1987): 57–70. On Mary Ann Angell Young's status in Brigham Young's family, see Turner, *Brigham Young: Pioneer Prophet*, 157, 189. The remark that Mary Ann Angell Young "preferred a more secluded existence" is from Turner, 377.

10. On Brigham Young's and Joseph Smith's wives, see Johnson, "Determining and Defining 'Wife,'" 65–70; Compton, *In Sacred Loneliness*, 4–9. On the psychological and emotional experiences of plural wives, see Harline, *The Polygamous Wives Writing Club*, 11–58.

11. B. H. Young, "Free Inhabitants in the County of Great Salt Lake, Deseret, United States Federal Census, Utah Territory" (US National Archives and Records Administration, 1850), microfilm 25540, Family History Library, Salt Lake City; Jesse C. Little, "Tax Assessment Rolls" (Salt Lake City [Utah] Assessor, 1856), series 4922, box 1, folder 1, Utah State Archives; Jesse C. Little, "Tax Assessment Rolls" (Salt Lake City [Utah] Assessor, 1858), series 4922, box 1, folder 3, Utah State Archives; Wolfinger, "A Test of Faith," 132, 160n15, 160n16.

12. Jeter Clinton, "Tax Assessment Rolls" (Salt Lake City [Utah] Assessor, 1859), images 2–4, series 4922, box 1, folder 4, Utah State Archives; Turner, *Brigham Young: Pioneer Prophet*, 228. On the relative desirability of laundry as employment, see Hunter, *To 'Joy My Freedom*, 57.

13. Historian Katherine Leonard Turner notes that by the early twentieth century, "Families who could afford to keep livestock were healthier and earned extra income; families who were healthier and had extra income to invest could more readily take on the challenges of raising livestock. By contrast, families who could not manage to keep livestock were noticeably poorer and tended to stay that way." *How the Other Half Ate: A History of Working-Class Meals at the Turn of the Century*, California Studies in Food and Culture 48 (Berkeley: University of California Press, 2014), 106. That Jane begged for milk is given in WPA Biographical Sketches, Utah State Historical Society, n.d., quoted in Wolfinger, "A Test of Faith," 159n13. On the Salt Lake community herd, see Arrington, *Great Basin Kingdom*, 91–92.

14. Jeter Clinton, "Tax Assessment Rolls" (Salt Lake City [Utah] Assessor, 1860), series 4922, box 1, folder 5, Utah State Archives; Jeter Clinton, "Tax Assessment Rolls" (Salt Lake City [Utah] Assessor, 1861), series 4922, box 1, folder 6, Utah State Archives; James, "Autobiography," Appendix, 147; Leonard Hill, "Account Book [Manuscript]: Nauvoo, Ill., 1843–1869," 29v–30r, Edward E. Ayer Manuscript Collection, Newberry Library, Chicago.

15. Ronald G. Coleman, "Blacks in Utah History," *Utah History to Go: Peoples of Utah*, http://historytogo.utah.gov/people/ethnic_cultures/the_peoples_of_utah/blacksinutahhistory.html; Young, "1850 Salt Lake Census"; United States Census Office, Utah Territorial Census, 1851, Schedule 2 ("Slave Colored Inhabitants Utah Co. Territory of Utah"), MS 2672, box 1, folder 6, LDS Church History Library; George D. Snider, "United States Federal Census, First Ward of Great Salt Lake City, County of Great Salt Lake, Territory of Utah" (US National Archives and Records Administration, 1860), microfilm 805313, Family History Library, Salt Lake City.

16. Kate B. Carter, *The Story of the Negro Pioneer* (Salt Lake City: Daughters of Utah Pioneers, 1965), 22, 28–29, 50–51.

17. Paul H. Peterson, "'Like a Fire in My Bones': The Reformation Correspondence between Brigham Young and George Q. Cannon," in *Regional Studies in Latter-Day Saint Church History: California*, Regional Studies in Latter-Day Saint Church History 1 (Provo: Department of Church History and Doctrine, Brigham Young University, 1998), 107, http://contentdm.lib.byu.edu/cdm/ref/collection/rsc/id/13334.

18. Peterson's description of the church's policy is from Paul H. Peterson, "Reformation (LDS) of 1856–1857," *Encyclopedia of Mormonism* (New York: Macmillan, 1992), 1197. Samuel W. Richards's comment comes from Richards, Letter to the Editor, October 7, 1856, *Millennial Star* 19 (January 17, 1857): 42, quoted in Lisle G. Brown, "'Temple Pro Tempore': The Salt Lake City Endowment House," *Journal of Mormon History* 34, no. 4 (Fall 2008): 19. Brigham Young's comments are from Brigham Young to George Q. Cannon, 4 July 1857, Brigham Young Letterbooks, Archive Division, Historical Department, The Church of Jesus Christ of Latter-day Saints, Salt Lake City, quoted in Peterson, "Like a Fire in My Bones," 114.

19. On the Utah War, see especially Richard D. Poll and William P. MacKinnon, "Causes of the Utah War Reconsidered," *Journal of Mormon History* 20, no. 2 (April 1994): 16–44; William P. MacKinnon, "Exodus and the Utah War: Tales from the Mormon Move South, 1858," *Overland Journal* 34, no. 3 (Fall 2016): 89–100; William P. MacKinnon, "Epilogue to the Utah War: Impact and Legacy," *Journal of Mormon History* 29, no. 2 (April 2003): 186–248; William P. MacKinnon, "Utah's Civil War(s): Linkages and Connections," *Utah Historical Quarterly* 80, no. 4 (Fall 2012): 296–313.

20. Turner, *Brigham Young: Pioneer Prophet*, 293, 298.

21. MacKinnon, "Exodus and the Utah War," 100; Richard D. Poll, "The Move South," *BYU Studies* 29, no. 4 (October 1989): 84; Turner, *Brigham Young: Pioneer Prophet*, 299; Little, "1858 Tax Rolls"; Clinton, "1859 Tax Rolls"; Brigham Young Office, "Ledger B, 1854 November–1859 June," 171, Brigham Young office files; Ledgers, 1849–1859, CR 1234 1, box 93, folder 1, LDS Church History Library.

22. MacKinnon, "Utah's Civil War(s)," 307; Richard E. Bennett, "'We Know No North, No South, No East, No West': Mormon Interpretations of the Civil War, 1861–65," in *Civil War Saints:*, ed. Kenneth L. Alford (Provo and Salt Lake City: Religious Studies Center, Brigham Young University, in cooperation with Deseret Book Company, 2012), 57, https://rsc.byu.edu/es/archived/civil-war-saints/we-know-no-north-no-south-no-east-no-west-mormon-interpretations-civil-war. On Utah's minimal participation in the conflict, see also MacKinnon, "Utah's Civil War(s)," 300; John Gary Maxwell, *The Civil War Years in Utah: The Kingdom of God and the Territory That Did Not Fight* (Norman: University of Oklahoma Press, 2016), 3–4.

23. *D&C*, 87: 3, 7, 8. For LDS interpretation of this revelation as applying to the American Civil War, see MacKinnon, "Utah's Civil War(s)," 302–3; Bennett, "'We Know No North, No South, No East, No West,'" 52–54.

24. Celia and Carrie Bankhead Leggroan interview, transcript, December 3, 1977, 22, Helen Zeese Papanikolas papers, box 2, folder 8, Marriott Library Special Collections, University of Utah.

25. Wells to Gen. G. D. Grant, Salt Lake Military District, Special Orders #3, August 2, 1861, Nauvoo Legion Letterbook, MS 1370, LDS Church History Library, Salt Lake City, quoted in Ephraim D. Dickson III, "Protecting the Home Front: The Utah Territorial Militia during the Civil War," in *Civil War Saints*, ed. Kenneth L. Alford (Provo: Religious Studies Center, Brigham Young University, 2012), 143, https://rsc.byu.edu/sites/default/files/pubs/pdf/chaps/CWS%2009%20Dickson.pdf; Richards to Harmon, quoted in Dickson III, 147; A.L. Fullmer, "Report of the 1st Regt., 2nd Brig. N.L. Commanded by A. L. Fullmer, Dec. 27, 1861," December 27, 1861, image 12, Utah, Territorial Militia Records, 1849–1877, Family History Library, Salt Lake City; Wolfinger, "A Test of Faith," 132.

26. Dickson III, "Protecting the Home Front," 144–45; Fullmer, "Report of the 1st Regt., 2nd Brig. N.L. Commanded by A. L. Fullmer, Dec. 27, 1861."

27. Reeve, *Religion of a Different Color*, 164; James in Gates, ed., "Joseph Smith, the Prophet," Appendix, 152.

28. *D&C*, 101: 77–80.

29. On Martin, see Peter E. Palmquist, *Pioneer Photographers of the Far West: A Biographical Dictionary, 1840–1865* (Stanford, CA: Stanford University Press, 2000), 382–83. For more on whether the woman photographed in Martin's studio was Jane, see Amy Tanner Thiriot, "The Things We Know: A Picture of Jane Manning James (Revisited)," *Keepapitchinin, the Mormon History Blog* (blog), November 29, 2017, http://www.keepapitchinin.org/2017/11/29/jane-james-picture-revisited/, in which Thiriot superimposed an 1897 line drawing of Jane over the photo. Thiriot determined that the two images matched so closely that they must depict the same person.

30. Laura Wexler, *Tender Violence: Domestic Visions in an Age of U.S. Imperialism*, Cultural Studies of the United States (Chapel Hill: University of North Carolina Press, 2000), 65, 2.

31. Teresa Zackodnik, "The 'Green-Backs of Civilization': Sojourner Truth and Portrait Photography," *American Studies* 46, no. 2 (Summer 2005): 119, 122–24.

Chapter 6

1. James, "Autobiography," Appendix, 147; Elias Smith, *Jane E. James v. Isaac James* (Salt Lake County Probate Court March 1870).

2. Wolfinger, "A Test of Faith," 161n21; Edwin Brown Firmage and Richard Collin Mangrum, *Zion in the Courts: A Legal History of the Church of Jesus Christ of Latter-Day Saints, 1830–1900* (Urbana: University of Illinois Press, 1988), 277. On interactions between probate and ecclesiastical courts on issues surrounding divorce, see Firmage and Mangrum, 329–31.

3. On probate court judges and their jurisdiction in Utah, see James B. Allen, "The Unusual Jurisdiction of County Probate Courts in the Territory of Utah," *Utah Historical Quarterly* 36, no. 2 (Spring 1968): 132–42.

4. On Utah's divorce laws, see Lisa Madsen Pearson and Carol Cornwall Madsen, "Innovation and Accommodation: The Legal Status of Women in Territorial Utah, 1850–1896," in *Women in Utah History: Paradigm or Paradox?* (University Press of Colorado, 2005), 44. Utah's divorce statistics were reported in Carroll D. Wright, ed., *Marriage and Divorce in the United States, 1867 to 1886*, Demography (New York: Arno Press, 1976), 414, 416. I calculated the frequency of divorce in the states and territories surrounding Utah using the number of divorces and the population reported for 1870 in Arizona, Colorado, Idaho, Nevada, New Mexico, and Wyoming. See Wright, 220, 236, 260, 352, 356, 440. On divorces granted by Brigham Young, see Eugene E. Campbell and Bruce L. Campbell, "Divorce among Mormon Polygamists: Extent and Explanations," *Utah Historical Quarterly* 46 (Winter 1978): 4–23.

5. Peggy Pascoe, *Relations of Rescue: The Search for Female Moral Authority in the American West, 1874–1939* (New York: Oxford University Press, 1990), 4; Talbot, "The Church Family in Nineteenth-Century America," 231; Rebecca de Schweinitz, "Preaching the Gospel of Church and Sex: Mormon Women's Fiction in the Young Woman's Journal, 1889–1910," *Dialogue: A Journal of Mormon Thought* 33, no. 4 (Winter 2000): 41–42, 45, 50–53.

6. Amy Hoyt and Sara M. Patterson, "Mormon Masculinity: Changing Gender Expectations in the Era of Transition from Polygamy to Monogamy, 1890–1920," *Gender & History* 23, no. 1 (April 1, 2011): 73; O. Kendall White Jr., "Boundary Maintenance, Blacks, and the Mormon Priesthood," *Journal of Religious Thought* 37 (Fall/Winter 1980–1981): 44.

7. Wolfinger, "A Test of Faith," 161n21.

8. Wolfinger, 162n28 and 161n21; "Eighth Ward Relief Society Minutes and Records (1867–1969)" (Salt Lake City, Utah), LR 2525 14, LDS Church History Library; Unsigned, "Saint without Priesthood: The Collected Testimonies of Ex-Slave Samuel D. Chambers," *Dialogue: A Journal of Mormon Thought* 12, no. 2 (Summer 1979): 13.

9. Entry for January 27, 1875, Emily Dow Partridge Young, "Emily P. Young Diary and Reminiscences, 1874 February–1899 November," MS 2845, folder 1, image 87, LDS Church History Library. On a blog post I wrote about Jane, Connell O'Donovan made the point that Smith would have mentioned Isaac's infidelity in his divorce decree if that had been a factor in the Jameses' divorce. See Connell O'Donovan, comment 19, February 20, 2013, 4:25 p.m., on Quincy D. Newell, "Black History Month at the JI: Talking about Jane (Newell)," *Juvenile Instructor* (blog), February 19, 2013, http://juvenileinstructor.org/black-history-month-at-the-ji-talking-about-jane-newell. I have not been able to verify the existence of the woman to whom Jane referred, let alone establish her identity.

10. On fortune-telling in the nineteenth-century United States, see Jamie L. Pietruska, *Looking Forward: Prediction and Uncertainty in Modern America* (Chicago: University of Chicago Press, 2017), 199–200, 204, 208. On the history of legislation against interracial marriage, see Nancy F. Cott, *Public Vows: A History of Marriage and the Nation* (Cambridge, MA: Harvard University Press, 2000), 44–45. On Brigham Young's opposition to interracial marriage, see Reeve, *Religion of a Different Color*, 158. On interracial marriage in Utah, see Patrick Q. Mason, "The Prohibition of Interracial Marriage in Utah, 1888–1963," *Utah Historical Quarterly* 76, no. 2 (Spring 2008): 108–31.

11. "A Growing and Dangerous Class," *New York Times*, February 4, 1867, quoted in Pietruska, *Looking Forward*, 212; Bolton, "Fortune-Telling in America To-Day," 299.

12. The quotation detailing fortune-tellers' methods comes from Pietruska, *Looking Forward*, 205–6. For an example of Young discussing the "wicked" fortune teller, see Brigham Young, "The Priesthood and Satan—the Constitution and Government of the United States— Rights and Policy of the Latter-Day Saints: A Discourse by President Brigham Young, Delivered in the Tabernacle, Great Salt Lake City, Feb. 18, 1855," in *Journal of Discourses by Brigham Young, President of the Church of Jesus Christ of Latter-Day Saints, His Two Counsellors, the Twelve Apostles, and Others*, ed. G. D. Watt, vol. 2 (Liverpool, England: F. D. Richards, 1855), 180, http://contentdm.lib.byu.edu/cdm/ref/collection/JournalOfDiscourses3/ id/9600. On fortune-telling and other forms of folk magic in early Mormonism, see D. Michael Quinn, *Early Mormonism and the Magic World View*, revised and enlarged ed. (Salt Lake City: Signature Books, 1998). On Lucy Stanton McCary, see Hudson, *Real Native Genius*, 168.

13. On the decline and subsequent reorganization of Relief Societies, see Laurel Thatcher Ulrich, *A House Full of Females: Plural Marriage and Women's Rights in Early Mormonism, 1835–1870* (New York: Knopf, 2017), 361–63. Records of Jane's Relief Society membership appear in a transcription of meeting minutes for a March 24, 1870, meeting in the First Ward, Park Stake, "First Ward Relief Society History [ca. 1941]" LR 2871 28, LDS Church History Library.

14. "Non-Population Census Schedules for Utah Territory and Vermont, 1870: Mortality" (US National Archives and Records Administration, 1870), 5, line 5, US Federal Census Mortality Schedules, 1850–1885 [database online]; Archive Collection: M1807; Archive Roll Number: 1; Census Year: 1870, Ancestry.com. I thank Amy Tanner Thiriot for sharing this source with me. On Corinne, see Brigham D. Madsen, *Corinne: The Gentile Capital of Utah* (Salt Lake City: Utah State Historical Society, 1980), 5–11, 71, 244–45. The visitor's description of Corinne is a quotation from M. LeBaron de Hübner, *A Ramble Round the World, 1871* (New York, 1875), 118, quoted in Madsen, 71. According to Madsen, the 1870 Census counted eighteen African Americans in Corinne. Though small in absolute terms, the black community in Corinne was larger, proportionally, than black populations elsewhere in Utah. Madsen wrote that "Most [African Americans in Corinne] worked as employees of the various hotels and saloons in the town" (245). No African American man with the last name "Robinson" is listed in the 1870 census of Corinne. The census record for Mary Ann is found in George B. Moulton, "United States Federal Census, Corinne City, Box Elder County, Utah Territory" (US National Archives and Records Administration, 1870), 11, household 102, microfilm 553,109, Family History Library, Salt Lake City. The suggestion that Mary Ann's surname concealed illicit sexual activity is based on Thiriot, "Mrs. Nellie Kidd, Courtesan," *Keepapitchinin, the Mormon History Blog* (blog), January 6, 2015, http://www.keepapitchinin.org/2015/01/06/mrs-nellie-kidd-courtesan. Death records for Mary Ann and Henry are in "Utah, Salt Lake County Death Records, 1849–1949" (Salt Lake City, Salt Lake, Utah, Management and Archives, n.d.), entries 4656 and 4660, microfilm 4,139,616, Family History Library, Salt Lake City. Records of financial assistance Jane received from the Relief Society are in "Eighth (Salt Lake City) Ward Relief Society Minute Book 'A,' 1867–1877," in "Eighth Ward Relief Society Minutes and Records (1867–1969)."

15. Hunter, *To 'Joy My Freedom*, 195.

16. Silas's death record is in "Utah, Salt Lake County Death Records, 1849–1949," entry 5143. See Hunter, *To 'Joy My Freedom*, 187–218 for an analysis of the racialization of tuberculosis in Atlanta and the postbellum South more broadly. The quotations in this paragraph are from Hunter, 194 and 195.

17. Wolfinger, "A Test of Faith," 140; John R. Winder, "Tax Assessment Rolls" (Salt Lake City [Utah] Assessor, 1875), image 28, series 4922, box 4, folder 1, Utah State Archives; John R. Winder, "Tax Assessment Rolls" (Salt Lake City [Utah] Assessor, 1876), image 36, series 4922, box 4, folder 3, Utah State Archives.

18. Nettie's and Miriam's death records are in "Utah, Salt Lake County Death Records, 1849– 1949," entries 6349 and 6632. For records of Jane's donations, see Eighth (Salt Lake City) Ward Relief Society Minute Book "A," 1867–1877, in "Eighth Ward Relief Society Minutes and Records (1867–1969)," entries for November 20, 1875 (pumpkins) and April 20, 1876

(soap); First Ward, Park Stake, "First Ward Relief Society History [ca. 1941]," transcript of minutes for May 26, 1870 (rags).

19. For evidence of Sylvester and Mary Ann's marriage, see "Utah, Salt Lake County Death Records, 1849–1949," entry 2596. On the legislature's disinclination to regulate marriage, see Pearson and Madsen, "Innovation and Accommodation," 43. For examples of Jane's transition to the "Perkins" surname, see "Eighth Ward Relief Society Minutes and Records (1867–1969)," Minute Book "A," 1867–1877. Although there were two women named Jane James in the Eighth Ward, donors were identified both by their name and by the block on which they lived. Jane Elizabeth Manning James lived on the "first block" of the Eighth Ward; the other Jane James lived on the third block.

20. Brown, "'Temple Pro Tempore,'" 20.

21. The biblical passage in which Latter-day Saints found evidence for the practice of baptisms for the dead is 1 Corinthians 5:29. On the LDS practice, see H. David Burton, "Baptism for the Dead: LDS Practice," Encyclopedia of Mormonism (New York: Macmillan, 1992), 95–96.

22. The record of the baptisms Jane and others did is Church of Jesus Christ of Latter-day Saints, Endowment House, "Colored Brethren and Sisters, Endowment House, Salt Lake City, Utah, Sept. 3, 1875" (Genealogical Society of Utah, 1961), image 23, microfilm 255498, Family History Library, Salt Lake City. For the weather conditions that day, see "Weather Report," Salt Lake Herald, September 4, 1875. For the physical characteristics of the Endowment House, see Brown, "'Temple Pro Tempore,'" 32, 33, 34, 37, 46.

23. Brown, "'Temple Pro Tempore,'" 47.

24. The 1820, 1830, and 1840 censuses of Wilton, CT, list the family of Morris Brown, a free African American man. Based on the census-taker's age estimates, Brown was born between 1775 and 1785. See Phinehas Miller, "United States Federal Census, Town of Wilton, Fairfield County, Connecticut" (US National Archives and Records Administration, 1820), 294, microfilm 281,234, Family History Library, Salt Lake City; Isaacs, "United States Federal Census, Town of Wilton, Fairfield County, Connecticut," 214; Dikeman, "United States Federal Census, Town of Wilton, Fairfield County, Connecticut," 170. Genealogical sources also reveal the existence of a woman named Susan Brown who married a free African American man named George Hicks. Susan Brown Hicks died in 1835 at the age of 21. See "Susan A Brown Hicks (Unknown-1835)," FindaGrave, https://www.findagrave.com/memorial/129868840. George Hicks appears to have remarried; in the 1840 census he appears in Stamford, living with a free African American woman in his age bracket, but without children. See James H. Minor, "United States Federal Census, Town of Stamford, Fairfield County, Connecticut" (US National Archives and Records Administration, 1840), 70, microfilm 3,018, Family History Library, Salt Lake City. Tonya Reiter suggests that the Susan Brown for whom Jane was baptized was married to Morris Brown, which is also a possibility. Tonya Reiter, "Black Saviors on Mount Zion: Proxy Baptisms and Latter-Day Saints of African Descent," Journal of Mormon History 43, no. 4 (2017): 108.

25. Brown, "'Temple Pro Tempore,'" 48; Leroy W. Hooten Jr., "Salt Lake City Old Water Conveyance Systems," October 8, 2009, http://www.slcdocs.com/utilities/NewsEvents/news2007/news6272007.htm.

26. Eighth (Salt Lake City) Ward Relief Society Minute Book "A," 1876–1877, in "Eighth Ward Relief Society Minutes and Records (1867–1969)," entry for April 20, 1876.

27. Eighth (Salt Lake City) Ward Relief Society Minute Book "A," 1867 to 1877, "Eighth Ward Relief Society Minutes and Records (1867–1969)," entries for July 6, 1876, and June 1, 1871.

28. Philes's death date is given in Church of Jesus Christ of Latter-day Saints, Logan Temple, "Baptisms for the Dead, 1884–1943," 320, entry 11463. Isaac Manning applied to receive Cato Treadwell's Revolutionary War pension in 1884 and gave his mother's death date as May 15, 1861. It may be that Jane only became aware of her mother's death fifteen years later, but Isaac may also have been mistaken about the date of his mother's death. He claimed in his application that all five of his sisters, including Jane, were dead—and Jane was very much alive at the time. Max Mueller uses census records and Jane's statements to argue that Jane could read and write, but that old age and infirmity later rendered her illiterate.

See Mueller, *Race and the Making of the Mormon People*, 137–38. Elizabeth McHenry's work on antebellum African American writers and readers suggests that the question is actually far more complicated than whether Jane was or was not "literate": reading and writing were less often the solitary endeavors that we might imagine, and far more often community activities that drew in a range of people whose individual abilities to read and/or write might vary widely. See Elizabeth McHenry, "Rereading Literary Legacy: New Considerations of the 19th-Century African-American Reader and Writer," *Callaloo* 22, no. 2 (Spring 1999): 477–82. I thank my colleague Erin Forbes for pointing me to this source. Isaac's signature is found in "In the Matter of the Estate of Jane Elizabeth James, Deceased, No. 5870" (District Court, Probate Division, In and For Salt Lake County, State of Utah).

29. Jane's and Frank's donations are recorded in Minutes, Teachers Meeting, October 14, 1874, in Eighth Ward, Liberty Stake, "Eighth Ward General Minutes" (Salt Lake City), LR 2525 11, LDS Church History Library. The St. George Temple was dedicated on April 6, 1877. Kirk M. Curtis, "History of the St. George Temple" (Brigham Young University, 1964), 92, https://scholarsarchive.byu.edu/cgi/viewcontent.cgi?referer=https://www.google.com/&httpsredir=1&article=5629&context=etd; Jane James spoke in the Eighth Ward Relief Society meeting on April 5, 1877. Eighth (Salt Lake City) Ward Relief Society Minute Book "A," 1867–1877, minutes for April 5, 1877, in "Eighth Ward Relief Society Minutes and Records (1867–1969)." For reporting on the dedication of the St. George temple, see, for example, James G. Bleak, "General Conference at St. George," *The Deseret News*, April 11, 1877; "The Conference," *Salt Lake Herald*, April 7, 1877; "Miscellaneous: The St. George Conference in Full Blast," *Salt Lake Daily Tribune*, April 7, 1877. Brigham Young shut the Endowment House in 1876, telling all Latter-day Saints to do temple work in the St. George Temple once it was completed. After Young's death, his successor John Taylor reopened the Salt Lake Endowment House. It remained open until 1889. Devery S. Anderson, ed., *The Development of LDS Temple Worship, 1846–2000: A Documentary History*, Smith-Pettit Foundation Book (Salt Lake City: Signature Books, 2011), xxx.

30. Jonathan Stapley, *The Power of Godliness: Mormon Liturgy and Cosmology* (New York: Oxford University Press, 2018), 17; Flake, "The Development of Early Latter-Day Saint Marriage Rites, 1831–53," 79, 88–89, 94, 98–99, 101–2.

31. It is important to note that church leaders and members were drawing on racial categorizations that were linked to Biblical lineages. Phenotype—physical appearance, including dark skin—was not the only determinant: many dark-skinned people in Mormon history faced no restrictions with regard to the priesthood or temple access. To use that fact as an argument that the LDS policy restricting the access of people of African descent was not racist, however, is misguided. For discussion and analysis of church leaders working to channel priesthood power away from people of African descent, see Reeve, *Religion of a Different Color*, 106–70, 188–214; Lester E. Bush, "Mormonism's Negro Doctrine: An Historical Overview," *Dialogue: A Journal of Mormon Thought* 8, no. 1 (1973): 11–68.

32. Turner, *Brigham Young: Pioneer Prophet*, 406–7.

Chapter 7

1. Isaac James's location is given in J. M. Sparrow, "United States Federal Census, Portland, Multnomah County, Oregon, Enumeration District 139" (US National Archives and Records Administration, 1880), microfilm 005162038, Family History Library, Salt Lake City; Frank Perkins appears in S. Suckley, "United States Federal Census, Salt Lake City 8th and 9th Wards, Salt Lake County, Utah, Enumeration District 42" (US National Archives and Records Administration, 1880), microfilm 1,255,337, Family History Library, Salt Lake City; William N. McCurdy, "United States Federal Census, Salt Lake City 13th Ward, Salt Lake County, Utah" (US National Archives and Records Administration, 1880), microfilm 1,255,337, Family History Library, Salt Lake City. Perkins lived with the family of Washington Anderson, whose address is corroborated in Marc W. Anderson, "Memories of My Grandparents" (FamilySearch.org), https://www.familysearch.org/photos/artifacts/11773712?p=4316647&returnLabel=Washington%20Franklin%20Anderson%20

(K27T-WZ1)&returnUrl=https%3A%2F%2Fwww.familysearch.org%2Ftree%2Fperson%2F memories%2FK27T-WZ1.

2. In the 1870 census, both Ellen and Malvina had the last name "James." By the 1880 census, Ellen was gone; Malvina was listed as "Robinson." Robinson was Mary Ann's "married" name and may have been given to Malvina as well to obscure her status as an illegitimate child. By 1880, Mary Ann had died, thus further obscuring Malvina's parentage. In the 1880 census, Jessie was given the last name "James," clearly connecting her to Jane but again obscuring her parentage. D. R. Firman, "United States Federal Census, 8th Ward Salt Lake City, County of Salt Lake, Territory of Utah" (US National Archives and Records Administration, 1870), microfilm 553,110, Family History Library, Salt Lake City; Suckley, "USFC, Salt Lake City 8th and 9th Wards, 1880."

3. Jane James to John Taylor, Salt Lake City, December 27, 1884, transcribed in Wolfinger, "A Test of Faith," 148.

4. The quotation from the office journal comes from Lester E. Bush, "Blacks and the Priesthood, Textual Excerpts from the George Albert Smith Papers and the Adam S. Bennion Papers, 1859–1954" (Provo), Lester E. Bush Papers, MS 685, box 10, folder 3, L. Tom Perry Special Collections, Harold B. Lee Library, Brigham Young University, quoting Gardo House Office Journal for Tuesday, March 20, 1883. Robert W. Sloan, *Utah Gazetteer and Directory of Logan, Ogden, Provo and Salt Lake Cities, for 1884* (Salt Lake City: Herald Printing and Publishing Company, 1884), 480–81, lists eleven people with the last name of Ellis in 1884. The tax rolls for 1883 also list five people with the last name of Ellis. We would expect the tax rolls to have a smaller number of Ellises, because they list only those with sufficient resources to be required to pay taxes.

5. Angus M. Cannon, Salt Lake City, to Jane E. James, Salt Lake City, June 16, 1888, transcribed in Wolfinger, "A Test of Faith," 148–49.

6. Details about the trip between Salt Lake and Logan come from George A. Crofutt, *Crofutt's Overland Tours* (Chicago: H. J. Smith and Co., 1889), 134–35, 160, 162–63. Details about Logan's population come from Edward N. Rowland, "United States Federal Census, Logan City Precinct, Cache County, Utah, Enumeration District 8" (US National Archives and Records Administration, 1880), microfilm 005162567, Family History Library, Salt Lake City.

7. Melvin A. Larkin, "The History of the L.D.S. Temple in Logan, Utah" (Utah State Agricultural College, 1954), 120; Church of Jesus Christ of Latter-day Saints, Logan Temple, "Baptisms for the Dead, 1884–1943," 320.

8. For Sylvester's excommunication, see Newell, "James, Jane E. M.—Miscellaneous Material." On Mormons' ecclesiastical courts, see Firmage and Mangrum, *Zion in the Courts*, 261–370. Taylor's remarks came in a speech at Manti, UT, May 19, 1883, reprinted as John Taylor, "Duties of the Latter-Day Saints—How Children Should Be Trained—An Academy for Sanpete—The Kind of Teachers to Select—Education Advocated—Intemperance Condemned—Sin to Be Exposed—Unworthy Men Not to Be Sustained in Office—Example of a Darkened Mind—Providence Over the Saints," in *Journal of Discourses by President John Taylor, His Counsellors, the Twelve Apostles, and Others*, vol. 24 (Liverpool, England: John Henry Smith, 1884), 171, http://jod.mrm.org/24/166.

9. For Ellen's and Malvina's presence in Jane's home, see Firman, "USFC, Salt Lake City 8th Ward, 1870." On the identity of "Mrs. Nellie Kidd," see Thiriot, "Mrs. Nellie Kidd, Courtesan." For the San Francisco conviction of Nellie Kidd, see "Untitled ('In the City Criminal Court to-Day')," *Daily Evening Bulletin*, June 28, 1879, Second edition.

10. On Jane's property transfers, see Wolfinger, "A Test of Faith," 140, 165n57. That Malvina went to California with Ellen is suggested by a list of letters waiting in the Sacramento Post Office in 1890 that names both Nellie Kidd and "Miss Melvina Jones," whom I believe to be Malvina James. "List of Letters," *Sacramento Daily Record-Union*, January 27, 1890.

11. Eighth Ward, Liberty Stake, "Eighth Ward General Minutes."

12. E. E. Frost, Acting Secretary, August 7, 1890, in "Eighth Ward Relief Society Minutes and Records (1867–1969)," 5: 99; Smith, *James v. James*.

13. "Old Folks' Day 1891," *Deseret Evening News*, June 19, 1891.

14. "Utah, Salt Lake County Death Records, 1849–1949," entry 1633; "Death of a Colored Pioneer," *Deseret Evening News*, November 20, 1891.

15. The report that it "was an ideal Christmas" comes from "Christmas Carols," *Salt Lake Herald*, December 26, 1891. For other stories of Christmas, see, for example, A. H. Gibson, "Christmas on Rocky Ridge," *Deseret Evening News*, December 24, 1891; "Peace on Earth," *Deseret Evening News*, December 24, 1891. On the changing meaning of Christmas in the United States, see especially Leigh Eric Schmidt, *Consumer Rites: The Buying & Selling of American Holidays* (Princeton, NJ: Princeton University Press, 1995), 148–91.

16. Jesse is listed as a porter in a hotel in the 1880 census. See Enos Anderson, "United States Federal Census, Salt Lake City 14th Ward, Salt Lake County, Utah, Enumeration District 45" (US National Archives and Records Administration, 1880), microfilm 1,255,337, Family History Library, Salt Lake City. The quotation about the hotels' "spreads" is from "Christmas Carols." Details on the Relief Society Christmas baskets are in "Eighth Ward Relief Society Minutes and Records (1867–1969)," 4: 14, 24–25, 28, 29, 30.

17. *Utah Gazetteer, 1892–93* (Salt Lake City: Stenhouse and Co., 1892), 489; E[lizabeth] J[efford] D[rake] Roundy, "Communicated," *Deseret Evening News*, April 17, 1911.

18. Roger D. Launius, *Invisible Saints: A History of Black Americans in the Reorganized Church* (Independence, MO: Herald Pub. House, 1988), 127; Eighth Ward, Liberty Stake, "Eighth Ward General Minutes."

19. Smith, "1889 Patriarchal Blessing." Hereafter, citations of this source will refer to the version reprinted in the Appendix.

20. H. Smith, Patriarchal Blessing (1844), Appendix, 140; J. Smith, Patriarchal Blessing (1889), Appendix, 141.

21. The letters quoted in this paragraph are: Jane E. James to Apostle Joseph F. Smith, Salt Lake City, 7 February 1890; Jane E. James to President John Taylor, Salt Lake City, 27 December 1884; and Zina D. H. Young to Apostle Joseph F. Smith, Salt Lake City, 15 January 1894, all reprinted in Wolfinger, "A Test of Faith," 149, 148, and 150, respectively. Jane's lament is found in James, "Autobiography," Appendix, 147.

22. Irving, "The Law of Adoption," 293–94; Jonathan A. Stapley, "Adoptive Sealing Ritual in Mormonism," *Journal of Mormon History* 37, no. 3 (Summer 2011): 59–60.

23. Irving, "The Law of Adoption," 310.

24. Jane's statement that Joseph Smith "used to be just like I was his child" is from James in Gates, ed. "Joseph Smith, the Prophet," Appendix, 150; see also James, "Autobiography," Appendix, 145–46. For Jane's request to have her brother and her husband sealed to Joseph Smith as children, see Zina D. H. Young to Apostle Joseph F. Smith, Salt Lake City, 15 January 1894, reprinted in Wolfinger, "A Test of Faith," 150. For Jane's request to be sealed to Lewis, see Jane E. James to Apostle Joseph F. Smith, Salt Lake City, 7 February 1890, reprinted in Wolfinger, 149. For more information on Lewis, see Connell O'Donovan, "The Mormon Priesthood Ban and Elder Q. Walker Lewis: 'An Example for His More Whiter Brethren to Follow,'" *John Whitmer Historical Association Journal* 26 (2006): 48–100; Reeve, *Religion of a Different Color*, 106–11.

25. *D&C*, 132: 16–17.

26. The official record of this ceremony is Adoption Record, Book A, 26, LDS Church History Library. This source is restricted and therefore not available to most researchers. I have examined photographs of this document. At least three other sources provide transcriptions of this record: David J. Buerger, "Confidential Research Files, 1950–1974" (Salt Lake City), folder 5, 4, David J. Buerger Papers, Special Collections and Archives, Marriott Library, University of Utah; Anderson, *Development of LDS Temple Worship*, 97–98; and Connell, "Chronology Pertaining to Blacks and the LDS Church | Jane M. James Sealed as Eternal Servant to Joseph Smith | Event View," http://www.xtimeline.com/evt/view. aspx?id=66094. Unfortunately, each of these transcriptions differs from the original and from the others. While most variations are cosmetic, encompassing details like punctuation and spelling, one is crucial: none of the available transcriptions names Zina D. H. Young as the proxy for Jane James. The original document clearly designates Young as Jane's proxy. "Chronology Pertaining to Blacks" names Bathsheba W. Smith as Jane's proxy. Anderson

claims that "in 1895, Church leaders revoked Manning's sealing"; that the sealing "was restored in 1902"; and that the 1902 ceremony was performed "with Bathsheba Smith acting as proxy" for Jane. Anderson, *Development of LDS Temple Worship*, 97n51. Anderson cites no source to support these claims and has since withdrawn them. Devery Anderson, personal communication with the author, March 6, 2017. Oddly, this ceremony was performed just about a month and a half after President Wilford Woodruff announced that he had received a revelation on adoption, clarifying the ritual. After Woodruff's revelation, Saints were not to be adopted to people other than their parents. Instead, Woodruff proclaimed at the April general conference that year, "We want the Latter-day Saints from this time to trace their genealogies as far as they can, and to be sealed to their fathers and mothers. Have children sealed to their parents, and run their chain through as far as you can get it." To be in compliance with Woodruff's revelation, Jane should have been sealed to her parents—but instead she was attached to Joseph Smith as a servant. Quotation in Irving, "The Law of Adoption," 312. Jonathan Stapley argues that "it is no coincidence that Manning's extraordinary sealing occurred mere weeks after Woodruff's" announcement. Stapley places Jane's sealing ceremony in the context of an understanding of sealing as creating the "family of God" and Brigham Young's abiding belief that "black Mormon women and men were not to be integrated into the material family of God." Stapley, *The Power of Godliness*, 21–22.

27. According to the minutes of a 1902 meeting of the Council of the Twelve Apostles, "President Woodruff, Cannon, and Smith . . . decided that she might be adopted into the family of Joseph Smith as a servant, which was done." Minutes of a meeting of the Council of the Twelve Apostles, 2 January 1902, as given in "Excerpts from the Weekly Council Meetings of the Quorum of Twelve Apostles, Dealing with the Rights of Negroes in the Church, 1849–1940," George Albert Smith Papers, University of Utah, reprinted in Wolfinger, "A Test of Faith," 151. This, then, was still adoption, but of a different sort. The term "adoption" was the one Latter-day Saints used in official records of sealings of children to nonbiological parents, but, Stapley wrote, "In common parlance and in official discourse [in Utah] . . . Church leaders and lay members tended to refer to all child-to-parent sealings as adoptions, regardless of biology." Stapley, "Adoptive Sealing Ritual in Mormonism," 64. These terminological slippages suggested, again, that the church leadership thought of this ritual as a sealing. For the 1902 meeting, see "Minutes of a Meeting of the Council of the Twelve Apostles, 2 January 1902," reprinted in Wolfinger, "A Test of Faith," 151. See also George Q. Cannon, *The Journals of George Q. Cannon, 1849–1901*, ebook (Salt Lake City: Church Historian's Press, 2018), entry for August 22, 1895, which deals with Jane's request for endowments, rather than sealings. I am grateful to Ardis E. Parshall for alerting me to this source and Matthew J. Grow for his help with it.

28. On the Retrenchment Society, see Carol Cornwall Madsen, "Retrenchment Association," *Encyclopedia of Mormonism* (New York: Macmillan, 1992), 1223–25. For Jane's request, see Lydia D. Alder, "Ladies' Semi-Monthly Meeting," *Woman's Exponent*, June 1, 1894. The text of this patriarchal blessing is reprinted in full in the Appendix, 140.

29. Jesse's death record is in "Utah, Salt Lake County Death Records, 1849–1949," entry 3911. Jesse's employment was listed in Anderson, "USFC, Salt Lake City 14th Ward, 1880." Jane's remarks are reported in "Eighth Ward Relief Society Minutes and Records (1867–1969)," 5: 151, meeting minutes for November 2, 1893. The story about Jane recognizing Joseph Smith from her dream is in James in Gates, ed., "Joseph Smith, the Prophet," Appendix, 150.

30. Jane's remarks are recorded in Lydia D. Alder, "Ladies' Semi-Monthly Meeting," *Woman's Exponent*, December 1, 1893. Jesse's rebaptism is documented in Eighth Ward, Liberty Stake, "Eighth Ward General Minutes."

31. "Utah, Salt Lake County Death Records, 1849–1949," entry 3911.

Chapter 8

1. "Salt Lake Temple Records, Baptisms for the Dead, Book D, 1894–1895," Family History Library, Salt Lake City.
2. "Eighth Ward Relief Society Minutes and Records (1867–1969)," 5: 138.

3. Jane's remarks in Relief Society meetings come from "Eighth Ward Relief Society Minutes and Records (1867–1969)," 5: 138, 151. Jane's Retrenchment Society meeting comments were reported in Lydia D. Alder, "Ladies' Semi-Monthly [sic] Meeting," *Woman's Exponent*, December 15, 1896. The Church leaders' statement comes from Meeting Minutes of the First Presidency and Twelve, *Journal History*, February 18, 1903, 4, quoted in Stapley and Wright, "Female Ritual Healing," 51.

4. "Old Folks' Day."

5. Vilate's death was reported in "Died," *Deseret Evening News*, March 4, 1897; her sick leave was noted in Missionary Society Methodist Episcopal Church, *Seventy-Fifth Annual Report of the Missionary Society of the Methodist Episcopal Church for the Year 1893* (New York, 1894), 22. Jane's Retrenchment Society meeting statement was reported in Alder, "Ladies' Semi-Monthly Meeting," December 1, 1893.

6. "Slavery in Utah," *Broad Ax*, March 25, 1899.

7. "A Pioneer Meeting," *Deseret Evening News*, July 26, 1897.

8. The literature on collective memory is vast. The foundational work is Maurice Halbwachs, *On Collective Memory*, The Heritage of Sociology (Chicago: University of Chicago Press, 1992). On Latter-day Saints' use of collective memory, see Kathleen Flake, "Re-Placing Memory: Latter-Day Saint Use of Historical Monuments and Narrative in the Early Twentieth Century," *Religion and American Culture: A Journal of Interpretation* 13, no. 1 (Winter 2003): 69–109.

9. All three of Jane's accounts may be found in the Appendix, 142–52. Barney's account corrected "First Negroes to Join Mormon Church," *Salt Lake Herald*, October 2, 1899.

10. Jane's remark about Joseph Smith's appearance is from James in Gates, ed., "Joseph Smith, the Prophet," Appendix, 151. The quotation stating that Smith "was a handsome man" is from Gates, "Joseph Smith, the Prophet," 548. See also the other interviews published in Gates, 548–58; and "Joseph Smith, the Prophet," 537–48. On the struggle over Mormons' place in the United States body politic, in which Latter-day Saints' gender performance and racial identity figured, see Gordon, *The Mormon Question*; Kathleen Flake, *The Politics of American Religious Identity: The Seating of Senator Reed Smoot, Mormon Apostle* (Chapel Hill: University of North Carolina Press, 2004); Reeve, *Religion of a Different Color*; and W. Paul Reeve, "All 'Mormon Elder-Berry's' Children: Race, Whiteness, and the Attack on Mormon 'Anglo-Saxon Triumphalism,'" in *Directions for Mormon Studies in the Twenty-First Century*, ed. Patrick Q. Mason (Salt Lake City: University of Utah Press, 2016), 152–75. Bartholow's report comes from United States Senate, *Statistical Report on the Sickness and Morality in the Army of the United States, compiled from the Records of the Surgeon General's Office; Embracing a Period of Five Years from January 1, 1855, to January, 1860*, Senate Executive Document 52, 36th Congress, 1st Session, 301–302, quoted in Reeve, *Religion of a Different Color*, 15, the work from which I also borrow the phrase "struggle for whiteness."

11. On the LDS desire to emulate Joseph Smith, see Grant Underwood, "The Prophetic Legacy in Islam and Mormonism: Some Comparative Observations," in *New Perspectives in Mormon Studies: Creating and Crossing Boundaries* (Norman: University of Oklahoma Press, 2013), 109–13. For examples of Jane speaking about her memories of Joseph Smith, see Zina Hyde, "Ladies' Semi-Monthly Meeting," *Woman's Exponent*, February 1, 1896, 110; A. T. Hyde, "Ladies Semi-Monthly Meeting," *Woman's Exponent*, September 1, 1896; Hannah M. Wright, "Ladies Semi-Monthly Meeting," *Woman's Exponent*, November 1, 1898, 62; and James in Gates, ed., "Joseph Smith, the Prophet," Appendix, 150–52. For Jane's insistence that Joseph Smith had offered to adopt her, see Jane E. James to President John Taylor, Salt Lake City, 27 December 1884; Jane E. James to Apostle Joseph F. Smith, Salt Lake City, 7 February 1890; Zina D. H. Young to Apostle Joseph F. Smith, Salt Lake City, 15 January 1894, all reprinted in Wolfinger, "A Test of Faith," 148, 149, 150. On the temple ritual of adoption, see Irving, "The Law of Adoption."

12. Bush, "Mormonism's Negro Doctrine," 31–34. Joseph F. Smith's conclusion was at odds with his own earlier statements and the fact that Abel acted as a priesthood holder to the end of his life, including participating in priesthood quorums in Utah and serving multiple missions for the church. See Reeve, *Religion of a Different Color*, 195–210.

13. Jane's request for prayer for her eyesight is in "Eighth Ward Relief Society Minutes and Records (1867–1969)," 5: 151. Jane's description of herself as "nearly blind" is in James, "Autobiography," Appendix, 148. Information about Jane's appearance and housekeeping is in Barney, "Jane Manning James," Appendix, 143; Henrietta Bankhead, paraphrased in Carter, *The Story of the Negro Pioneer*, 9; and Lawrence, Henrietta Leggroan Bankhead interview, 27. The quotation about Jane's household furnishings is also from this interview.

14. The quotation from Roundy's biographer, and much of the biographical information in this paragraph, is from Andrew Jenson, "Roundy, Elizabeth Jefford Drake," *Latter-Day Saint Biographical Encyclopedia* (Salt Lake City: Andrew Jenson History Company, 1901), 809–11, quotation on 810. Roundy's poem, "The Prophet Joseph Smith" [1897] is found in "Elizabeth J. Drake Roundy Papers, 1860–1913" (Salt Lake City), folder 1, item 12, LDS Church History Library. The letter from one of Joseph Smith's plural wives is Lucy Walker Kimball Smith to Sister Roundy, Salt Lake City, January 12, 1909, folder 1, item 14, folio 1v–2r. That Jane's autobiography was "written from her verbal statement" is in James, "Autobiography," Appendix, 144. The account Roundy gathered from Isaac Manning was published with his obituary. See Roundy, "Communicated."

15. The quotation about Jane making cushions comes from "Funeral of Isaac Manning," *Deseret Evening News*, April 17, 1911. The quotation about "seeing two Negroes sitting on the stand" is from Anna Shipp, quoted in Carter, *The Story of the Negro Pioneer*, 9. Jane's obituary was printed as "Death of Jane Manning James: Servant in Family of Prophet Joseph Smith at Nauvoo Passes Away Today," *Deseret Evening News*, April 16, 1908. For earlier references to Jane as "Aunt" Jane, see "Record Train of Old Folks," *Salt Lake Herald*, June 23, 1905; James in Gates, ed., "Joseph Smith, the Prophet," Appendix, 150.

16. The editorial on Zina Young's funeral was "Aunt Zina D. H Young," *Young Woman's Journal* 12, no. 10 (October 1901): 472–73; the poetic tribute to Zina Young was Rhoda B. Nash, "Aunt Zina," *Young Woman's Journal* 12, no. 10 (October 1901): 439; the speaker at Zina Young's funeral was Apostle Lund, quoted in "Aunt Zina D. H Young," 473. The profile of Bathsheba Smith was Lucy Woodruff Smith, "Past Three Score Years and Ten," *Young Woman's Journal* 12, no. 10 (October 1901): 440. On the meaning and use of the term "mother in Israel," see Sydney Smith Reynolds, "Mother in Israel," *Encyclopedia of Mormonism* (New York: Macmillan, 1992), 963. For Jane's patriarchal blessing promising her she would be known as a "mother in Israel," see J. Smith, Patriarchal Blessing (1889), Appendix, 141.

17. This discussion of the implications of the generally honorific term "aunt" are drawn from Quincy D. Newell, "Black Jane/Aunt Jane: Negotiating Race and Gender in the Nineteenth-Century LDS Church" (American Society of Church History Winter Meeting, San Diego, CA, 2010).

18. Patricia J. Sotirin and Laura L. Ellingson, *Where the Aunts Are: Family, Feminism, and Kinship in Popular Culture* (Waco, TX: Baylor University Press, 2013), 39; Stone, *African American Connecticut*, 41; "Old Youngsters in a Merry Whirl," *Salt Lake Herald*, June 27, 1906.

19. That Josephine checked on Jane is in Henrietta Bankhead, paraphrased in Carter, *The Story of the Negro Pioneer*, 9. Historian Lisa Dillon has found that in 1900 "only a quarter of elderly [i.e., over age 65] American widows who had seen 6 children survive [to adulthood] lived in a household without any children present." Instead, Jane's residence with Isaac put her in a group of five to seven percent of elderly American widows who lived neither with children nor with nonrelatives as boarders or lodgers, but "in other situations, such as with a sibling or employer." Lisa Dillon, *The Shady Side of Fifty: Age and Old Age in Late Victorian Canada and the United States* (Montreal: McGill-Queen's University Press, 2008), 162, 166–67, 179.

20. Mrs. Jane Elizabeth James, Salt Lake City, to President Joseph F. Smith, August 31, 1903, reprinted in Wolfinger, "A Test of Faith," 151.

21. Jane's postscript is in Jane E. James, Salt Lake City, to Apostle Joseph F. Smith, 7 February 1890, reprinted in Wolfinger, 149. Jane's conversation with Barney is recounted in Barney, "Jane Manning James," Appendix, 142–43. My interpretation of Jane's comment that she was "white with the exception of the color of [her] skin" is inspired by Darlene Clark Hine's argument that black women purchased cosmetic products from Madame C. J. Walker in the

early twentieth century because "Black women desired what whiteness represented. They did not wish to be white, for to do so meant abandoning the culture and institutions they had created to ensure the survival and progress of their people." Darlene Clark Hine, "'In the Kingdom of Culture': Black Women and the Intersection of Race, Gender, and Class," in *Lure and Loathing: Essays on Race, Identity, and the Ambivalence of Assimilation*, ed. Gerald Early (New York: Penguin Books, 1994), 347.

22. The remarks made about Jane in Relief Society are in "Eighth Ward Relief Society Minutes and Records (1867–1969)," 10: 29. That Ellen had married is in Thiriot, "Mrs. Nellie Kidd, Courtesan." Jane's decision to transfer property to Ellen is in Wolfinger, "A Test of Faith," 166n58.

23. "Death of Jane Manning James: Servant in Family of Prophet Joseph Smith at Nauvoo Passes Away Today"; "Aged Servant Is Dead," *Salt Lake Herald*, April 17, 1908; "'Aunt Jane' Laid to Rest," *Deseret Evening News*, April 21, 1908. The letter Jane wrote to Smith is Jane E. James, Salt Lake City, to Joseph F. Smith, 7 February 1890, reprinted in Wolfinger, "A Test of Faith," 149. The "prominent church member" was Matthias F. Cowley, who recounted Smith's words in *Wilford Woodruff, Fourth President of the Church of Jesus Christ of Latter-Day Saints: History of His Life and Labors, as Recorded in His Daily Journals* (Salt Lake City: Deseret News, 1909), 587.

24. Details of Jane's funeral are in "'Aunt Jane' Laid to Rest." Information about Hunter, and details about his funeral, are in "Funeral Services for Bro. Oscar F. Hunter" (George Cannon Family Association), Official George Q. Cannon Family History Website, http://www.georgeqcannon.com/Family%20History%20Database/All%20Family%20History%20Files/Cannon%20Family/William%20W%20Hunter%20Family/Documents/Funeral%20of%20Oscar%20F%20Hunter.pdf. For more on Hunter, see Andrew Jenson, "Hunter, Oscar Fitzallen," *Latter-Day Saint Biographical Encyclopedia* (Salt Lake City: Andrew Jenson History Company, 1914). Information on Mindwell Chipman's involvement with the Relief Society is in Salt Lake Liberty Stake, "Salt Lake Liberty Stake Relief Society Minutes and Records," 1904–1973, 252, LDS Church History Library.

25. Frank Perkins's death record is at "Utah, Salt Lake County Death Records, 1849–1949," entry 14267. Details of Jane's funeral, including that many black people attended, are in "'Aunt Jane' Laid to Rest." For the stories surrounding news of Jane's funeral, see the *Deseret Evening News*, April 21, 1908, 2.

26. "Eighth Ward Relief Society Minutes and Records (1867–1969)," 9: 47; Ellen M. McLean, claim, March 1, 1910, in "In the Matter of the Estate of Jane Elizabeth James, Deceased, No. 5870."

27. James, "Autobiography," Appendix, 148; Wolfinger, "A Test of Faith," 165n58; Ellen M. McLean, receipt, November 14, 1910; Sylvester James, receipt, November 14, 1910; Isaac Manning, agreement and receipt, October 26, 1910, all in "In the Matter of the Estate of Jane Elizabeth James, Deceased, No. 5870"; "Funeral of Isaac Manning."

Epilogue

1. *D&C*, Official Declaration 2; Linda King Newell and Valeen Tippetts Avery, "Jane Manning James: Black Saint, 1847 Pioneer," *Ensign*, August 1979, 29.

2. For complete development of this argument, see Newell, *Narrating Jane*.

3. For Jane's LDS Conference Center appearances, see M. Russell Ballard, "The Trek Continues!" (Church of Jesus Christ of Latter-day Saints General Conference, Salt Lake City, October 1, 2017), http://www.lds.org/general-conference/2017/10/the-trek-continues?lang=eng; and Larry Richman, "Video: Be One Celebration of the 40th Anniversary of the LDS Revelation on the Priesthood," LDS Media Talk: Resources from LDS Church & Mormons worldwide, June 1, 2018, https://ldsmediatalk.com/2018/06/01/video-be-one-celebration-of-the-40th-anniversary-of-the-lds-revelation-on-the-priesthood. The painting that Elspeth Young explicitly identified as a depiction of Jane is *Till We Meet Again*, 2013, oil paint, 32.75" by 61", 2013. According to Young's gallery representative, that painting is displayed in the LDS Conference Center. Al R. Young, "Till We Meet Again by Elspeth Young Featured

at LDS Conference Center," Al Young Studios Newsroom, February 2, 2015, https://www.alyoung.com/content/content-0.51.0000.099.html. According to Dana Dodini, Young's original painting *And Thou Didst Hear Me* hangs in the Johannesburg, South Africa temple. Reproductions hang in multiple US temples, including the temples in Payson, UT; Hartford, CT; and Ogden, UT. Dana Dodini, "Local Artist Celebrates Pioneers through Art in Payson Temple," The Daily Universe, June 5, 2015, http://universe.byu.edu/2015/06/05/local-artist-celebrates-pioneers-through-art-in-payson-temple. Elspeth Young makes no claim that the woman depicted in this painting is Jane James, but observers frequently identify her as Jane. The artist's notes indicate that the same model was used for both *And Thou Didst Hear Me* and *Till We Meet Again*. Elspeth Young, "And Thou Didst Hear Me," Temple Fine Art Collection, https://www.alyoung.com/art/work-and_thou_didst_hear_me.html. For identification of the woman in *And Thou Didst Hear Me* as Jane, see, for example, Rebecca Lane, "8 Utah Valley Artists with Pieces in the Payson Utah Temple," UtahValley360, May 19, 2015, https://utahvalley360.com/2015/05/19/8-utah-valley-artists-pieces-payson-utah-temple; "LDS Black Saints," Amasa Mason Lyman: "A Labor of Love," http://www.amasamasonlyman.com/lds-black-saints.html; JaNae Francis, "First Look: Tour inside Ogden LDS Temple," Standard-Examiner, July 29, 2014, http://www.standard.net/Faith/2014/07/29/30-Ogden-Temple-tour. For Jane's pop culture appearances, see "Illuminating Ladies: A Coloring Book of Mormon Women | Exponent II," *Exponent II* (blog), http://www.exponentii.org/product/illuminating-ladies-a-coloring-book-of-mormon-women; and Matt Page, "Mormon Prayer Candles," *Mattpagedotcom.Com* (blog), October 29, 2017, http://mattpagedotcom.com/portfolio/items/mormon-prayer-candles/.

Appendix

1. The LDS Church will only release copies of patriarchal blessings to direct descendants of the blessing recipients. I am grateful to Louis Duffy, Jane's great-great-grandson, for sharing copies of Jane's patriarchal blessings with me and granting permission for them to be published here.
2. Text in **bold italic font** appears to have been inserted at some point after the writing of the original manuscript. Text enclosed in <triangular brackets> appears above the main line of text in the original manuscript. Damage and erasure of the original manuscript is noted in [square brackets].

BIBLIOGRAPHY

Manuscript Sources

Church of Jesus Christ of Latter-day Saints Church History Library, Salt Lake City.
  Albert Merrill family record, circa 1845–1917.
  Brigham Young Office Files, 1832–1878.
  Camp of Israel Schedules and Reports, 1845–1849.
  "City Wall around Great Salt Lake City Constructed by the Utah Pioneers around 1853 and 1854 [Map]." Compiled and copyrighted by Nicholas Morgan; map work by J. B. Ireland.
  Daniel Spencer Letter, Salt Lake City, Utah to Brother Grove, October 5, 1848.
  Emily P. Young Diary and Reminiscences, 1874 February–1899 November.
  Eighth Ward General Minutes.
  Eighth Ward Relief Society Minutes and Records (1867–1969).
  Elizabeth J. Drake Roundy Papers, 1860–1913.
  Erastus Snow Journals, 1835–1851; 1856–1857.
  First Ward Relief Society History ca. 1941.
  General Church minutes, 1839–1877.
  George A. Smith historical photograph collection.
  George Parker Dykes to Diantha, Alcina, and Cynthia Dykes, 1846 July–September.
  Isaac C. Haight Journal, 1842 June–1850 April.
  Jane Manning James autobiography, circa 1902.
  Joseph F. Smith papers, 1854–1918.
  Nauvoo (Ill.) records, 1841–1845.
  Nauvoo Stake ward census, 1842.
  Patriarchal blessings.
  Sally Randall letters, 1843–1852.
  Salt Lake Liberty Stake Relief Society minutes and records, 1904–1973.
  Utah Territorial Census, 1851.
Church of Jesus Christ of Latter-day Saints Family History Library, Salt Lake City.
  Church of Jesus Christ of Latter-day Saints, Logan Temple. "Baptisms for the Dead, 1884–1943."
  Church of Jesus Christ of Latter-day Saints, Endowment House. "Colored Brethren and Sisters, Endowment House, Salt Lake City, UT, Sept. 3, 1875."
  Church of Jesus Christ of Latter-day Saints, Salt Lake Temple. "Salt Lake Temple Records, Baptisms for the Dead, Book D, 1894–1895."
  Congregational Church, New Canaan, CT. *Church Records, 1733–1899.* 2 vols.
  Salt Lake County Management and Archives. "Utah, Salt Lake County Death Records, 1849–1949."

Trumbull, Connecticut Registrar of Vital Statistics. "Records of Births, Marriages, and Deaths, v. 1–2, 1848–1906."

US National Archives and Records Administration, 1820 United States Federal Census.

US National Archives and Records Administration, 1830 United States Federal Census.

US National Archives and Records Administration, 1840 United States Federal Census.

US National Archives and Records Administration, 1850 United States Federal Census.

US National Archives and Records Administration, 1860 United States Federal Census.

US National Archives and Records Administration, 1870 United States Federal Census.

US National Archives and Records Administration, 1880 United States Federal Census.

Utah, Territorial Militia Records, 1849–1877.

Wilton, Connecticut Registrar of Vital Statistics. "Records of Births, Marriages, and Deaths, 1776–1901."

Wilton, Connecticut Town Clerk. "Land Records, 1802–1902, Vol. 4: 1816–1826."

Wilton, Connecticut, Town Clerk. "Land Records, 1802–1902, Vol. 9: 1843–1851."

Connecticut State Library, Hartford, CT.

New Canaan, Connecticut Congregational Church Records Vol. 1A, 1806–1853.

Carl A. Kroch Library, Division of Rare and Manuscript Collections, Cornell University, Ithaca, NY.

Greenleaf, Joseph, et al. *Historical Account of the Celebration of the One Hundred and Fiftieth Anniversary of the Organization of the Congregational Church, of New Canaan, Conn., June 20, 1883.* Stamford, CT: Gillespie Brothers, 1883.

Department of Rare Books and Special Collections, Princeton University, Princeton, NJ.

Photographs Collection (GC131); Graphic Arts Collection.

L. Tom Perry Special Collections, Harold B. Lee Library, Brigham Young University, Provo.

Lester E. Bush Papers.

Library of Congress, Washington, DC

Anderson, George. "Pioneers of 1847 at the Utah Pioneer Jubilee, Salt Lake City, Utah, July 24th 1897. LC-USZ62-6377. Prints and Photographs Division.

"Baptismal Font, Mormon Temple, Salt Lake City, Utah, 1911-1912." LOT 3275. Prints and Photographs Division.

Historic American Buildings Survey. "Mansion House, Main & Water Streets, Nauvoo, Hancock County, IL." Prints and Photographs Division.

Marriott Library Special Collections and Archives, University of Utah, Salt Lake City.

Helen Zeese Papanikolas papers.

Linda King Newell Papers.

David J. Buerger Papers.

New Canaan Historical Society Library, New Canaan, CT.

Smith, Rev. Theophilus. "Pastoral Book." Typescript.

Slaves and Free Blacks in Canaan Parish and New Canaan to 1880.

Newberry Library, Chicago.

Edward E. Ayer Manuscript Collection.

Official George Q. Cannon Family History Website (www.georgeqcannon.com)

"Funeral Services for Bro. Oscar F. Hunter."

Utah State Archives, Salt Lake City.

Smith, Elias. *Jane E. James v. Isaac James.* Salt Lake County Probate Court, March 1870.

District Court, Probate Division, In and For Salt Lake County, State of Utah. "In the Matter of the Estate of Jane Elizabeth James, Deceased, No. 5870."

Salt Lake City (Utah) Assessor. Tax Assessment Rolls. 1856.

Salt Lake City (Utah) Assessor. Tax Assessment Rolls. 1858.

Salt Lake City (Utah) Assessor. Tax Assessment Rolls. 1859.

Salt Lake City (Utah) Assessor. Tax Assessment Rolls. 1860.

Salt Lake City (Utah) Assessor. Tax Assessment Rolls. 1861.

Salt Lake City (Utah) Assessor. Tax Assessment Rolls. 1875.

Salt Lake City (Utah) Assessor. Tax Assessment Rolls. 1876.

Utah State Archives Indexes, Department of Health. Office of Vital Records and Statistics
  Death certificates.
Utah State Historical Society, Salt Lake City.
Classified Photograph Collection.

Newspapers and Magazines

Broad Ax (Salt Lake City)
Daily Evening Bulletin (San Francisco)
Deseret Evening News (Salt Lake City)
Millennial Star
Nauvoo Neighbor
New York Herald
Sacramento Daily Record-Union
Saints' Herald (Plano, IL)
Salt Lake Daily Tribune
Salt Lake Herald
Times and Seasons
Woman's Exponent
Young Woman's Journal

Online Databases

A Century of Black Mormons (www.centuryofblackmormons.org)
Ancestry (www.ancestry.com)
  "Non-Population Census Schedules for Utah Territory and Vermont, 1870: Mortality." US
    National Archives and Records Administration, 1870. US Federal Census Mortality
    Schedules, 1850–1885 [database online]; Archive Collection: M1807; Archive Roll
    Number: 1; Census Year: 1870.
FamilySearch (www.familysearch.org)
  Anderson, Marc W. "Memories of My Grandparents."
  Canada Census, 1871.
  "Ontario Births, 1869-1912."
Find A Grave (www.findagrave.com)
  Susan A. Brown Hicks.
  Hannah Sperry Fitch.
  Joseph Fitch Sr.
Joseph Smith Papers (www.josephsmithpapers.org)
  Bond to Elijah Able, 8 December 1839.
  Smith, Lucy Mack. History, 1844–1845.
Utah Digital Newspapers (https://digital newspapers.org)
  Deseret Evening News.
  Salt Lake Herald.
  Salt Lake Daily Tribune.

Books, Articles, Theses, Dissertations, Internet Sources, and Unpublished Papers

Ahlstrom, Sydney E. *A Religious History of the American People*. New Haven, CT: Yale University
  Press, 1972.
Allen, James B. "The Unusual Jurisdiction of County Probate Courts in the Territory of Utah."
  Utah Historical Quarterly 36, no. 2 (Spring 1968): 132–42.
Amott, Teresa L., and Julie A. Matthaei. *Race, Gender, and Work: A Multicultural Economic History
  of Women in the United States*. Boston: South End Press, 1991.

Anderson, Devery S., ed. *The Development of LDS Temple Worship, 1846–2000: A Documentary History*. Smith-Pettit Foundation Book. Salt Lake City: Signature Books, 2011.

Appleby, Joyce, Eileen K. Cheng, and Joanne L. Goodwin, eds. *Encyclopedia of Women in American History*. New York: Routledge, 2015.

Armitage, Susan H., and Elizabeth Jameson, eds. *The Women's West*. Norman: University of Oklahoma Press, 1987.

Arrington, Leonard J. *Great Basin Kingdom: Economic History of the Latter-Day Saints, 1830–1900*. Lincoln: University of Nebraska Press, 1958.

Arrington, Leonard J., and Davis Bitton. *The Mormon Experience: A History of the Latter-Day Saints*. New York: Knopf, 1979.

Ballard, M. Russell. "The Trek Continues!" General Conference talk presented at the Church of Jesus Christ of Latter-day Saints General Conference, Salt Lake City, UT, October 1, 2017. http://www.lds.org/general-conference/2017/10/the-trek-continues?lang=eng.

Bates, Irene M. "Patriarchal Blessings and the Routinization of Charisma." *Dialogue: A Journal of Mormon Thought* 26, no. 3 (Fall 1993): 11–29.

Beecher, Lyman. *The Autobiography of Lyman Beecher*. Edited by Barbara M. Cross. Cambridge, MA: Harvard University Press, 1961.

Bennett, Richard E. "'We Know No North, No South, No East, No West': Mormon Interpretations of the Civil War, 1861–65." In *Civil War Saints*, edited by Kenneth L. Alford, 51–63. Provo and Salt Lake City: Religious Studies Center, Brigham Young University, in cooperation with Deseret Book Company, 2012.

Berkin, Carol, and Mary Beth Norton. *Women of America: A History*. Boston: Houghton Mifflin, 1979.

Black, Susan Easton. "How Large Was the Population of Nauvoo." *BYU Studies* 35, no. 2 (April 1, 1995): 91–94.

Boles, Richard J. "Documents Relating to African American Experiences of White Congregational Churches in Massachusetts, 1773–1832." *New England Quarterly* 86, no. 2 (2013): 310–23.

Bolton, Henry Carrington. "Fortune-Telling in America To-Day. A Study of Advertisements." *Journal of American Folklore* 8, no. 31 (1895): 299–307.

Bracks, Lean'tin, Jessie Carney Smith, and Linda T. Wynn. *The Complete Encyclopedia of African American History*. 3 vols. Canton, OH: Visible Ink Press, 2015.

Bringhurst, Newell G. *Saints, Slaves, and Blacks: The Changing Place of Black People within Mormonism*. Contributions to the Study of Religion 4. Westport, CT: Greenwood Press, 1981.

Brown, Lisle G. "'Temple Pro Tempore': The Salt Lake City Endowment House." *Journal of Mormon History* 34, no. 4 (Fall 2008): 1–68.

Brown, Samuel M. "Early Mormon Adoption Theology and the Mechanics of Salvation." *Journal of Mormon History* 37, no. 3 (Summer 2011): 3–52.

Brown, Samuel M. *In Heaven as It Is on Earth: Joseph Smith and the Early Mormon Conquest of Death*. New York: Oxford University Press, 2012.

Buerger, David J. "The Development of the Mormon Temple Endowment Ceremony." *Dialogue: A Journal of Mormon Thought* 20 (Winter 1987): 33–76.

Burton, H. David. "Baptism for the Dead: LDS Practice." In *Encyclopedia of Mormonism*, edited by Daniel H. Ludlow, 95–96. New York: Macmillan, 1992.

Bush, Barbara. "African Caribbean Slave Mothers and Children: Traumas of Dislocation and Enslavement across the Atlantic World." *Caribbean Quarterly* 56, no. 1/2 (June 2010): 69–94.

Bush, Lester E. "Mormonism's Negro Doctrine: An Historical Overview." *Dialogue: A Journal of Mormon Thought* 8, no. 1 (1973): 11–68.

Bushman, Richard L. *Joseph Smith: Rough Stone Rolling*. New York: Knopf, 2005.

Bushnell, Horace. *Nature and the Supernatural as Together Constituting the One System of God*. 5th ed. New York: Charles Scribner, 1861.

Campbell, Eugene E., and Bruce L. Campbell. "Divorce among Mormon Polygamists: Extent and Explanations." *Utah Historical Quarterly* 46 (Winter 1978): 4–23.

Cannon, George Q. *The Journals of George Q. Cannon, 1849–1901*. E-book. Salt Lake City: Church Historian's Press, 2018.

Cant, Michael A., and Rufus A. Johnstone. "Reproductive Conflict and the Separation of Reproductive Generations in Humans." *Proceedings of the National Academy of Sciences of the United States of America* 105, no. 14 (2008): 5332–36.

Carby, Hazel V. *Reconstructing Womanhood: The Emergence of the Afro-American Woman Novelist.* New York: Oxford University Press, 1987.

Carroll, Brett E. *The Routledge Historical Atlas of Religion in America.* New York: Routledge, 2000.

Carter, Kate B. *The Story of the Negro Pioneer.* Salt Lake City: Daughters of Utah Pioneers, 1965.

Church of Jesus Christ of Latter-day Saints. *The Doctrine and Covenants of the Church of Jesus Christ of Latter-Day Saints.* Salt Lake City: Church of Jesus Christ of Latter-day Saints, 1981.

Church of Jesus Christ of Latter-day Saints Newsroom. "Temple Garments." Mormon News Room, September 16, 2014. http://www.mormonnewsroom.org/article/temple-garments.

Christian, Charles Melvin. *Black Saga: The African American Experience.* Boston: Houghton Mifflin, 1995.

Coleman, Ronald G. "Blacks in Utah History." Utah History to Go: Peoples of Utah. http://historytogo.utah.gov/people/ethnic_cultures/the_peoples_of_utah/blacksinutahhistory.html.

Coleman, Ronald G. "'Is There No Blessing for Me?': Jane Elizabeth Manning James, a Mormon African American Woman." In *African American Women Confront the West: 1600–2000,* edited by Quintard Taylor and Shirley Ann Wilson Moore, 144–62. Norman: University of Oklahoma Press, 2003.

Compton, Todd. *In Sacred Loneliness: The Plural Wives of Joseph Smith.* Salt Lake City: Signature Books, 1997.

Connell. "Chronology Pertaining to Blacks and the LDS Church | Jane M. James Sealed as Eternal Servant to Joseph Smith | Event View." http://www.xtimeline.com/evt/view.aspx?id=66094.

Copeland, Lee. "Speaking in Tongues in the Restoration Churches." *Dialogue: A Journal of Mormon Thought* 24, no. 1 (Spring 1991): 13–33.

Cott, Nancy F. *Public Vows: A History of Marriage and the Nation.* Cambridge, MA: Harvard University Press, 2000.

Cowley, Matthias F. *Wilford Woodruff, Fourth President of the Church of Jesus Christ of Latter-Day Saints: History of His Life and Labors, as Recorded in His Daily Journals.* Salt Lake City: Deseret News, 1909.

Crofutt, George A. *Crofutt's Overland Tours.* Chicago: H. J. Smith and Co., 1889.

Cruson, Daniel. *The Slaves of Central Fairfield County: The Journey from Slave to Freeman in Nineteenth-Century Connecticut.* Charleston, SC: The History Press, 2007.

Cullen-DuPont, Kathryn. *The Encyclopedia of Women's History in America.* New York: Facts on File, 1996.

Curtis, Kirk M. "History of the St. George Temple." MA thesis, Brigham Young University, 1964.

Daynes, Kathryn M. *More Wives than One: Transformation of the Mormon Marriage System, 1840–1910.* Urbana: University of Illinois Press, 2001.

Desgrées-du-Loû, Annabel, and Hermann Brou. "Resumption of Sexual Relations Following Childbirth: Norms, Practices and Reproductive Health Issues in Abidjan, Côte d'Ivoire." *Reproductive Health Matters* 13, no. 25 (May 2005): 155–63.

Deverell, William, ed. *A Companion to the American West.* Blackwell Companions to American History. Malden, MA: Blackwell, 2004.

Dickson III, Ephraim D. "Protecting the Home Front: The Utah Territorial Militia during the Civil War." In *Civil War Saints,* edited by Kenneth L. Alford, 143–59. Provo: Religious Studies Center, Brigham Young University, 2012. https://rsc.byu.edu/sites/default/files/pubs/pdf/chaps/CWS%2009%20Dickson.pdf.

Dillon, Lisa. *The Shady Side of Fifty: Age and Old Age in Late Victorian Canada and the United States.* Montreal: McGill-Queen's University Press, 2008.

Dinger, John S. *The Nauvoo City and High Council Minutes.* Salt Lake City: Signature Books, 2011.

Dodini, Dana. "Local Artist Celebrates Pioneers through Art in Payson Temple." *The Daily Universe,* June 5, 2015. http://universe.byu.edu/2015/06/05/local-artist-celebrates-pioneers-through-art-in-payson-temple.

Dunbar, Erica Armstrong. *A Fragile Freedom: African American Women and Emancipation in the Antebellum City.* New Haven, CT: Yale University Press, 2008.

Dunbar, Erica Armstrong. *Never Caught: The Washingtons' Relentless Pursuit of Their Runaway Slave, Ona Judge.* New York: 37 Ink/Atria, 2017.

Dykstra, Robert R. "White Men, Black Laws." *The Annals of Iowa* 46, no. 6 (Fall 1982): 403–40.

Eblen, Jack Ericson. "New Estimates of the Vital Rates of the United States Black Population during the Nineteenth Century." In *Studies in American Historical Demography*, edited by Maris A. Vinovskis, 339–57. New York: Academic Press, 1979.

Eighth Ward, Liberty Stake. "History of the Eighth Ward: In Commemoration of Laying Cornerstone of the New Chapel, Saturday, March Twenty-sixth, Nineteen Hundred Twenty-one." [Pamphlet.] Salt Lake City: 1921.

Faragher, John Mack. *Women and Men on the Overland Trail.* 2nd ed. Yale Nota Bene. New Haven, CT: Yale University Press, 2001.

Farmer, Jared. *On Zion's Mount: Mormons, Indians, and the American Landscape.* Cambridge, MA: Harvard University Press, 2008.

Finkelman, Paul, ed. *Encyclopedia of African American History, 1619–1895: From the Colonial Period to the Age of Frederick Douglass.* New York: Oxford University Press, 2006.

Firmage, Edwin Brown, and Richard Collin Mangrum. *Zion in the Courts: A Legal History of the Church of Jesus Christ of Latter-Day Saints, 1830–1900.* Urbana: University of Illinois Press, 1988.

Flake, Kathleen. "The Development of Early Latter-Day Saint Marriage Rites, 1831–53." *Journal of Mormon History* 41, no. 1 (2015): 77–102.

Flake, Kathleen. *The Politics of American Religious Identity: The Seating of Senator Reed Smoot, Mormon Apostle.* Chapel Hill: University of North Carolina Press, 2004.

Flake, Kathleen. "Re-Placing Memory: Latter-Day Saint Use of Historical Monuments and Narrative in the Early Twentieth Century." *Religion and American Culture: A Journal of Interpretation* 13, no. 1 (Winter 2003): 69–109.

Flanders, Robert Bruce. *Nauvoo: Kingdom on the Mississippi.* Urbana: University of Illinois Press, 1975.

Fleming, Stephen J. "'Sweeping Everything before It': Early Mormonism in the Pine Barrens of New Jersey." *BYU Studies* 40, no. 1 (2001): 72–104.

Fluhman, J. Spencer. *"A Peculiar People": Anti-Mormonism and the Making of Religion in Nineteenth-Century America.* Chapel Hill: University of North Carolina Press, 2012.

Francis, JaNae. "First Look: Tour inside Ogden LDS Temple." *Standard-Examiner*, July 29, 2014. http://www.standard.net/Faith/2014/07/29/30-Ogden-Temple-tour.

Frey, Sylvia R., and Betty Wood. *Come Shouting to Zion: African American Protestantism in the American South and British Caribbean to 1830.* Chapel Hill: University of North Carolina Press, 1998.

Gates, Henry Louis, Jr., and Donald Yacovone. *The African Americans: Many Rivers to Cross.* Carlsbad, CA: SmileyBooks, 2013.

Gaustad, Edwin S., and Mark A. Noll, eds. *A Documentary History of Religion in America.* 3rd ed. Vol. 2: To 1877. Grand Rapids, MI: William B. Eerdmans Publishing Company, 2003.

Gassan, Richard H. "Tourists and the City: New York's First Tourist Era, 1820–1840." *Winterthur Portfolio* 44, no. 2/3 (2010): 221–46.

Gentry, Leland H. "The Mormon Way Stations: Garden Grove and Mt. Pisgah." *BYU Studies* 21, no. 4 (Fall 1981): 445–61.

German, James. "Economy." In *Themes in Religion and American Culture*, edited by Philip Goff and Paul Harvey. Chapel Hill: University of North Carolina Press, 2004.

Gertz, Elmer. "The Black Laws of Illinois." *Journal of the Illinois State Historical Society (1908–1984)* 56, no. 3 (1963): 454–73.

Givens, Terryl. *People of Paradox: A History of Mormon Culture.* New York: Oxford University Press, 2007.

Glaude, Eddie S. *African American Religion: A Very Short Introduction.* Very Short Introductions 397. New York: Oxford University Press, 2014.

Glymph, Thavolia. *Out of the House of Bondage: The Transformation of the Plantation Household.* New York: Cambridge University Press, 2008.

Goldsmith, Judith. *Childbirth Wisdom: From the World's Oldest Societies.* Brookline, MA: East West Health Books, 1990.

Goodwin, Robert H. "Among the Poorest of Saints: Mormon Migration to and through Burlington, Iowa, 1846–1887." *Mormon Historical Studies* 4, no. 2 (Fall 2003): 97–112.

Gordon, Sarah Barringer. *The Mormon Question: Polygamy and Constitutional Conflict in Nineteenth-Century America.* Studies in Legal History. Chapel Hill: University of North Carolina Press, 2002.

Halbwachs, Maurice. *On Collective Memory.* The Heritage of Sociology. Chicago: University of Chicago Press, 1992.

Harline, Paula Kelly. *The Polygamous Wives Writing Club: From the Diaries of Mormon Pioneer Women.* New York: Oxford University Press, 2014.

Harper, Steven C. "Infallible Proofs, Both Human and Divine: The Persuasiveness of Mormonism for Early Converts." *Religion and American Culture: A Journal of Interpretation* 10, no. 1 (2000): 99–118.

Harris, Matthew L., and Newell G. Bringhurst, eds. *The Mormon Church and Blacks: A Documentary History.* Urbana: University of Illinois Press, 2015.

Hartley, William G. "Mormons, Crickets, and Gulls: A New Look at an Old Story." *Utah Historical Quarterly* 38 (1970): 224–39.

Hartley, William G. "The Pioneer Trek." *Ensign,* June 1997. https://www.lds.org/ensign/1997/06/the-pioneer-trek-nauvoo-to-winter-quarters?lang=eng.

Hartman, Saidiya. "Venus in Two Acts." *Small Axe* 12, no. 2 (2008): 1–14.

Hayden, Dolores. "Biddy Mason's Los Angeles 1856–1891." *California History* 68, no. 3 (1989): 86–99.

Hewitt, Nancy A., ed. *A Companion to American Women's History.* Blackwell Companions to American History. Malden, MA: Blackwell, 2002.

Hine, Darlene Clark. "'In the Kingdom of Culture': Black Women and the Intersection of Race, Gender, and Class." In *Lure and Loathing: Essays on Race, Identity, and the Ambivalence of Assimilation,* edited by Gerald Early, 337–51. New York: Penguin Books, 1994.

Hine, Robert V., and John Mack Faragher. *The American West: A New Interpretive History.* New Haven, CT: Yale University Press, 2000.

Hobson, Janell. "The Rape of Harriet Tubman." *Meridians: Feminism, Race, Transnationalism* 12, no. 2 (2014): 161–68.

Hodges, Graham Russell. *David Ruggles: Radical Black Abolitionist and the Underground Railroad in New York City.* John Hope Franklin Series in African American History and Culture. Chapel Hill: University of North Carolina Press, 2010.

Hodges, Graham Russell. *Slavery and Freedom in the Rural North: African Americans in Monmouth County, New Jersey, 1665–1865.* Madison, WI: Madison House, 1997.

Holloway, Joseph E. "Names and Naming, African." In *Encyclopedia of African-American Culture and History,* edited by Colin A. Palmer, 2nd ed., 4: 1572–74. Detroit: Macmillan, 2006.

Holmes, Linda Janet. "African American Midwives in the South." In *The American Way of Birth,* edited by Pamela Eakins, 273–91. Health, Society, and Policy. Philadelphia: Temple University Press, 1986.

Hooten Jr., Leroy W. "Salt Lake City Old Water Conveyance Systems." October 8, 2009. http://www.slcdocs.com/utilities/NewsEvents/news2007/news6272007.htm.

Horton, James Oliver. *Hard Road to Freedom: The Story of African America.* New Brunswick, NJ: Rutgers University Press, 2001.

Howard, Angela, and Frances M. Kavenik, eds. *Handbook of American Women's History.* 2nd ed. Thousand Oaks, CA: Sage Publications, 2000.

Hoyt, Amy, and Sara M. Patterson. "Mormon Masculinity: Changing Gender Expectations in the Era of Transition from Polygamy to Monogamy, 1890–1920." *Gender & History* 23, no. 1 (April 1, 2011): 72–91.

Hudson, Angela Pulley. *Real Native Genius: How an Ex-Slave and a White Mormon Became Famous Indians.* Chapel Hill: University of North Carolina Press, 2015.

Hunter, Tera W. *Bound in Wedlock: Slave and Free Black Marriage in the Nineteenth Century.* Cambridge, MA: The Belknap Press of Harvard University Press, 2017.

Hunter, Tera W. *To 'Joy My Freedom: Southern Black Women's Lives and Labors after the Civil War.* Cambridge, MA: Harvard University Press, 1997.

"Illuminating Ladies: A Coloring Book of Mormon Women | Exponent II." *Exponent II* (blog). http://www.exponentii.org/product/illuminating-ladies-a-coloring-book-of-mormon-women.

Irving, Gordon. "The Law of Adoption: One Phase of the Development of the Mormon Concept of Salvation, 1830–1900." *Brigham Young University Studies* 14 (Spring 1974): 291–314.

Jackson, William Kesler. *Elijah Abel: The Life and Times of a Black Priesthood Holder.* Springville, UT: CFI, an imprint of Cedar Fort, Inc., 2013.

Jacobs, Harriet. "Incidents in the Life of a Slave Girl." In *The Classic Slave Narratives,* edited by Henry Louis Gates Jr., 333–515. New York: Penguin Books, 1987.

Jacobs, Harriet, John S. Jacobs, Louisa Matilda Jacobs, and Jean Fagan Yellin. *The Harriet Jacobs Family Papers.* Chapel Hill: University of North Carolina Press, 2008.

Jameson, Elizabeth, and Susan H. Armitage, eds. *Writing the Range: Race, Class, and Culture in the Women's West.* Norman: University of Oklahoma Press, 1997.

Jenson, Andrew. "Hunter, Oscar Fitzallen." *Latter-Day Saint Biographical Encyclopedia.* Salt Lake City: Andrew Jenson History Company, 1914.

Jenson, Andrew. "Roundy, Elizabeth Jefford Drake." *Latter-Day Saint Biographical Encyclopedia.* Salt Lake City: Andrew Jenson History Company, 1901.

Johnson, Jeffery Ogden. "Determining and Defining 'Wife': The Brigham Young Households." *Dialogue: A Journal of Mormon Thought* 20, no. 3 (Fall 1987): 57–70.

Johnson, Sharon P. "Cultural Blindness and Ambiguity: Reading (for) and Writing about Rape." *French Cultural Studies* 27, no. 2 (May 2016): 113–34.

Kelley, Robin D. G., and Earl Lewis. *To Make Our World Anew: A History of African Americans.* 2 vols. New York: Oxford University Press, 2000.

Kerber, Linda K., Alice Kessler-Harris, and Kathryn Kish Sklar, eds. *U.S. History as Women's History: New Feminist Essays.* Gender & American Culture. Chapel Hill: University of North Carolina Press, 1995.

Kerber, Linda K., Alice Kessler-Harris, and Jane Sherron De Hart. *Women's America: Refocusing the Past.* 6th ed. New York: Oxford University Press, 2004.

King, Mary Louise. *Portrait of New Canaan: The History of a Connecticut Town.* Chester, PA: New Canaan Historical Society; printed by John Spencer, Inc., 1981.

King, Wilma. "'Prematurely Knowing of Evil Things': The Sexual Abuse of African American Girls and Young Women in Slavery and Freedom." *Journal of African American History* 99, no. 3 (Summer 2014): 173–96.

Korshak, Yvonne. "The Liberty Cap as a Revolutionary Symbol in America and France." *Smithsonian Studies in American Art* 1, no. 2 (Autumn 1987): 52–69.

Kusmer, Kenneth L. *A Ghetto Takes Shape: Black Cleveland, 1870–1930.* Blacks in the New World. Urbana: University of Illinois Press, 1976.

Laderman, Gary. "Locating the Dead: A Cultural History of Death in the Antebellum, Anglo-Protestant Communities of the Northeast." *Journal of the American Academy of Religion* 63, no. 1 (1995): 27–52.

Lane, Rebecca. "8 Utah Valley Artists with Pieces in the Payson Utah Temple." *Utah Valley 360,* May 19, 2015. https://utahvalley360.com/2015/05/19/8-utah-valley-artists-pieces-payson-utah-temple.

Larkin, Melvin A. "The History of the L.D.S. Temple in Logan, Utah." MA thesis, Utah State Agricultural College, 1954.

Larson, Gustive O. *Prelude to the Kingdom: Mormon Desert Conquest, a Chapter in American Cooperative Experience.* Francestown, NH: M. Jones Co., 1947.

Launius, Roger D. *Invisible Saints: A History of Black Americans in the Reorganized Church.* Independence, MO: Herald Publishing House, 1988.

"LDS Black Saints." Amasa Mason Lyman: "A Labor of Love." http://www.amasamasonlyman.com/lds-black-saints.html.

Library of Congress. "A Century of Lawmaking for a New Nation: U.S. Congressional Documents and Debates, 1774–1875." *American Memory.* https://memory.loc.gov/cgi-bin/ampage?collI d=llsl&fileName=009/llsl009.db&recNum=480.

Limerick, Patricia Nelson. *The Legacy of Conquest: The Unbroken Past of the American West.* New York: Norton, 1987.

MacKay, Michael Hubbard, and Nicholas J. Frederick. *Joseph Smith's Seer Stones.* Provo and Salt Lake City: Religious Studies Center, Brigham Young University, in cooperation with Deseret Book Company, 2016.

MacKinnon, William P. "Epilogue to the Utah War: Impact and Legacy." *Journal of Mormon History* 29, no. 2 (April 2003): 186–248.

MacKinnon, William P. "Exodus and the Utah War: Tales from the Mormon Move South, 1858." *Overland Journal* 34, no. 3 (Fall 2016): 89–100.

MacKinnon, William P. "Utah's Civil War(s): Linkages and Connections." *Utah Historical Quarterly* 80, no. 4 (Fall 2012): 296–313.

Madsen, Brigham D. *Corinne: The Gentile Capital of Utah.* Salt Lake City: Utah State Historical Society, 1980.

Madsen, Carol Cornwall. "Retrenchment Association." *Encyclopedia of Mormonism.* New York: Macmillan, 1992.

Mankiller, Wilma Pearl, ed. *The Reader's Companion to U.S. Women's History.* Boston: Houghton Mifflin, 1998.

Marable, Manning, ed. *Freedom on My Mind: The Columbia Documentary History of the African American Experience.* New York: Columbia University Press, 2003.

Marquardt, H. Michael, ed. *Early Patriarchal Blessings of the Church of Jesus Christ of Latter-Day Saints.* Salt Lake City: Smith-Pettit Foundation, 2007.

Marsden, George M. *The Evangelical Mind and the New School Presbyterian Experience: A Case Study of Thought and Theology in Nineteenth-Century America.* Yale Publications in American Studies 20. New Haven, CT: Yale University Press, 1970.

Mason, Patrick Q. "The Prohibition of Interracial Marriage in Utah, 1888–1963." *Utah Historical Quarterly* 76, no. 2 (Spring 2008): 108–31.

Mauss, Armand L. *All Abraham's Children: Changing Mormon Conceptions of Race and Lineage.* Urbana: University of Illinois Press, 2003.

Maxwell, John Gary. *The Civil War Years in Utah: The Kingdom of God and the Territory That Did Not Fight.* Norman: University of Oklahoma Press, 2016.

McDannell, Colleen. *Material Christianity: Religion and Popular Culture in America.* New Haven, CT: Yale University Press, 1995.

McHenry, Elizabeth. "Rereading Literary Legacy: New Considerations of the 19th-Century African-American Reader and Writer." *Callaloo* 22, no. 2 (Spring 1999): 477–82.

Methodist Episcopal Church, Missionary Society. *Seventy-Fifth Annual Report of the Missionary Society of the Methodist Episcopal Church for the Year 1893.* New York, 1894.

Milner, Clyde A., II., ed. *A New Significance: Re-Envisioning the History of the American West.* New York: Oxford University Press, 1996.

Milner, Clyde A., II., Carol A. O'Connor, and Martha A. Sandweiss, eds. *The Oxford History of the American West.* New York: Oxford University Press, 1994.

Moynihan, Ruth Barnes, Cynthia Eagle Russett, and Laurie Crumpacker, eds. *Second to None: A Documentary History of American Women.* Lincoln: University of Nebraska Press, 1993.

Mueller, Max Perry. *Race and the Making of the Mormon People.* Chapel Hill: University of North Carolina Press, 2017.

Myres, Sandra L. *Westering Women and the Frontier Experience, 1800–1915.* Histories of the American Frontier. Albuquerque: University of New Mexico Press, 1982.

The New-York State Guide; Containing an Alphabetical List of Counties, Towns, Cities, Villages, Post-Offices, &c. with the Census of 1840; Canals and Railroads, Lakes and Rivers; Steamboat Routes, Canal Routes, Stage Routes, and Tables of Distances; with Railroad, Steamboat and Canal Arrangements, &c. &c. Compiled from Authentic Sources. Albany, NY: J. Disturnell, 1843.

Newell, Linda King, and Valeen Tippetts Avery. "Jane Manning James: Black Saint, 1847 Pioneer." *Ensign,* August 1979.

Newell, Linda King, and Valeen Tippetts Avery. *Mormon Enigma: Emma Hale Smith.* 2nd ed. Urbana: University of Illinois Press, 1994.

Newell, Quincy D. "The Autobiography and Interview of Jane Elizabeth Manning James." *Journal of Africana Religions* 1, no. 2 (2013): 251–91.

Newell, Quincy D. "Black History Month at the JI: Talking about Jane (Newell)." *Juvenile Instructor* (blog), February 19, 2013. http://juvenileinstructor.org/black-history-month-at-the-ji-talking-about-jane-newell.

Newell, Quincy D. "Black Jane/Aunt Jane: Negotiating Race and Gender in the Nineteenth-Century LDS Church." Paper presented at the American Society of Church History Winter Meeting, San Diego, CA, January 2010.

Newell, Quincy D. "'Is There No Blessing for Me?' Jane James's Construction of Space in Latter-Day Saint History and Practice." In *New Perspectives in Mormon Studies: Creating and Crossing Boundaries,* edited by Quincy D. Newell and Eric F. Mason, 41–65. Norman: University of Oklahoma Press, 2013.

Newell, Quincy D. "Jane James's Agency." In *Women and Mormonism: Historical and Contemporary Perspectives,* edited by Kate Holbrook and Matthew Bowman, 136–48. Salt Lake City: University of Utah Press, 2016.

Newell, Quincy D. *Narrating Jane: Telling the Story of an Early African American Mormon Woman.* Leonard J. Arrington Mormon History Lecture 21. Logan: Utah State University Press, 2016.

Newell, Quincy D. "What Jane James Saw." In *Directions for Mormon Studies in the Twenty-First Century,* edited by Patrick Q. Mason, 135–51. Salt Lake City: University of Utah Press, 2016.

Newman, Simon P. *Parades and the Politics of the Street: Festive Culture in the Early American Republic.* Philadelphia: University of Pennsylvania Press, 2010.

Newton, Marjorie. *Hero or Traitor: A Biographical Study of Charles Wesley Wandell.* John Whitmer Historical Association Monograph Series. Independence, MO: Independence Press, 1992.

Oaks, Dallin H. "The Suppression of the *Nauvoo Expositor.*" *Utah Law Review* 9 (Winter 1965): 862–903.

O'Donovan, Connell. "The Mormon Priesthood Ban and Elder Q. Walker Lewis: 'An Example for His More Whiter Brethren to Follow.'" *John Whitmer Historical Association Journal* 26 (2006): 48–100.

Page, Matt. "Mormon Prayer Candles." *Mattpagedotcom.Com* (blog), October 29, 2017. http://mattpagedotcom.com/portfolio/items/mormon-prayer-candles.

Painter, Nell Irvin. *Creating Black Americans: African-American History and Its Meanings, 1619 to the Present.* New York: Oxford University Press, 2006.

Painter, Nell Irvin. *Sojourner Truth: A Life, a Symbol.* New York: Norton, 1996.

Palmquist, Peter E., and Thomas R. Kailbourn. *Pioneer Photographers of the Far West: A Biographical Dictionary, 1840–1865.* Stanford, CA: Stanford University Press, 2000.

Pascoe, Peggy. *Relations of Rescue: The Search for Female Moral Authority in the American West, 1874–1939.* New York: Oxford University Press, 1990.

Pearson, Lisa Madsen, and Carol Cornwall Madsen. "Innovation and Accommodation: The Legal Status of Women in Territorial Utah, 1850–1896." In *Women in Utah History: Paradigm or Paradox?,* 36–81. Boulder: University Press of Colorado, 2005.

Peterson, Paul H. "'Like a Fire in My Bones': The Reformation Correspondence between Brigham Young and George Q. Cannon." In *Regional Studies in Latter-Day Saint Church History: California,* 107–16. Regional Studies in Latter-Day Saint Church History 1. Provo: Department of Church History and Doctrine, Brigham Young University, 1998.

Peterson, Paul H. "Reformation (LDS) of 1856–1857." In *Encyclopedia of Mormonism,* edited by Daniel H. Ludlow, 1197–98. New York: Macmillan, 1992.

Pietruska, Jamie L. *Looking Forward: Prediction and Uncertainty in Modern America.* Chicago: University of Chicago Press, 2017.

Poll, Richard D. "The Move South." *BYU Studies* 29, no. 4 (October 1989): 65–88.

Poll, Richard D., and William P. MacKinnon. "Causes of the Utah War Reconsidered." *Journal of Mormon History* 20, no. 2 (April 1994): 16–44.

Pryor, Elizabeth Stordeur. *Colored Travelers: Mobility and the Fight for Citizenship before the Civil War*. John Hope Franklin Series in African American History and Culture. Chapel Hill: University of North Carolina Press, 2016.

Quinn, D. Michael. *Early Mormonism and the Magic World View*. Revised and enlarged ed. Salt Lake City: Signature Books, 1998.

Raboteau, Albert J. *Slave Religion: The "Invisible Institution" in the Antebellum South*. New York: Oxford University Press, 1978.

Radke-Moss, Andrea G. "Silent Memories of Missouri: Mormon Women and Men and Sexual Assault in Group Memory and Religious Identity." In *Mormon Women's History: Beyond Biography*, edited by Rachel Cope, Amy Easton-Flake, Keith A. Erekson, and Lisa Olsen Tait, 49–81. Vancouver: Fairleigh Dickinson University Press, 2017.

Reeve, W. Paul. "All 'Mormon Elder-Berry's' Children: Race, Whiteness, and the Attack on Mormon 'Anglo-Saxon Triumphalism.'" In *Directions for Mormon Studies in the Twenty-First Century*, edited by Patrick Q. Mason, 152–75. Salt Lake City: University of Utah Press, 2016.

Reeve, W. Paul. *Religion of a Different Color: Race and the Mormon Struggle for Whiteness*. New York: Oxford University Press, 2015.

Reeve, W. Paul, Christopher B. Rich Jr., and LaJean Carruth. *"Enough to Cause the Angels in Heaven to Blush": Race, Servitude, and Priesthood at the 1852 Utah Legislature*, forthcoming.

Reiter, Tonya. "Black Saviors on Mount Zion: Proxy Baptisms and Latter-Day Saints of African Descent." *Journal of Mormon History* 43, no. 4 (2017): 100–23.

Reynolds, Sydney Smith. "Mother in Israel." In *Encyclopedia of Mormonism*, edited by Daniel H. Ludlow, 963–64. New York: Macmillan, 1992.

Rich, Christopher B. "The True Policy for Utah: Servitude, Slavery, and 'An Act in Relation to Service.'" *Utah Historical Quarterly* 80, no. 1 (Winter 2012): 54–74.

Richman, Larry. "Video: Be One Celebration of the 40th Anniversary of the LDS Revelation on the Priesthood." *LDS Media Talk: Resources from LDS Church & Mormons worldwide*, June 1, 2018. https://ldsmediatalk.com/2018/06/01/video-be-one-celebration-of-the-40th-anniversary-of-the-lds-revelation-on-the-priesthood.

Richter, Amy G., ed. *At Home in Nineteenth-Century America: A Documentary History*. New York: New York University Press, 2015.

Roberts, B. H. *A Comprehensive History of the Church of Jesus Christ of Latter-Day Saints Century I*. Salt Lake City: Deseret News Press, 1930.

Rosen, Hannah. *Terror in the Heart of Freedom: Citizenship, Sexual Violence, and the Meaning of Race in the Postemancipation South*. Gender and American Culture. Chapel Hill: University of North Carolina Press, 2009.

Ruíz, Vicki, and Ellen Carol DuBois, eds. *Unequal Sisters: A Multicultural Reader in U.S. Women's History*. 2nd ed. New York: Routledge, 1994.

Russell, Robert H. *Wilton, Connecticut: Three Centuries of People, Places, and Progress*. Wilton, CT: Wilton Historical Society, 2004.

St. John, Samuel. *Historical Address, Delivered in the Congregational Church of New Canaan, Conn., July 4th, 1876*. Stamford, CT: Wm. W. Gillespie & Co., 1876.

"Saint without Priesthood: The Collected Testimonies of Ex-Slave Samuel D. Chambers." *Dialogue: A Journal of Mormon Thought* 12, no. 2 (Summer 1979): 13–21.

Sandoval-Strausz, A. K. *Hotel: An American History*. New Haven, CT: Yale University Press, 2007.

Scharff, Virginia. *Twenty Thousand Roads : Women, Movement, and the West*. Berkeley: University of California Press, 2003.

Schlesinger, Arthur M. "Liberty Tree: A Genealogy." *New England Quarterly* 25, no. 4 (December 1952): 435–58.

Schmidt, Leigh Eric. *Consumer Rites: The Buying & Selling of American Holidays*. Princeton, NJ: Princeton University Press, 1995.

Schweinitz, Rebecca de. "Preaching the Gospel of Church and Sex: Mormon Women's Fiction in the Young Woman's Journal, 1889–1910." *Dialogue: A Journal of Mormon Thought* 33, no. 4 (Winter 2000): 27–54.

Scott, Joan W. "Gender: A Useful Category of Historical Analysis." *American Historical Review* 91, no. 5 (December 1986): 1053–75.

Selleck, Charles Melbourne. *Norwalk*. Norwalk, CT: The author, 1896.

Sensbach, Jon. *Rebecca's Revival: Creating Black Christianity in the Atlantic World*. Cambridge, MA: Harvard University Press, 2005.

Sessions, Patty Bartlett, and Donna Toland Smart. *Mormon Midwife: The 1846–1888 Diaries of Patty Bartlett Sessions*. Logan: Utah State University Press, 1997.

Shepherd, Gordon, Gary Shepherd, and Natalie Shepherd. "Gender Differences in the Early Patriarchal Blessings of the LDS Church, 1834–1845." *John Whitmer Historical Association Journal* 30 (2010): 39–65.

Shipps, Jan. *Mormonism: The Story of a New Religious Tradition*. Urbana: University of Illinois Press, 1985.

Shipps, Jan. *Sojourner in the Promised Land: Forty Years among the Mormons*. Urbana: University of Illinois Press, 2000.

Skolnick, M., L. Bean, D. May, V. Arbon, K. De Nevers, and P. Cartwright. "Mormon Demographic History I: Nuptiality and Fertility of Once-Married Couples." *Population Studies* 32, no. 1 (March 1978): 5–19.

Sloan, Robert W. *Utah Gazetteer and Directory of Logan, Ogden, Provo and Salt Lake Cities, for 1884*. Salt Lake City: Herald Printing and Publishing Company, 1884.

Smith, Joseph, III *The Memoirs of President Joseph Smith III (1832–1914): The Second Prophet of the Church*. Edited by Mary Audentia Smith Anderson. Independence, MO: Price Publishing Company, 2001.

Smith, John Calvin. *The Western Tourist, and Emigrant's Guide, with a Compendious Gazetteer of the States of Ohio, Michigan, Indiana, Illinois, and Missouri, and the Territories of Wisconsin, and Iowa*. New York: J. H. Colton, 1839.

Smith, William H. *Smith's Canadian Gazetteer*. Toronto: H. & W. Rowsell, 1846. https://archive.org/details/smithscanadianga00smit.

Smucker, Samuel Mosheim. *The Religious, Social and Political History of the Mormons, Or Latter-Day Saints, from Their Origin to the Present Time*. Hurst & Company, 1881.

Sotirin, Patricia J., and Laura L. Ellingson. *Where the Aunts Are: Family, Feminism, and Kinship in Popular Culture*. Waco, TX: Baylor University Press, 2013.

Spafford, Horatio Gates. *A Pocket Guide for the Tourist and Traveller along the Line of the Canals and the Interior Commerce of the State of New York*. New York: T. and J. Swords, 1824.

Spillers, Hortense J. *Black, White, and in Color: Essays on American Literature and Culture*. Chicago: University of Chicago Press, 2003.

Stapley, Jonathan A. "Adoptive Sealing Ritual in Mormonism." *Journal of Mormon History* 37, no. 3 (Summer 2011): 53–117.

Stapley, Jonathan A. *The Power of Godliness: Mormon Liturgy and Cosmology*. New York: Oxford University Press, 2018.

Stapley, Jonathan A., and Kristine Wright. "Female Ritual Healing in Mormonism." *Journal of Mormon History* 37, no. 1 (Winter 2011): 1–85.

Stevenson, Brenda E. *Life in Black and White: Family and Community in the Slave South*. New York: Oxford University Press, 1996.

Stone, Frank Andrews. *African American Connecticut: The Black Scene in a New England State; Eighteenth to Twenty-First Century*. Deland, FL: Global Research Center, continuing the Isaac N. Thut World Education Center, 2008.

Sundhagen, Rebecca. "Breastfeeding and Child Spacing." In *Childbirth across Cultures: Ideas and Practices of Pregnancy, Childbirth and the Postpartum*, edited by Helaine Selin and Pamela K. Stone, 23–32. Science across Cultures: The History of Non-Western Science 5. New York: Springer, 2009.

Stuart, Joseph. "Holy Races: Race in the Formation of Mormonism and the Nation of Islam." MA thesis, University of Virginia, 2014.

Sutherland, Daniel E. *Americans and Their Servants: Domestic Service in the United States from 1800 to 1920*. Baton Rouge: Louisiana State University Press, 1981.

Talbot, Christine. "The Church Family in Nineteenth-Century America: Mormonism and the Public/Private Divide." *Journal of Mormon History* 37, no. 4 (Fall 2011): 208–57.

Tate, Gayle T. *Unknown Tongues: Black Women's Political Activism in the Antebellum Era, 1830–1860*. Black American and Diasporic Studies. East Lansing: Michigan State University Press, 2003.

Taves, Ann. "Spiritual Purity and Sexual Shame: Religious Themes in the Writings of Harriet Jacobs." *Church History* 56, no. 1 (March 1987): 59–72.

Taylor, John. "Duties of the Latter-Day Saints—How Children Should Be Trained—An Academy for Sanpete—The Kind of Teachers to Select—Education Advocated—Intemperance Condemned—Sin to Be Exposed—Unworthy Men Not to Be Sustained in Office—Example of a Darkened Mind—Providence Over the Saints." In *Journal of Discourses by President John Taylor, His Counsellors, the Twelve Apostles, and Others*, 24: 166–72. Liverpool, England: John Henry Smith, 1884.

Taylor, Quintard. *In Search of the Racial Frontier: African Americans in the American West, 1528–1990*. New York: Norton, 1998.

Thiriot, Amy Tanner. "Mrs. Nellie Kidd, Courtesan." *Keepapitchinin, the Mormon History Blog* (blog), January 6, 2015. http://www.keepapitchinin.org/2015/01/06/mrs-nellie-kidd-courtesan.

Thiriot, Amy Tanner. "The Things We Know: A Picture of Jane Manning James (Revisited)." *Keepapitchinin, the Mormon History Blog* (blog), November 29, 2017. http://www.keepapitchinin.org/2017/11/29/jane-james-picture-revisited.

Turley Jr., Richard E., Robin S. Jensen, and Mark Ashurst-McGee. "Joseph the Seer." *Ensign*, October 2015.

Turner, John G. *Brigham Young: Pioneer Prophet*. Cambridge, MA: The Belknap Press of Harvard University Press, 2012.

Turner, Katherine Leonard. *How the Other Half Ate: A History of Working-Class Meals at the Turn of the Century*. California Studies in Food and Culture 48. Berkeley: University of California Press, 2014.

Ulrich, Laurel Thatcher. *A House Full of Females: Plural Marriage and Women's Rights in Early Mormonism, 1835–1870*. New York: Knopf, 2017.

Underwood, Grant. *The Millenarian World of Early Mormonism*. Urbana: University of Illinois Press, 1993.

Underwood, Grant. "The Prophetic Legacy in Islam and Mormonism: Some Comparative Observations." In *New Perspectives in Mormon Studies: Creating and Crossing Boundaries*, 101–18. Norman: University of Oklahoma Press, 2013.

Utah Gazetteer, 1892–93. Salt Lake City: Stenhouse and Co., 1892.

Van Hoosear, David Hermon. "Annals of Wilton: Negroes of Wilton." *Wilton Bulletin*. March 16, 1939.

Van Hoosear, David Hermon. "Annals of Wilton: Negroes of Wilton (Concluded)." *Wilton Bulletin*. March 30, 1939.

Van Hoosear, David Hermon. "Annals of Wilton: Negroes of Wilton (Continued)." *Wilton Bulletin*. March 23, 1939.

Van Wagoner, Richard S. *Mormon Polygamy: A History*. 2d ed. Salt Lake City: Signature Books, 1989.

Vandewater, Robert J. *The Tourist, or Pocket Manual for Travellers on the Hudson River, the Western and Northern Canals and Railroads; the Stage Routes to Niagara Falls; and down Lake Ontario and the St. Lawrence to Montreal and Quebec. Comprising Also the Routes to Lebanon, Ballston, and Saratoga Springs, with Many New and Interesting Details*. 9th edition. New York: Harper Brothers, 1841.

Vermillion, Mary. "Reembodying the Self: Representations of Rape in *Incidents in the Life of a Slave Girl* and *I Know Why the Caged Bird Sings*." *Biography: An Interdisciplinary Quarterly* 15, no. 3 (Summer 1992): 243–60.

Walker, Ronald. "Young 'Tony' Ivins." Presented at the Juanita Brooks Lecture Series, St. George, UT, March 15, 2000. https://library.dixie.edu/special_collections/juanita_brooks_lectures/2000.html.

Walvin, James. *Atlas of Slavery*. New York: Routledge, 2014.

Weed, Samuel Richards. *Norwalk after Two Hundred & Fifty Years: An Account of the Celebration of the 250th Anniversary of the Charter of the Town*. South Norwalk, CT: C. A. Freeman, 1902.

Weisenfeld, Judith. *New World A-Coming: Black Religion and Racial Identity during the Great Migration*. New York: New York University Press, 2016.

Wexler, Laura. *Tender Violence: Domestic Visions in an Age of U.S. Imperialism*. Cultural Studies of the United States. Chapel Hill: University of North Carolina Press, 2000.

White, O. Kendall, Jr "Boundary Maintenance, Blacks, and the Mormon Priesthood." *Journal of Religious Thought* 37 (Fall/Winter 1980–81): 30–44.

White, Richard. *"It's Your Misfortune and None of My Own": A History of the American West*. 1st ed. Norman: University of Oklahoma Press, 1991.

Wigmore, Gregory. "Before the Railroad: From Slavery to Freedom in the Canadian-American Borderland." *Journal of American History* 98, no. 2 (2011): 437–54.

Williams, George H., and Edith Waldvogel. "A History of Speaking in Tongues and Related Gifts." In *The Charismatic Movement*, edited by Michael P. Hamilton, 61–113. Grand Rapids, MI: William B. Eerdmans Publishing Company, 1975.

Winks, Robin W. *The Blacks in Canada: A History*. 2nd ed. Montreal: McGill-Queen's University Press, 1997.

Wolfinger, Henry J. "A Test of Faith: Jane Elizabeth James and the Origins of the Utah Black Community." In *Social Accommodation in Utah*, edited by Clark S. Knowlton, 126–72. American West Center Occasional Papers. Salt Lake City: University of Utah, 1975.

Wright, Carroll D., ed. *Marriage and Divorce in the United States, 1867 to 1886*. Demography. New York: Arno Press, 1976.

Young, Al R. "Till We Meet Again by Elspeth Young Featured at LDS Conference Center." *Al Young Studios Newsroom*, February 2, 2015. https://www.alyoung.com/content/content-0.51.0000.099.html.

Young, Brigham. "The Priesthood and Satan—the Constitution and Government of the United States—Rights and Policy of the Latter-Day Saints: A Discourse by President Brigham Young, Delivered in the Tabernacle, Great Salt Lake City, Feb. 18, 1855." In *Journal of Discourses by Brigham Young, President of the Church of Jesus Christ of Latter-Day Saints, His Two Counsellors, the Twelve Apostles, and Others*, edited by G. D. Watt, 2: 179–91. Liverpool, England: F. D. Richards, 1855.

Young, Elspeth. "And Thou Didst Hear Me." *Temple Fine Art Collection*. https://www.alyoung.com/art/work-and_thou_didst_hear_me.html.

Young, Elspeth. *Till We Meet Again*. 2013. Oil paint, 32.75" by 61".

Young, Margaret Blair, and Darius Aidan Gray. *Bound for Canaan*. 1st ed. Standing on the Promises 2. Salt Lake City: Bookcraft, 2000.

Young, Margaret Blair, and Darius Aidan Gray. *Bound for Canaan*. Revised and expanded ed. Standing on the Promises 2. Provo: Zarahemla Books, 2013.

Young, Margaret Blair, and Darius Aidan Gray. *The Last Mile of the Way*. 1st ed. Standing on the Promises 3. Salt Lake City: Bookcraft, 2003.

Young, Margaret Blair, and Darius Aidan Gray. *The Last Mile of the Way*. Revised and expanded ed. Standing on the Promises 3. Provo: Zarahemla Books, 2013.

Young, Margaret Blair, and Darius Aidan Gray. *One More River to Cross*. 1st ed. Standing on the Promises 1. Salt Lake City: Bookcraft, 2000.

Young, Margaret Blair, and Darius Aidan Gray. *One More River to Cross*. Revised and expanded ed. Standing on the Promises 1. Provo: Zarahemla Books, 2013.

Zackodnik, Teresa. "The 'Green-Backs of Civilization': Sojourner Truth and Portrait Photography." *American Studies* 46, no. 2 (Summer 2005): 117–43.

INDEX

promoted Quorum of the Twelve Apostles as
    LDS Church leaders after Joseph Smith's
    death, 56–57
racist comments by, 75
Salt Lake Valley settlement, 67
seer stones, 45
Utah Territory "Act in Relation to Service,"
    74–75, 84
Utah War, 81–82

Young, Eliza Partridge, 46, 47, 146
Young, Elspeth, 137
Young, Emily Dow Partridge, 46, 47, 76,
    92, 146
Young, Mary Ann Angell, 73, 76
Young, Zina D. H., 113, 115, 128–29

Zackodnik, Teresa, 88